COUNTERPUBLICS AND THE STATE

SUNY series in Communication Studies
Edited by Dudley D. Cahn

Counterpublics
and the State

EDITED BY
Robert Asen
AND
Daniel C. Brouwer

STATE UNIVERSITY OF NEW YORK PRESS

Published by
State University of New York Press, Albany

© 2001 State University of New York

For information, address State University of New York Press,
90 State Street, Suite 700, Albany, NY 12207

Production by Cathleen Collins
Marketing by Patrick Durocher

Library of Congress Cataloging-in-Publication Data

Counterpublics and the state / edited by Robert Asen and Daniel C. Brouwer.
    p. cm. — (SUNY series in communication studies)
    Includes bibliographical references and index.
    ISBN 0-7914-5161-5 (alk. paper) — ISBN 0-7914-5162-3 (pb : alk. paper)
      1. Social movements. 2. Dissenters. 3. Marginality, Social. 4. Political persecution.
I. Asen, Robert, 1968– II. Brouwer, Daniel C., 1970– III. Series.

HN17.5 .C686 2001
303.48′4—dc21
                                                        00-054747

10 9 8 7 6 5 4 3 2 1

Contents

Acknowledgments

M any people, places, and events influenced the development of this manuscript. Primary among these was our mutual reliance on each other. We wish to indicate that the labor for this book, from conceptualizing to organizing to writing to editing, was equally shared. Through many emails, faxes, and phone calls, we have become entangled as colleagues and as friends. We like this very much.

We are indebted to G. Thomas Goodnight and Jean Goodwin of Northwestern University, both of whom have contributed significantly to our intellectual conceptualization of relations between publics, counterpublics, and states. Both individuals participated as cheerleaders and gadflies in the development of this manuscript. Those who read, listened to, and offered critical commentary about portions of the manuscript include Elizabeth Lozano and B. Hannah Rockwell at Loyola University Chicago; Susan Zaeske at the University of Wisconsin, Madison; Lawrence R. Frey at Memphis University; David S. Birdsell at Baruch College; J. Robert Cox and graduate students in his course at the University of North Carolina, Chapel Hill; Cara A. Finnegan and graduate students in her course at the University of Illinois, Urbana-Champaign; Jean Goodwin and graduate students at colloquia at Northwestern University; and three reviewers for SUNY Press. We further thank colleagues at Loyola University Chicago; the University of Wisconsin, Madison; and Arizona State University for their encouragement and faith. Lawrence R. Frey, James Darsey of Georgia State University, David Zarefsky of Northwestern University, Stephen E. Lucas of the University of Wisconsin, Madison, and Rochelle Klaskin provided invaluable editorial advice and guidance at various stages of the project. At annual meetings of the National Communication Association, Rosa A. Eberly of the University of Texas, Austin, Catherine Helen Palczewski of the University of Northern Iowa, Valeria Fabj of Northern Illinois University, and Matthew J. Sobnosky of the College of

vii

William and Mary organized and facilitated seminars at which portions of the manuscript were incubated and presented. In many ways and in multiple settings, these various colleagues demonstrated care, concern, and support toward this project that sustained our optimism through the years of its development. The better portions of the manuscript bear their traces.

We express our profound thanks and admiration to each of the volume's contributors. Their enthusiasm, commitment, patience, and understanding continually reminded us that this was a project worth doing and worth doing with them. We have been personally and intellectually enriched through our collaboration with our contributors. Our editor at SUNY Press, Priscilla Ross, was a model of efficiency and clarity. For extending to us the opportunity to see this project through to fruition, we heartily thank her. Copyeditor Laura Glenn's keen eyes and diligence helped us to avoid many mistakes, and production editor Cathleen Collins's foresight and rapid responses to queries enabled us to stay on track with the production schedule. At Arizona State University, Janet Soper and Mary Fran Draisker of the Publication Assistance Center of the College of Public Programs assisted in the creation of the index for this volume.

To those people who struggle to survive, organize, and assert themselves on public and state stages, we express our solidarity.

Introduction

Reconfigurations of the Public Sphere

ROBERT ASEN AND DANIEL C. BROUWER

Social transformation often creates doubt and generates unpredictability for social actors. New developments elicit scrutiny toward established ways of understanding and acting. Scrutiny, in turn, enables examination of social institutions, practices, and relations. In democratic societies, doubt and unpredictability wrought by social change may be especially acute for those ideas and arrangements perceived as "public," in the various senses of public as accessible to, relevant to, known to, directed to, and/or constituted by members of a political community. For "public" seems at once both a necessary and a fragile notion for democratic orders. In the United States, the best-known expression of concern for the public in the face of social transformation may be John Dewey's 1927 work *The Public and Its Problems*. Dewey wrote famously of a public in eclipse. Increasing social complexity threatened the collective perception and practical judgment of a functioning public of citizens.

Dewey did not regard the public as a stable entity always located in the aggregated physical bodies of persons. Rather, he viewed the public as an ephemeral phenomenon built through collective perception. Dewey's pragmatic orientation led him to seek the conditions and forms of community life in social action. Some human acts produced consequences that extended beyond the parties directly involved in the action, and the "public" arose in the perception by affected others of these indirect consequences. Technological developments, however, cast doubt on the ability of the public to realize its standing. Dewey expressed concern that "the machine age has so enormously expanded, multiplied, intensified and

1

complicated the scope of the indirect consequences, . . . [has] formed such immense and consolidated unions in action, on an impersonal rather than a community basis, that the resultant public cannot identify and distinguish itself" ([1927] 1954, 126). Apathy characterized a bewildered public unable to find and organize itself.

The eclipse of the public upset the proper relationship between the public and the state. The public came into being as members of a political community perceived their affected status by the indirect consequences of human actions. To protect themselves and their interests, members of this public organized a state. According to Dewey, "the perception of consequences which are projected in important ways beyond the persons and associations directly concerned in them is the source of a public; and . . . its organization into a state is effected by establishing special agencies to care for and regulate these consequences" (39). The state served as an instrument of the public only to the extent to which the latter articulated its interests. Thus, with a public no longer capable of perceiving, articulating, and organizing its interests, crises emerged in the relations between public and state.

Our own time, like Dewey's, presents challenges for the public, however we wish to understand the term. In the mass media celebration and mystification of technology resound promises to restructure social relations. New communication technologies increase the speed of communication at a rate unimaginable for Dewey and his contemporaries. These technologies bring together dispersed persons and extend the reach of the "public" even further. If Dewey worried that "there are too many publics and too much of public concern for our existing resources to cope with" (126), then new communication technologies threaten to exacerbate this problem. Many publics arise as well from the demands made by long-suppressed and marginalized groups for the rights and responsibilities of political membership, collective sovereignty, or both. Groups drawing on axes of race, gender, class, sexuality, and ethnicity have sought to redeem the promises of democracy. These groups have demanded from those who enjoy fuller privileges of citizenship and from those agents of state authority varying levels of autonomy and power.

Yet if current technological advancement and putative dispersal of "the public" suggest parallels with Dewey's time, this volume engages an important shift in the problem from public and the state to *counter*publics and the state. Once this move has been made, Dewey's conceptual ordering of "public" and "state" functions neither as a model of what has been eclipsed nor what may be reconstituted. For counterpublics derive their "counter" status in significant respects from varying degrees of exclusion from prominent channels of political discourse and a corresponding lack of political power. The power frequently denied counterpublics consists not only in the capacity to induce or compel actions from others, but power in the Arendtian (1958) sense of that which arises when citizens act jointly. However, exclusion is neither fixed nor total. Sometimes, ostensibly inaccessible means and venues provide opportunities for counterpublic and state interaction. Other times, alternative modes and sites engender such interaction. In various ways, the contributors to this volume explore counterpublic and state engagement amid obstacles that complicate their relations. Sometimes counterpublic and state relations are informed by an element of tension and conflict. Gerard Hauser, Erik Doxtader, Daniel Brouwer, Catherine Squires, and Robert Asen pursue these conflicted relations through topics of prison writing, religious dissidence, AIDS activism, newspaper reporting, and alleged government wrongdoing. New communication technologies (NCTs) and processes of globalization further shape engagements between counterpublics and the state. In this volume, Catherine Palczewski and Todd McDorman explore the significance of NCTs for the advocacy campaigns of counterpublics and social movements in the United States. In a different vein, Marie Mater investigates the possibility of a computer-mediated global public sphere, while our final contributor Dana Cloud examines the impact of globalization on counterpublic and state engagements in Indonesia.

In its multifarious manifestations in various settings, counterpublic and state engagement is embedded in the lively and disruptive forces of political and social discourse. Such engagement compels critical scholarly reflection concerning how we understand inclusion and exclusion, how we construe relations among publics, and what we regard as constitutive of public authority and its organization in the state for the achievement of shared ends. Counterpublic and state engagement illuminates not only discourse in the public sphere but public sphere studies as an academic enterprise. In the remainder of this introduction, we explicate the background notion of a bourgeois public sphere, investigate developments in public sphere theory, and highlight the key themes of this volume.

THE BOURGEOIS PUBLIC SPHERE AND ITS CRITICS

Studying the interactions of counterpublics and the state invokes a wider context of studies in the public sphere. These studies extend a lineage of work in this area that includes Dewey's book as well as other important titles such as Walter Lippmann's (1925) *The Phantom Public*, to which Dewey explicitly acknowledges his debt, and Hannah Arendt's (1958) *The Human Condition*. In recent years, interest in the public sphere from scholars in a range of disciplines has grown sharply. Exemplifying current calls for interdisciplinary scholarship, this interest has brought together communication scholars with those in history, sociology, political science, philosophy, English, and other fields. Through journal articles, books, convention papers, conference panels, and seminars, scholars have debated the presuppositions, practices, and ends of the public sphere. These debates have entered the classroom as graduate and undergraduate courses in the public sphere now appear regularly in course listings. Increases in all of these measures indicate that interest in the public sphere has not yet peaked. As Goodnight and Hingstman (1997) note, growing interest in the public sphere has coalesced an important interdisciplinary line of inquiry. Indeed, Goodnight's own work in the field of communication has articulated critical themes and tensions in public sphere studies. Goodnight (1982, 1987) has called attention to the ways that argumentative practices and grounds construct issues as personal, technical, and public as well as engender discursive shifts in understanding among these spheres.

In the U.S. academic context, interdisciplinary debates have been spurred in large measure by the 1989 English translation of Jürgen Habermas's 1962 *Strukturwandel der Öffentlichkeit, The Structural Transformation of the Public Sphere.*[1] The book explicates the historical and critical concept of the bourgeois public sphere (see also Habermas 1974). As a historical concept, the bourgeois public sphere describes the emergence in civil society of a realm in which citizens came together as private persons to form a public that, acting in an advisory capacity, debated the activities of the state. Sustained through political pamphlets and coffeehouses, the bourgeois public sphere flourished in Europe in the seventeenth and eighteenth centuries. The bourgeois public sphere was instantiated through critical discourse and presupposed a rational debating public. Bourgeois subjectivity arose from a world of letters to assume a political form. A political consciousness developed as the bourgeoisie opposed absolute sovereignty with demands for abstract and universal laws and ultimately asserted itself as the only legitimate source for these laws. Economic autonomy and familial socialization enabled the development of the bourgeois political subject. As a critical concept, the bourgeois public sphere signifies an open forum of debate and an egalitarian community of citizens implicit in the practice of the bourgeoisie and explicit in their justifications of the public sphere. Three qualities characterize this critical public sphere: access is guaranteed to all citizens; citizens debate openly; and citizens debate matters of general interest.

Significant contradictions plagued this realm. Most prominently, participation in this public sphere conflated bourgeois and *homme.* Habermas explains that "*the fully developed bourgeois public sphere was based on the fictitious identity of the two roles assumed by the privatized individuals who came together to form a public: the role of property owners and the role of human beings pure and simple* [emphasis in original]" (1989, 56). Presupposing that social and economic conditions presented "everyone" with an equal opportunity to achieve an educated and propertied standing (private autonomy), bourgeois ideology regarded actual exclusion from the public sphere to be warranted by a principle of publicity that, in turn, assumed that educated and propertied persons were best-able to advance the general interest. The bourgeoisie experienced no break between their humanity and their status as citizens. They did not need to "leave their private existence behind to exercise their public role" (87). The homogenous class standing of the bourgeoisie engendered a shared vision of the good that blocked as potential topics of deliberation the arrangements that sustained actual exclusions from the public sphere.

Habermas's original account has been the subject of considerable debate and has been criticized for perpetuating its own exclusions by failing to explore the contemporaneous functioning of alternative modes of publicity. Attention has focused particularly on women's exclusion from the public sphere, and feminist criticism has been instrumental in elucidating this lacuna. Along these lines, some historiographers have traced how women participated in public life despite the restrictions and obstructions of bourgeois publicity (e.g., Ryan 1990). Others have challenged the bourgeois public sphere directly, arguing that women's exclusion functioned constitutively for the articulation of bourgeois publicity (Landes 1988; Pateman 1988; Fleming 1993). From this perspective, bourgeois notions of reason and universality arose in contrast to female subjugation in the domestic sphere.[2] A related critique of *Structural Transformation* concerns the exclusion of laborers from the bourgeois public sphere (Eley 1992; Aronowitz 1993). In a prominent alternative study, Oskar Negt and Alexander Kluge attempt in *Public Sphere and Experience* to fill-in some of the gaps in Habermas's account by explicating the development of a proletarian public sphere. Negt and Kluge view the bourgeois public sphere as deriving "its entire substance from the existence of owners of private property" (1993, 10). Capitalists participated in this sphere to bolster their hegemonic socioeconomic position through the invocation of a public good that furthered their individual interests. They experienced the bourgeois public sphere as a realm for enacting a "dominant knowledge": "a specialized knowledge of how to exploit this sphere properly" (1993, 11).

Habermas has responded to these charges of exclusion. Reflecting on his earlier work, Habermas (1992, 428) concedes that "the exclusion of women had structuring significance" for the bourgeois public sphere by determining its relation to the private sphere in a sex-specific fashion. Still, he sees the tensions of bourgeois publicity as potentials for self-transformation. With regard to laborers' exclusion from the bourgeois public sphere, Habermas (1992) regards such exclusion as contingent, and he situates the proletarian public sphere as a historical parallel of the bourgeois public sphere. Regardless of the extent to which Habermas concedes the exclusionary nature of the bourgeois public sphere, the import of these charges is that in failing to explore the contemporaneous functioning of alternative public spheres, he ends up idealizing the bourgeois public sphere (Fraser 1992a). In the view of some commentators, this idealization constructs a history of fulfillment then fall told through rose-colored glasses (Schudson 1992; Willard 1996).

RECONFIGURATIONS IN PUBLIC SPHERE THEORY

Recognition of the historical and conceptual exclusions of the bourgeois public sphere has motivated efforts to rethink the public sphere more inclusively without abandoning its promise of a critical publicity. We maintain that these efforts have proceeded through three key moves: to discern the multiplicity of the public sphere; to loosen boundaries and appreciate the permeability of borders; and to reconsider the separation of the public sphere and the state. In explicating these three key moves, we both review and critique critical developments, noting the problems they address as well as the issues they raise.

Multiplicity of the Public

The first key move in rethinking the public sphere more inclusively entails discerning the public sphere as a multiplicity of dialectically related public spheres rather than a single, encompassing arena of discourse. Reformulations along these lines take aim at the ideology of the bourgeois public sphere, which advances the circumscription of public deliberation to a single overarching arena as a positive and desirable bolstering of democracy and conversely regards the expansion of deliberation through a multiplicity of publics as a negative and undesirable departure from democracy (Fraser 1992a). Undoing this conceptual hierarchy, scholars have theorized alternative, nondominant publics amid wider publics to elucidate the complex discursive practices and constellatory relations among these realms. Gerard Hauser (1998), one of the contributors to this volume, describes the public sphere as a reticulate structure of discursive arenas spread across civil society (see also, e.g., Taylor 1995). Similarly, Seyla Benhabib (1996) envisions an "anonymous public conversation" arising from mutually interlocking and overlapping networks of opinion formation and dissemination, and Habermas in his recent work (1996) links the vitality of constitutional democracies to the good health of a public sphere functioning through widely diverse and relatively autonomous publics.

An invigorating line of inquiry concerning alternatives to dominant public spheres has proceeded under the term "counterpublics." Rita Felski and Nancy Fraser have been prominent articulators of this concept. Appearing around the time of the English translation of *Structural Transformation*, their early work in this area advocates recognition of the "current plurality of public spheres" (Felski 1989, 155) and the "plurality of competing publics" (Fraser 1992a, 122). Felski describes counterpublic spheres as critical oppositional forces that seek to disrupt the homogenizing and universalizing processes of a global mass-communication culture that promotes an uncritical consumerism. Counterpublic spheres voice oppositional needs and values not by appealing to the universality of the bourgeois public sphere but by affirming specificity of race, gender, sexuality, ethnicity, or some other axis of difference. In an oft-cited definition, Fraser (1992a, 123) identifies counterpublics as "parallel discursive arenas where members of subordinated social groups invent and circulate counterdiscourses to formulate oppositional interpretations of their identities, interests, and needs." Once formed, counterpublics enable their constituents to engage in communicative processes beyond the supervision of dominant groups. These definitions open up the study of counterpublics to a vast array of associations, marginal populations, social movements, and coalitions.

Common to Fraser and Felski's conceptions is an imperative to practice both inward and outward address as a response to the experience and discernment of exclusion. Discussing the feminist counterpublic sphere, Felski (1989, 167) explains that "the experience of discrimination, oppression, and cultural dislocation provides the impetus for the development of a self-consciously oppositional identity. Yet insofar as it is a *public* sphere, its arguments are also directed outward, toward a dissemination of feminist ideas and values throughout society as a whole." Similarly, Fraser asserts that counterpublics assume a publicist orientation and thus reveal a dual character. She observes that "on the one hand, they function as spaces of withdrawal and regroupment; on the other hand, they also function as bases and training grounds for agitational activities directed toward wider publics" (1992a, 124). For both theorists, the emancipatory potential of counterpublics emerges in this dialectical movement of withdrawal and reengagement with wider publics. Jane Mansbridge (1996) employs the term "oscillation" to capture counterpublic movement across varying arenas. She cautions that the dangers for counterpublic agents of remaining sequestered in an enclave—breeding of intolerance for others, difficulty of translating interests, detachment from healthy criticism—compel counterpublic oscillation. One may add that only through reengagement can constituents hope to redeem the promise of a critical publicity implicit in the practice and sometimes explicit in the justifications of wider publics. The dialectical movement of counterpublics underscores their publicist aspirations; counterpublics do not seek separatism or isolation.

Our discussion thus far has treated "counterpublic" as an unproblematic concept, yet developments in counterpublic theory raise questions even as they enrich the movement toward multiplicity in models of the public sphere. An important question deferred in many discussions of counterpublic theory concerns the quality of relations among publics: what is "counter" about counterpublics? This question is worth asking, for scholars sometimes write about counterpublics with a frustrating vagueness. This issue cannot be resolved by fixing counterpublics ontologically. But prominent candidates may be brought forth and evaluated for their conceptual value.[3] The first candidate appears in the group identity of counterpublic agents. As Fraser and Felski's notions of counterpublic suggest, unequal access to power and uneven distribution of symbolic and material resources advantage dominant social groups and disadvantage subordinate groups in public discourse. Taking this circumstance into account, one may locate the "counter" of counterpublics in the identity of the persons who articulate oppositional discourse. This approach offers a useful way of explicating historical experiences of exclusion and oppression and incorporating recent developments such as new social movements (NSMs). Theorists of NSMs claim that a primary goal of these movements is the affirmation of identities suppressed or distorted by regimes of power and legitimation.[4] In this sense, nascent counterpublics emerge when collectives assert, "we are Black," "we are queer," "we are wimmin." Contributors to the recent volume *The Black Public Sphere* (Black Public Sphere Collective 1995), for example, have engaged public sphere theory to contribute to the ongoing project of Black emancipation. A group-identity approach also recognizes that oppression and subordination are rarely suffered randomly. Certain groups of people have been more likely than others to be subordinated and oppressed, to perceive themselves as such, and to organize in opposition to subordination and oppression. Yet some theorists (e.g., Young 1997) have argued that group identities such as "black" and "women," which may reify into essential identities, mask important differences among individual group members. Moreover, inhabitors of marginal identities do not always oppose domination in their activities in wider publics; to insist that oppositionality inheres in marginal identities is to overlook these peoples' mundane or hegemonically complicit activities. Finally, an exclusive focus on identity may displace political and economic stratification as informing counterdiscourse and require the conceptual countenance of less-than-emancipatory counterpublics, which may undermine the larger aims of counterpublic theory.

Another approach may be to locate the "counter" of counterpublics in topics that have been introduced into wider public agendas through counterpublicity. This strategy promises to reveal a history of discursive contestation and transformation; it may disclose the processes through which topics once viewed by many as "private issues" or "special interests" become construed as matters that potentially affect many persons, as "public problems." Along these lines, Fraser references the efforts of counterpublic agents to force onto wider agendas neglected women's concerns by circulating such terms as "sexism" and "sexual harassment." Yet a topical orientation risks reifying the same rigid distinctions that it seeks to dispel by suggesting that some topics are necessarily public while others are necessarily counterpublic. Furthermore, it draws critical attention only to those movements from margin to center, thus neglecting the ways in which dominant or public topics are rendered marginal or private. One also may locate the "counter" of counterpublics in places that have fostered counterpublic discourse, a move seemingly warranted by the spatializing addition of "sphere" to the term "counterpublic." This approach foregrounds the situational traits or institutional arrangements that may advantage or disadvantage participants even in the absence of stated rules of entry. But certain locations may not necessarily be more hospitable to counterpublic discourse than others. And we limit our vision of emancipatory practice in this manner by foreclosing the possibility of counterpublic discourse emerging in wider fora. These candidates for the "counter" in counterpublics raise questions of the emergence and stability of counterpublics. They envision discursively and nondiscursively constituted as well as ephemeral and institutionally secured counterpublics.

Multiple meanings of *public* connoted in the term *counterpublic* complicate these questions. Public, as indicated earlier, may indicate something potentially open to all (as in the bourgeois public sphere), potentially concerning all (as in matters of public interest), potentially known to all (as in public information), potentially constituted by all (as in the general public), and potential movement toward all (as in attempts to publicize matters). Prefixing "counter" to these multiple meanings of "public" instigates a rich and varied set of conceptual understandings. In our framing, particular couplings of "counter" and "public" may resolve some of the issues and tensions noted above and yet exacerbate others. For example, formulations of counter seeking to elucidate responses of persons subject to exclusions may overcome charges of separatism by emphasizing publicity in the active efforts of such persons to engage others. But as this formulation addresses concerns about separatism, it raises the problem of essential group identities. Alternative formulations may address concerns regarding essentialism by highlighting how persons of diverse backgrounds may join together in common cause through counterpublic spheres to force formerly marginal issues onto a national agenda. Yet these formulations run the risk of valorizing particular spaces as necessarily inventive. The point to emphasize here is that a wide variety of couplings may be generated, none of which resolves once and for all the tensions of counterpublic theory. As a result, counterpublics will differ with regard to density, complexity, breadth, and access to resources and power; they may be episodic, enduring, or abstract (Calhoun 1998, 374; Habermas 1996, 374). The task of scholars is to attend to the contingent, particular constructions of counter entered into by participants in the public sphere.

Permeable Boundaries

As a second reconfiguration, boundaries and borders have been loosened by removing the restriction of deliberation in the public sphere to the common good, for this restriction assumes a priori distinctions of public and private. "Public" and "private" are not fixed, content-specific categories that structure the public sphere prior to discourse. Rather, "public" and "private" emerge in social action and dialogue even as collectively held conceptions of each shape the conditions of their emergence. Boundary drawing and maintenance constitute perpetual performances enacted through public discourse. In his recent work, Habermas (1996) holds that the thematization of boundary questions represents important moments of political debate. Similarly, Seyla Benhabib (1992) observes that in important respects public dialogue consists of challenging and redefining established notions of the common good.

Accepting as decided an already established ordering of public and private often leads to silencing the concerns of certain excluded groups. Benhabib proclaims that "all struggles against oppression in the modern world begin by redefining what had previously been considered 'private,' non-public and non-political issues as matters of public concern, as issues of justice, as sites of power which need discursive legitimation" (1992, 100). These struggles unfold in various directions as antagonists encounter one another in the multiple sites of the public sphere. In various case studies (see, e.g., Fraser 1992b; McClure 1996), scholars have demonstrated how the assertion of "public" and "private" function as discursive strategies that offer advantage to one participant or another. To various case studies, one may add the controversy surrounding President Clinton's illicit affair with former White House intern Monica Lewinsky. After repeatedly denying sexual relations with Lewinsky, the president addressed the nation on 17 August 1998, to acknowledge that "I did have a relationship with Ms. Lewinsky that was not appropriate" (1998, 1638). Clinton admitted regret for misleading people, but he countered that it was time for the national government to move beyond an Independent Counsel investigation that had delved into private matters. Indeed, Clinton insisted that the episode was "private." He vowed to "reclaim my family life for my family. It's nobody's business but ours. Even Presidents have private lives. It is time to stop the pursuit of personal destruction and the prying into private lives and get on with our national life" (1998, 1638). As this excerpt suggests, Clinton does not appeal in this first "apology" speech to some preexisting category of private. Rather, he attempts to assert against his antagonists that the scandal *should* be viewed by the citizenry as private.

Although borders may be permeable, doing away with distinctions between public and private altogether would constitute critical neglect of important qualities of public discourse. Among those who disavow such distinctions, Jodi Dean (1992, 305; see also 1996) seeks to "move beyond the distinction between the public and private spheres" by theorizing civil society as a series of interconnected discursive spheres that nevertheless call on a notion of critical publicity. Cindy Griffin (1996, 38) wonders how, in light of developments in postmodern and feminist rhetorical theory, "scholars justify the division of the two spheres at all" (see also Phillips 1996). However, participants deploy these distinctions regularly in public debates and controversies; such controversies turn in significant respects on how participants draw lines of public and private. Distinctions between public and private hold prescriptive as well as explanatory value, for constructions of private can offer respite from the glare of publicity. The siege laid by members of the mass media on families who have suffered tragedies demonstrates the need for such "private" spaces. Defending the normative value of privacy, Jean Cohen (1996) constructs a concept of the private as a corollary of a differentiated public that entails freedom from official intrusion as well as decision-making autonomy. Cohen argues that such a conception values difference in pluralist societies and enables the constitution of one's own identity. For these reasons, complexities of public and private ought not lead to calls for their dissolution. Rather, they should drive public sphere scholars to pay attention to struggles over demarcation as valuable sites of study. Boundaries mark relations of power that often inform discourse obliquely. In various instances, scholars can reveal how traditional modes of drawing the distinction between public and private have been part of a discourse of domination.

As scholars have loosened the restriction of discourse in the public sphere to the common good, so too have they sought to undo the status-bracketing requirements of the bourgeois public sphere. Nancy Fraser explains that the bourgeois conception of the public sphere envisioned an arena in which interlocutors set aside status inequalities and spoke to one another as if they were equal in social and economic standing. Yet even in the absence of formal exclusions, social inequality can infect deliberation as modes of discussion and engagement mark inequalities. Fraser calls instead for discourse in the public sphere to address and thematize inequalities as explicit topics of debate. Fraser's call participates in a larger effort to articulate difference as a resource for public deliberation and discourse in the public sphere. Iris Marion Young describes difference as "a necessary resource for a discussion-based politics in which participants aim to cooperate, reach understanding, and do justice" (1997, 385; see also 1996). Young holds that viewing difference as a resource facilitates inclusion of diverse perspectives in democratic discussion and decision-making and engenders among participants a more comprehensive account of social relations, consequences of actions, and relative advantage and disadvantage. However, the challenge remains for public sphere scholars to construct common enough frameworks so that participants may raise questions of justice and fairness.

Scholars also have sought to loosen boundaries and borders by arguing that consensus need not be viewed as the end of discourse in the public sphere. Besides deliberation oriented toward agreement, discourse in the public sphere may serve a number of purposes, including expressing identity, raising awareness, celebrating difference, and enabling play. In contexts of agreement (e.g., policy-making fora), rethinking consensus in a plural mode has emerged as a response to the fact of irreducible value pluralism. Thomas McCarthy explains that a background consensus may motivate members of diverse political communities to assent to collective decisions with which they disagree: "Their background agreement with the operative political conception of justice may *rationally motivate* them to consent to laws they regard as unwise or unjust in the hope, perhaps, that they will be able to use the same resources to change them" (1992, 68). Various efforts of McCarthy and others (e.g., Estlund 1997) lead toward what James Bohman has called a "plural public reason," which does not presuppose a single norm of reasonableness and recognizes instead that participants may agree with one another for different publicly accessible reasons (1996, 83). Along these lines, some proponents of consensus do not necessarily regard its absence as an indicator of failed deliberation. Joshua Cohen (1989) has explicated an influential ideal deliberative procedure that aims for a rationally motivated consensus. However, Cohen notes that in situations where "the decision is made by majority rule, participants may appeal to considerations that are quite generally recognized as having considerable weight, and as a suitable basis for collective choice, even among people who disagree about the right result" (1997, 414).

Elucidation of the nonconsensual ends of the public sphere has focused attention on the varied functions of public discourse, layered conceptions of reason and alternative agreements, and situations where action must be taken in the absence of agreement. Yet some attempts to overcome consensus have produced performative contradictions and totalizing replacements. As an instance of the former, Jean-François Lyotard (1984) gainsays consensus and the metaprescriptives—rules governing dialogue—on which consensus-oriented discourse putatively relies. Lyotard calls instead for a turn to dissension and heteromorphous local language games. But in renouncing terror—the threatened or actual elimination of a player from a language game—Lyotard appeals to the prescriptives, such as open access and debate, that he seeks to deny. Kendall Phillips (1996) seeks to recuperate dissent in studies of the public sphere; however, Phillips presents a totalizing account of the public sphere as consensus-based. Both performative contradictions and totalizing replacements point to the danger that in seeking to loosen boundaries and borders, we may reinscribe a binary logic on our theory and criticism. G. Thomas Goodnight, who appears in Phillips's retelling of public sphere theory, warns against the construction of binary categories. He observes that "gestures of consent and dissent are contingent inventions spun from human conditions of uncertainty. Differences that make a difference sometimes emerge from rhetorical engagements because, and in spite, of attributed consensus" (1997, 270). From this understanding, we are better able to recognize that "public" and "consensus" need not be set against "private" and "dissent."

Imbrications of State and Public

The third key move in public sphere theory involves reconsideration of the separation of the public sphere and the state. This revision gains impetus from lively debates over the degree to which state institutions inform public discourse and publics influence state institutions. The liberal political tradition from which Habermas (1989) derives his original theory of the bourgeois public sphere insisted on a conceptual distinction between the public sphere and the state on one side and the official economy on the other. Unencumbered by the constraints of either realm, the bourgeois public sphere could engender rational-critical discourse that would serve as a critical check on the state. In significant respects, Habermas attributes the decline of the historical bourgeois public sphere to the interpenetration of public and private realms since the era of liberal capitalism as the state has intervened in the affairs of civil society and society has increasingly assumed tasks previously accomplished under state authority.

In her well-known critique, Fraser (1992a) holds that the strict separation of the bourgeois public sphere from the state promotes "weak publics," publics whose deliberations consist of opinion formation but not decision-making authority. She regards this ascription of functions as inadequate for understanding contemporary political arrangements, which, since the achievement of parliamentary sovereignty, have blurred lines separating civil society and the state. Indeed, a sovereign parliament functions as a public sphere within the state, a "strong public" whose deliberations entail opinion formation and decision-making authority. In an ambitious U.S. effort, James Fishkin (1991, 1995) proposes "deliberative opinion polls" as a means of linking opinion formation with decision-making. For instance, in the selection of primary candidates for president, he envisions a "national caucus" that would charge participants with selecting a certain number of at-large delegates to the national conventions of the two major parties. A national sample of citizens would spend a few days at a single site interacting with candidates of the Democratic and Republican parties. After debating the issues with the candidates and each other, participants would be polled on their preferences.

Habermas in his more recent work proposes a two-track model of deliberative democracy that dislocates the state as the instigator of social action. This dislocation recognizes the significance for a healthy democracy of interplay between state and non-state actors. Yet Habermas's model sustains a clear separation between the public sphere and the state; he distinguishes parliamentary bodies as a "context of justification" from the "context of discovery" of a procedurally unregulated public sphere. Deliberations in the former have "less to do with becoming sensitive to new ways of looking at problems than with justifying the selection of a problem and the choice among competing proposals for solving it" (1996, 307). Habermas holds that "the communicative structures of the public sphere constitute a far-flung network of sensors that react to the pressure of society-wide problems and stimulate influential opinions," but this "communicative power cannot 'rule' of itself but can only point the use of administrative power in specific directions" (1996, 300). He concludes that "only the political system can act" (1996, 360).

Gainsaying strict separations, Michael Schudson argues that the state should be seen as part of the public sphere and not as a distinct dimension of social life. He understands the public sphere to include "a set of activities that constitute a democratic society's self-reflection and self-governance" (1994, 530). Schudson holds that legislatures themselves are privileged public spheres operating within the state. And he points to the news media and political parties as prominent examples of the ways in which civil society institutions exist both inside and outside the state. Further, democratic governments offer multiple forums and various points of access for citizens. In addition to constituting aspects of the public sphere, the state informs the shape of civil society generally. Schudson asserts that particular forms of political representation give rise to particular types of public space. This claim serves as an important call for public sphere scholars to account for the specific conditions in which discursive practices take place.

The "separatist" model of the public sphere and the state, we argue, discounts the capacity of an activist state to intervene in society in an effort to improve conditions for citizen participation in opinion-forming and decision-making activities. In this respect, Schudson's model better admits of the work done in the last two decades by theorists proposing state-initiated structural innovations to foster better societal conditions for deliberation. For instance, Lani Guinier (1994) advances a controversial "proportionality principle" that displaces majority rule decision-making by institutionalizing "turn-taking" between majority and minority groups; through turn-taking, minority groups accustomed to "losing" against the majority are able to influence outcomes that benefit them. Such an approach, she argues, while failing to achieve consensus consistently, would better distribute political satisfaction (104, 112). Campaign finance reform gains unique expression in Bruce Ackerman's (1993) federally funded "voucher" system, a system in which the government credits each registered voter with a sum of money to be spent during an election, and political candidates earn finances by persuading voters to transfer funds to their campaign. Ackerman defends his economic innovation as mitigating colonization of the political public sphere by market forces while simultaneously affirming the value of market forces in promoting political debate. More broadly, Joshua Cohen (1997, 427) calls for the implementation of "a strategy of associative democracy that would use public powers to encourage the development of the right kinds [depending on circumstances and unmet needs] of secondary association." Such a strategy would require the kind of collaborative, proactive state that Schudson's model portrays.

Though it draws attention to the activist and ameliorative potential of the state, Schudson's model neglects the emergence of relatively autonomous publics formed because their members have found inaccessible—or have been denied outright—certain rights, responsibilities, and resources offered or secured through state power. On this score, Habermas's model better accounts for counterpublics positioned antagonistically against the state. Further, states are not always the primary audience of counterpublic activities. In this way, attributions of primacy to the state cannot account adequately for instances of communal and chosen self-isolation or exclusion. Although he announces his intention to resist a state-centered theory of politics, Schudson in significant respects reinscribes the state as the central political actor as he explicates its structuring position in relation to society as a whole. This positioning produces a lingering tension in his model. Moreover, in any explication of a potentially activist state, attempts to foster multiple publics ought to be approached cautiously. Political dissidents have long recognized that participation in a state-sponsored forum can be a precarious experience that runs the risk of co-optation—a theme explored variously in some of the essays in this volume.

Debate over the relative autonomy of publics from the state and varying state influence of public discourse will only become more lively as the new millennium proceeds, for the state itself is undergoing transformations that portend important developments in relations between states and publics. The stability of the state as an entity is under duress from two directions: forces of globalization and robust civil societies within state borders. The growing trend toward international decision-making bodies and the increasing stature of multinational corporations challenge state autonomy, sovereignty, and legitimacy. Saskia Sassen (1996) argues that the international dispersal of factories, offices, and service outlets in an integrated corporate system in conjunction with the rise of global financial and stock markets have interconnected and transformed the economies of developed and developing nations. She sees in globalization processes an emergent form of "economic citizenship" that enables particular actors to demand accountability from governments. This economic citizenship summons a new rights-bearer: "Economic citizenship does not belong to citizens. It belongs to firms and markets, particularly the global financial markets, and is located not in individuals, not in citizens, but in global economic actors" (1996, 38; cf., Bauman 1998). Yet Sassen recognizes that although state sovereignty has been decentered, globalization is not a simple, one-way process of diminished state authority in a new age. For states themselves have worked to ease the flow of capital, labor, and goods across borders, and state legal systems remain the most important enforcers of global rights and property. Craig Calhoun (1998, 382) concurs that states overwhelmingly constitute the "most important arenas for democratic collective action" for addressing social, economic, political, and cultural issues. States and their representatives create a palpable, if not actual, presence in public discourse by influencing national agenda-setting, mass media, and the formation and maintenance of some discursive fora.

From within national borders, states find themselves increasingly pressured and held accountable to citizens' groups. In the United States, the extraordinary number of popular referenda in recent elections evidences the increasing level of political organizing and agenda-setting engaged in by civil associations within the United States. But the United States is hardly alone. In Indonesia, one can find over 2,000 independent environmental groups as compared to one such group twenty years ago, and the Philippines has witnessed a more than threefold increase in the number of registered nonprofit organizations through the early and middle 1990s (Bornstein 1999). As citizen associations grow in number and influence, states find their legitimacy increasingly challenged. More volatile than associations are separatist movements that challenge not only the legitimacy but also the integrity of the state. Arjun Appadurai (1996) observes that efforts by minority ethnic groups to establish sovereign nations within extant states strain the relationship between the two venerated entities named in the phrase "nation-state." In separatist movements, the "nation" seeks utter disidentification with the "state." Perceiving an increase in conflict between "nation" and "state" fueled in part by globalization, Appadurai explains that "the hyphen that links them is now less an icon of conjuncture than an index of disjuncture. . . . There is a battle of the imagination, with state and nation seeking to cannibalize one another" (1996, 39). From within and from without, states are under duress: the significance of globalization, robust civil societies, and separatism and their influence on states, social and political practices, and public discourse cannot be underestimated.

Thus far, we have summarized and critiqued what we argue are important developments in public sphere theory, specifically the move toward multiplicity, the move to loosen borders, and the move to reconsider separations between states and publics. Contributors to this volume intervene amid the vibrancy of debate over these developments. In the remaining sections, we introduce our two lines of inquiry, the themes and issues that emerge from these lines of inquiry, and some of the conclusions and insights from our contributors.

LINES OF INQUIRY

Examining practical occurrences yields insights into the status and potential of the contemporary public sphere. Counterpublics often encounter the state as one of their wider and most important publics. They approach the state in the form of social movement protests, demonstrations, demands for greater participation, or all of these. States themselves often express interest in counterpublics, whether in the form of placing particularly agitational counterpublics under surveillance, deliberating with counterpublics that approach them, approaching counterpublics, or actively extending a forum to counterpublics. Whether episodically or enduringly, openly or secretly, counterpublics and states encounter each other in complex, multiform relations. We have organized the essays in this book along two main lines of inquiry: first, conflicted encounters; second, new communication technologies and globalization.

Conflicted Encounters

In this first line of inquiry, the authors investigate counterpublic and state relations on a range of topics in multiple settings and in different historical moments. One quality that these diverse encounters share is an element of tension and conflict. Borne out of a history of exclusion, an unfamiliarity that breeds potential unease and mistrust, encounters of counterpublic agents and state officials sometimes are informed even in their cordial moments by this quality. In this first group of chapters, tension and conflict appear variously through overt, systematic suppression by state officials, duplicitous action by state officials that masks a latent hostility, internal conflict among counterpublic agents over whether relations should proceed at all, and invitation from counterpublic agents that evokes historical betrayals and animosities.

A fascinating literature represented by such writers as Mikhail Bakhtin (1968), James C. Scott (1985, 1990), Smadar Lavie (1990), and Anna Lowenhaupt Tsing (1993) explores the social and cultural practices by which profoundly marginal populations register dissent or opposition through inversion, grotesque humor, symbolic degradation, arrogation, and expressions of *Schadenfreude*. Those for whom direct public expressions of dissent engender extraordinary risk often exhibit a creativity in their interactions with state (or empire, or dynasty) officials. In less oppressive societies, dissidents typically benefit from a broader range of public means for registering their opposition. We in the United States are familiar with the wide variety of public activities ventured by members of the civil rights movement, including boycotts, picketing, marches, and "creative suffering." Other groups then and since have employed blockades, traffic disruptions, die-ins, and occupation of restricted spaces as means for dramatizing their claims and creating their own fora. Commentary on such tactics is abundant: In the 1960s and later, practices of civil disobedience in the United States and Europe were viewed by some as anarchic, antideliberative, or narcissistic (see, e.g., Gregg 1971) and by others as crucial for engendering self-criticism in a healthy nation-state. Habermas's (1985) announcement that the tactics of the New Social Movements force a reevaluation of civil disobedience as "an element of a mature political culture" (99) exemplifies this latter perspective.

When engagement with counterpublic agents provokes too many risks such as the threat of poignant critique, loss of credibility, exposure of villainy or corruption, or instigation of antigovernment uprising, states may act by removing the agitator(s) from public view. Typically achieved through exile, excommunication (sectarian and secular), or imprisonment, such removal places extraordinary limitations on dissident political activities. In the face of such limitation, dissidents engage in what Gerard Hauser calls "rhetorical resistance in a subterranean arena." Modes of artful opposition to the Communist regime in Poland in the 1980s are the focus of Hauser's contribution. In particular, Hauser finds in Adam Michnik's prison letter from Bialoleka an extraordinary vision of a civil society in which broad-based socialist reforms are constituted from deep inventional reservoirs of cultural memory. In Hauser's reading, the letter performs the necessary task of articulating a form of social identity that is more than coherent enough to sustain a social movement; the letter both guides the formation of this social identity and hastens the creation of a civil society not colonized by the Communist martial government. Whence its power? In part, while Michnik's imprisonment ostensibly squelches his voice, his imprisonment also "bestows a perverse imprimatur" on both Michnik and his letter, elevating their political-mythical significance as death can turn dissidents into martyrs.

Religious institutions and people of faith often impress themselves on stages of social controversy. Under conditions of apartheid in South Africa, pressure from religious institutions within the country hastened the birth of a new civil society. In his chapter, Erik Doxtader studies South Africa's transition toward a democratic state and focuses in particular on the ways in which the interdenominational *Kairos Document* of 1985 helped to constitute realms of civil society and public life in the nation's emergent democracy. Doxtader argues that the success of South Africa's transition derived largely from the ability of oppositional forces to channel the animosity bred from years of incredible violence and other forms of injustice into processes of oppositional argument and deliberation. Simultaneously motivated and agitated by Fraser's (1992a) innovative but vague account of the activities of counterpublics, Doxtader finds in the example of South Africa an opportunity to ground claims in the events characteristic of an emergent, actually existing democracy. Formulating such claims, he argues, necessitates a rhetorical turn in public sphere studies.

Perhaps the most recognizable way in which counterpublics approach the state (at least in relatively democratic states) is in the form of protest groups or social movements. The AIDS Coalition to Unleash Power (ACT UP) is a radical activist group that frequently directs its complaints and critiques against state officials and institutions. ACT UP's strident, disruptive, and often highly theatrical public demonstrations since its formation in 1987 have gained the attention of legislators, "the general public," other activist groups, and academics. Yet, as Dan Brouwer notes, the testimony of ACT UP members in congressional hearings has been overlooked. He argues that congressional hearings are not deliberative forums per se but rather serve a predeliberative function. Furthermore, participation in a state-sponsored forum is an act fraught with tension for any radical group that is skeptical of the state and worried about co-optation. In the face of this tension, Brouwer argues, the major reason for ACT UP participation in the state-sponsored forum of the hearings is the access to stronger, decision-making fora that it promises.

Between imprisonment and invitation, state responses to counterpublic agents take other forms. It is a common tactic, for example, even in advanced democracies, for states secretly to penetrate radical groups for purposes of surveillance. Intimidation tactics and special restrictions against counterpublic activities have also worked well. Catherine Squires's chapter on the history of the Black press in the United States between the World Wars examines the impact of these latter two tactics as practiced by federal and state governments. Extending Jane Mansbridge's (1996) concept of "oscillation," Squires argues that during this time period, the Black press exhibited traits of an "oscillating" public that projects its previously private or enclaved claims toward wider publics. Indeed, the publication of these claims invited intimidation and restrictions. The real and imagined power of Black mass media to generate social unrest compelled officials to request, publicly and privately, cessation of certain types of expression. Furthermore, as Squires notes, various state and federal entities created artificial shortages of the means of production, thus exacerbating the Black press's already tenuous relationship to structural access to the public sphere.

In contrast to the events that Squires examines, we should recognize instances where states initiate plausibly beneficial interactions with counterpublics. Elected or appointed representatives, for example, may appear before constituencies in order to inform or explain, to defend or evoke, to foster dialogue and gain insight. On those occasions when states are called on to explain or justify their actions, they necessarily engage in representation. Robert Asen explores "a fundamental tension in representation between absence and presence, between standing for something and embodying that something" as that tension inflects the speech of then-CIA director John Deutch before South Central Los Angeles community members. Amid allegations that the U.S. Central Intelligence Agency had backed a drug cartel that introduced crack cocaine into Los Angeles, Deutch's speech appears as one striking moment in the controversy. Asen studies the character of the rhetorical situation of Deutch's encounter with South Central community members and judges Deutch to have seriously miscalculated the parameters and constraints of the situation. More broadly, Asen argues that this encounter between Deutch and South Central residents exposes the inadequacy of current strands of public sphere theory to account for such encounters.

In the five concrete engagements that we have thus far introduced, one can discern relations between counterpublics and states inflected variously by inequities in power and resources, by competing claims about moral authority, by historical relations and critical memory, and by perceived conditions of safety and danger. Relations between counterpublics and states are further inflected by two related phenomena, New Communication Technologies (NCTs) and globalization. The remaining essays in this volume examine ways in which these two phenomena influence—sometimes facilitating, sometimes complicating—engagements.

New Communication Technologies and Globalization

Currently, the Internet is the most recognizable and familiar NCT. Globally, the Internet is growing faster than any past communication technology. In 1994, only four years after it became widely accessible, the Internet supported a usership of fifty million people.[5] By mid-1998, the Internet had over 140 million users with a predicted usership of 700 million (nearly one-twelfth of the world's population) by 2001 (United Nations Development Programme [UNDP] 1999, 58). Given such an astounding and unprecedented rate of growth, it is not surprising that many have expressed and continue to express optimism about the ability of the Internet to enhance communication, to invigorate already existing collectives, and to create new kinds of collectives. Tempering such optimism, however, is the fact that structural exclusions often alienate marginal peoples from the very technologies that could enable their amelioration.[6] In work that is becoming increasingly vital to studies in the public sphere, practitioners and scholars continue to investigate the ways in which counterpublics and states employ NCTs in their engagements with each other, the types of discursive fora to which NCTs give rise, and the degree to which such fora resemble or exemplify "publics."

The rapid ascent of NCTs has spurred discussion of the possibility of a "global" public sphere; indeed, the possibility of an emergent global public sphere is one of the many issues that congregate around the concept of "globalization." The United Nations defines globalization as "the growing interdependence of the world's people" and a "process integrating not just the economy but culture, technology and governance" (UNDP, 1). Economic, social, political, and cultural ties between nations are hardly new. But what has recently reinvigorated discussion about these ties is that there are significantly more of them and they are significantly more intense (UNDP, 31; Smith 1995). To the extent that the growing calls for more global governance (UNDP, 73; Köhler 1998; Held 1998) are heeded, we can anticipate more—and more intense—interactions between transnational publics and transnational political or economic entities. Those investigating the impact of globalization on relations between counterpublics and states address such questions as: Through globalization, does the state diminish as a relevant or efficacious site of appeal for political, economic, and cultural redress? What is to be gained from counterpublics' appeals to global, not state, audiences? And, can we even talk about "publics" or "counterpublics" without reference to a state? In the following paragraphs, we amplify the ways in which four of our contributors address these queries about globalization and NCTs.

In the mid-1990s, the Zapatistas in Mexico became "the first armed revolutionaries known to have solicited public sympathy for their struggle by publishing their communiqués over the Internet" (Harmon 1998, A5). Other collectives have made use of Internet technology for informing, organizing, and protesting. Communication scholars, sociologists, political scientists, and others must take heed when "hacktivism," "e-marches," and "cyber protest" become part of the popular vocabulary, for the terminology announces the transposition of familiar human activity through a new medium. Such is one claim of Catherine Palczewski in her chapter, "Cyber-movements, New Social Movements, and Counterpublics." Whereas many scholars focus on the impact of NCTs on direct political participation—activities in the political public sphere—Palczewski demonstrates how New Social Movement, counterpublic, and controversy-based rhetorical theories converge to draw attention to the organizational forms of social movements. To what extent do NCTs alter the internal rhetorical dynamics of social movements, and to what extent do altered rhetorical dynamics alter organizational forms? Through theoretical fusion and reference to case studies, Palczewski argues that NCTs occasion only a minor change in rhetorical dynamics and organizational forms.

Analysis of the use of web sites, listservs, and e-mail by right-to-die advocates in the United States leads Todd McDorman to argue that such technologies can have a significant positive impact on social movements. About right-to-die advocates' cyberdiscourse, McDorman offers three main arguments—that computer-mediated communication establishes a forum in which to foster resistant subjectivities more easily and more directly; that the fluidity of norms promotes more egalitarian communication; and that political mobilization is enhanced. McDorman encounters an interesting case of practice (almost) following theory: after the defeat of a ballot initiative in Michigan in 1998, right-to-die advocates created a listserv to discuss their regrets and complaints but also to assess reasons for their defeat and plot for greater success in the future. In this action, they exemplified one moment in the dialectic of counterpublicity: withdrawal into a forum in which "those who lose in each coercive move can rework their ideas and their strategies, gathering their forces and deciding in a more protected space in what way or whether to continue the battle" (Mansbridge 1996, 47). Notably, however, the right-to-die advocates in Michigan established their (cyber-) forum themselves, without the kind of state assistance that Mansbridge proposes.

In the details of McDorman's article, readers will find evidence that web sites and listservs were able to bring people together in what resemble communities of "situational intimacy" (Cerulo and Ruane 1998, 407–410), but we should ask: How large and dispersed can a population be and still resemble an enduring "community," and to what extent can communication technologies facilitate such a community? Bruce Robbins (1993) ends his introduction to *The Phantom Public Sphere* with a nod toward the future: "In the immediate aftermath of the cold war, before the North has settled into a definitive, equally polar antagonism with the South, it will be interesting to see whether room indeed exists for an international public sphere—for instance, in the universalizing language of 'human rights'—in which decolonization would become a discursive reality" (xxiii–xxiv). It has been just a few short years since Robbins's musing, but in those years several scholars have actively debated and theorized the possibility of and the minimal conditions for an international public sphere. Whether construed as an international public sphere, a "global public sphere" (Beck 1997; Habermas 1998), a "cosmopolitan public sphere" (Köhler 1998), or "cosmopolitan democracy" (Held 1998), the notion of a forum wherein vastly dispersed individuals of a multitude of ranks, roles, and races might come together for deliberation has captured the attention of many.

Marie Mater's essay addresses the possibilities of a global public sphere emergent through NCTs. While much has been made of NCTs' abilities to facilitate almost instantaneous communication between the geographically dispersed, most political experiments with NCTs have occurred at more local levels of municipalities (Tsagarousianou 1998, 168). And while Habermas has noted that an entity such as a transnational public sphere would require more and more developed structural apparatuses, Habermas does not explicitly thematize NCTs as part of this necessary apparatus. Mater does. She chastens Habermas for his failure to cultivate the seeds of his own thinking about a global public sphere and shares Karl-Otto Apel's optimism about a real, global communication community. Mater examines cooperation between the United Nations, the Association of Progressive Communications, and various nongovernmental organizations during four conferences during the 1990s—the Conference on Environment and Development, the Fourth World Conference on Women, Earth Summit+5, and Beijing+5. On the basis of her analysis of these NCT-facilitated collaborations, Mater argues that the United Nations is facilitating a reconfiguration between procedural publics and general publics in ways that bespeak the promises of globalization.

The promises and premises of globalization are not, however, without their detractors. With regard to the diminution of the state, there seem to be as many defenders of the ineluctability of the state in the face of global forces as there are prognosticators of states' declines (e.g., Smith 1995). Our final contributor, Dana Cloud, forcefully argues that theories of the effects of globalization can hardly account for the quality of events that took place in Indonesia in 1998. Then, a mass coalition of students, workers, and the poor protested the government of President Suharto and succeeded in wresting him from power. Whereas some globalization theorists would assert that postcapital states are no longer central sites for redress and that modern patterns of social organization and movement are anachronistic, Cloud argues that states must remain central sites and targets for social change. Her analysis of the events in Indonesia also leads Cloud to challenge New Social Movements theory, with its emphasis on symbolic and identity politics. Conceding few potential gains of symbolic politics and foregrounding the intertwinings of economy and state, Cloud insists on the continued salience of explicitly materialist politics that aim at redistributive justice.

CONCLUSION

The two lines of inquiry that structure this book converge in their interest in interactions between counterpublics and the state. In this way, the essays in this volume participate in a larger dialogue of public sphere studies that we have characterized as reconfigurations of the public sphere. The following chapters contribute to the movement toward multiplicity by showing how concrete engagements engender multiple, diverse publics, by illuminating how these multiple publics do not only engage each other but confront state power, and by noting that these relations with the state are as varied as relations with other publics. Contributors also address the movement toward multiplicity through treatment of instances of counterpublics' inward and outward address and through appreciation of the promise that critical publicity holds for greater inclusion in democratic processes. The authors in this volume contribute to the move to recognize permeable boundaries by amplifying the agonistics between counterpublics and states to shape the terrain of civil society and by foregrounding counterpublic agents' efforts to transform notions of the common good and to reprioritize items on public and official agendas. Furthermore, our authors' examination of diverse modes of discourse—poetic, rhetorical, demonstrative—shows that counterpublic agents often do not engage state authority in a deliberative mode, but that eschewal of deliberation does not necessarily constitute a failure on the part of counterpublic agents. Finally, the essays in this volume facilitate reconsideration of the separation between public sphere and state by revealing that structural relations between these two entities cannot be reduced to either complete separation or complete conflation. Through examination of specific encounters, our contributors demonstrate that different arrangements of state power may give rise to different kinds of publics, and newly emergent publics, as Dewey reminds us, may reconfigure state institutions.

In any field of academic inquiry, predicting future trends is a tricky endeavor. However, if the studies in this volume provide any indication, then public sphere studies ought to remain vibrant for the foreseeable future, for scholars and activists are likely to generate further reconfigurations in the public sphere. The following chapters engage public sphere studies at the intersection of theory and practice. They offer much needed case studies that make plain issues at stake in interactions between counterpublics and the state: political legitimacy, group and individual identity, political and economic transformation, personal rights and liberties, and social stability. The authors explore these issues through specific, often dramatic case studies that enable theoretical innovation as the complexities of counterpublic and state interactions disclose gaps and limitations in contemporary theory. Such explorations offer a pointed retort to those who bemoan the decline of public discourse (e.g., Sennett 1976; Lasch 1990). The discovery of engaged discourse in the public sphere is not the easiest of tasks, but the following chapters reveal that counterpublic and state interactions are sometimes the liveliest sites of such discourse.

NOTES

1. Hereafter cited as *Structural Transformation*. *Strukturwandel der Öffentlichkeit* has figured prominently in German debates regarding reconfigurations of first-generation Frankfurt School critical theory. On the German reception of Habermas's book prior to its English translation, see Hohendahl (1982).

2. This line of analysis has generated its own debates. Keith Michael Baker (1992), for instance, holds that Joan Landes reduces French revolutionary discourse to its Rousseauian variants, which defined the public sphere as essentially male and the private sphere as essentially female, and ignores alternative expressions that sought women's inclusion in public life, such as Condorcet's defense of women's political rights. Similarly, Dena Goodman (1992) charges that Landes's critique relies on too simple an opposition of public and private. In more recent work, Landes (1996, 296) acknowledges the existence of competing discourses on women's roles, but counters that none of the participants "wholly met the challenge of gender equality."

3. Our concern here for conceptual clarity earns further elaboration in Asen (2000).

4. New Social Movement theory has emerged from the larger body of public sphere theory, spurred largely by the publication of an article by Habermas in 1981 titled "New Social Movements." Other theorists of NSMs such as Alberto Melucci (1985, 1996) and Claus Offe (1985) have discerned a notable contrast between "old" and "new" social movements, particularly a move away from redistributive politics and toward symbolic politics.

5. To reach the same level of usership, it took radio thirty-eight years, personal computers sixteen years, and the television thirteen years (cited in United Nations Development Programme [UNDP] 1999, 58).

6. Consider, for example, that 93.3 percent of users are residents of the top fifth of the world's richest countries (UNDP 2), a figure that dramatizes the extraordinary difficulty that residents in developing and non-developed nations have in gaining access. Even if these residents did gain access, they would find that 80 percent of web sites and interfaces employ the language of English, a language that only one in ten people in the world speak (62). Statistics specific to the United States betray similar kinds of impediments to access. The 1999 National Telecommunications and Information Administration (NTIA) report shows that while all types of demographic groupings have greater access to telephony, computers, and the Internet, the rates of increase differ, sometimes dramatically, along the usual suspect demographic lines. Forty-two percent of those surveyed

owned personal computers (PCs); almost as many, 32.7 percent, had access to the Internet, with 26.2 percent having Internet access from home. But rates of PC ownership and Internet access were significantly differentiated along lines of race and ethnicity (Blacks and Hispanics were less likely to own and have access), income, education level, household type (single-parent families fared less well), age, region, and state. Availability of, access to, and competency with NCTs are all necessary considerations in efforts to account for the role of NCTs in social and political life. But these considerations presuppose that individuals actually *want access to* and *want to use* the technologies. The NTIA report cites a 1998 finding that among U.S. households that had never had Internet access, occupants of 25.7 percent of those households indicated that they "didn't want" Internet access. "Cost" accounted for 16.8 percent of respondents' reasons for not acquiring Internet access (NTIA, 5–8, 17).

REFERENCES

Ackerman, Bruce. 1993. Crediting the voters: A new beginning for campaign finance. *The American Prospect*, 21 March. http://epn.org/prospect/13/13acke.html (20 September 1999).
Appadurai, Arjun. 1996. *Modernity at large: Cultural dimensions of globalization.* Minneapolis: University of Minnesota Press.
Arendt, Hannah. 1958. *The human condition.* Chicago: University of Chicago Press.
Aronowitz, Stanley. 1993. Is democracy possible? The decline of the public in the American debate. In *The phantom public sphere*, edited by Bruce Robbins. Minneapolis: University of Minnesota Press.
Asen, Robert. 2000. Seeking the "counter" in counterpublics. *Communication Theory* 10:424–446.
Baker, Keith Michael. 1992. Defining the public sphere in eighteenth-century France: Variations on a theme by Habermas. In *Habermas and the public sphere*, edited by Craig Calhoun. Cambridge: Massachusetts Institute of Technology Press.
Bakhtin, Mikhail M. 1968. *Rabelais and his world.* Translated by Hélène Iswolsky. Cambridge: Massachusetts Institute of Technology Press.
Bauman, Zygmunt. 1998. *Globalization: The human consequences.* New York: Columbia University Press.
Beck, Ulrich. 1997. *The reinvention of politics: Rethinking modernity in the global social order.* Translated by Mark Ritter. Cambridge, England: Polity Press.

Benhabib, Seyla. 1992. *Situating the self: Gender, community, and postmodernism in contemporary ethics.* New York: Routledge.

———. 1996. Toward a deliberative model of democratic legitimacy. In *Democracy and difference: Contesting the boundaries of the political,* edited by Seyla Benhabib. Princeton, NJ: Princeton University Press.

Black Public Sphere Collective, ed. 1995. *The black public sphere: A public culture book.* Chicago: University of Chicago Press.

Bohman, James. 1996. *Public deliberation: Pluralism, complexity, and democracy.* Cambridge: Massachusetts Institute of Technology Press.

Bornstein, David. 1999. A force now in the world, citizens flex social muscle. *New York Times,* 10 July.

Calhoun, Craig. 1998. Community without propinquity revisited: Communications technology and the transformation of the urban public sphere. *Sociological Inquiry* 68:373–397.

Cerulo, Karen A., and Janet M. Ruane. 1998. Coming together: New taxonomies for the analysis of social relations. *Sociological Inquiry* 68:398–425.

Clinton, William Jefferson. 1998. Address to the nation on testimony before the independent counsel's grand jury. *Weekly Compilation of Presidential Documents* 34:1638–1639.

Cohen, Jean. 1996. Democracy, difference, and the right of privacy. In *Democracy and difference: Contesting the boundaries of the political,* edited by Seyla Benhabib. Princeton, NJ: Princeton University Press.

Cohen, Joshua. 1989. Deliberation and democratic legitimacy. In *The good polity: Normative analysis of the state,* edited by Alan Hamlin and Philip Pettit. Oxford: Blackwell.

———. 1997. Procedure and substance in deliberative democracy. In *Deliberative democracy: Essays on reason and politics,* edited by James Bohman and William Rehg. Cambridge: Massachusetts Institute of Technology Press.

Dean, Jodi. 1992. Including women: The consequences and side effects of feminist critiques of civil society. *Philosophy and Social Criticism* 18:379–406.

———. 1996. *Solidarity of strangers: Feminism after identity politics.* Berkeley: University of California Press.

Dewey, John. [1927] 1954. *The public and its problems.* Reprint, Athens, OH: Swallow Press.

Eley, Geoff. 1992. Nations, publics, and political cultures: Placing Habermas in the nineteenth century. In *Habermas and the public sphere,* edited by Craig Calhoun. Cambridge: Massachusetts Institute of Technology Press.

Estlund, David. 1997. Beyond fairness and deliberation: The epistemic dimension of public authority. In *Deliberative democracy: Essays on reason and politics*, edited by James Bohman and William Rehg. Cambridge: Massachusetts Institute of Technology Press.

Felski, Rita. 1989. *Beyond feminist aesthetics: Feminist literature and social change*. Cambridge: Harvard University Press.

Fishkin, James. 1991. *Democracy and deliberation: New directions for democratic reform*. New Haven, CT: Yale University Press.

———. 1995. *The voice of the people: Public opinions and democracy*. New Haven, CT: Yale University Press.

Fleming, Marie. 1993. Women and the "public use of reason." *Social Theory and Practice* 19:27–50.

Fraser, Nancy. 1992a. Rethinking the public sphere: A contribution to the critique of actually existing democracy. In *Habermas and the public sphere*, edited by Craig Calhoun. Cambridge: Massachusetts Institute of Technology Press.

———. 1992b. Sex, lies, and the public sphere: Some reflections on the confirmation of Clarence Thomas. *Critical Inquiry* 18:595–612.

Goodman, Dena. 1992. Public sphere and private life: Toward a synthesis of current historiographical approaches to the Old Regime. *History and Theory* 31:1–20.

Goodnight, G. Thomas. 1982. The personal, technical, and public spheres of argument: A speculative inquiry into the art of deliberation. *Journal of the American Forensic Association* 18:214–227.

———. 1987. Public discourse. *Critical Studies in Mass Communication* 4:428–432.

———. 1997. Opening up 'the spaces of public dissension.' *Communication Monographs* 64:270–275.

Goodnight, G. Thomas, and David B. Hingstman. 1997. Studies in the public sphere. *Quarterly Journal of Speech* 83:351–370.

Gregg, Richard B. 1971. The ego-function of the rhetoric of protest. *Philosophy & Rhetoric* 4:71–90.

Griffin, Cindy. 1996. The essentialist roots of the public sphere: A feminist critique. *Western Journal of Communication* 60:21–39.

Guinier, Lani. 1994. *The tyranny of the majority*. New York: Free Press.

Habermas, Jürgen. 1974. The public sphere: An encyclopedia article (1964). *New German Critique* 1:49–55.

———. 1981. New social movements. *Telos* 49:32–37.

———. 1985. Civil disobedience: Litmus test for the democratic constitutional state. *Berkeley Journal of Sociology* 30:95–116.

————. 1989. *The structural transformation of the public sphere: An inquiry into a category of bourgeois society.* Translated by Thomas Burger and Frederick Lawrence. Cambridge: Massachusetts Institute of Technology Press.

————. 1992. Further reflections on the public sphere. In *Habermas and the public sphere*, edited by Craig Calhoun. Cambridge: Massachusetts Institute of Technology Press.

————. 1996. *Between facts and norms: Contributions to a discourse theory of law and democracy.* Translated by William Rehg. Cambridge: Massachusetts Institute of Technology Press.

————. 1998. *The inclusion of the other: Studies in political theory.* Edited by Ciaran Cronin and Pablo De Greiff. Cambridge: Massachusetts Institute of Technology Press.

Harmon, Amy. 1998. 'Hacktivists' of all persuasions take their struggle to the web. *New York Times*, 31 October.

Hauser, Gerard A. 1998. Civil society and the principle of the public sphere. *Philosophy & Rhetoric* 31:19–40.

Held, David. 1998. Democracy and globalization. In *Re-imagining political community: Studies in cosmopolitan democracy*, edited by Daniele Archibugi, David Held, and Martin Köhler. Stanford, CA: Stanford University Press.

Hohendahl, Peter Uwe. 1982. *The institution of criticism.* Ithaca, NY: Cornell University Press.

Köhler, Martin. 1998. From the national to the cosmopolitan public sphere. In *Re-imagining political community: Studies in cosmopolitan democracy*, edited by Daniele Archibugi, David Held, and Martin Köhler. Stanford, CA: Stanford University Press.

Landes, Joan. 1988. *Women and the public sphere in the age of the French Revolution.* Ithaca, NY: Cornell University Press.

————. 1996. The performance of citizenship: Democracy, gender, and difference in the French Revolution. In *Democracy and difference: Contesting the boundaries of the political*, edited by Seyla Benhabib. Princeton, NJ: Princeton University Press.

Lasch, Christopher. 1990. Journalism, publicity, and the lost art of political argument. *Gannett Center Journal* 4:1–11.

Lavie, Smadar. 1990. *The poetics of military occupation: Mzeina allegories of Bedouin identity under Israeli and Egyptian rule.* Berkeley: University of California Press.

Lippmann, Walter. 1925. *The phantom public.* New York: Harcourt, Brace.

Lyotard, Jean-François. 1984. *The postmodern condition: A report on knowledge.* Translated by Geoff Bennington and Brian Massumi. Minneapolis: University of Minnesota Press.

Mansbridge, Jane. 1996. Using power/fighting power: The polity. In *Democracy and difference: Contesting the boundaries of the political*, edited by Seyla Benhabib. Princeton, NJ: Princeton University Press.

McCarthy, Thomas. 1992. Practical discourse: On the relation of morality to politics. In *Habermas and the public sphere*, edited by Craig Calhoun. Cambridge: Massachusetts Institute of Technology Press.

McClure, Kevin. 1996. The institutional subordination of contested issues: The case of Pittsburgh's steelworkers and ministers. *Communication Quarterly* 44:487–501.

Melucci, Alberto. 1985. The symbolic challenge of contemporary movements. *Social Research* 52:789–816.

———. 1996. *Challenging codes: Collective action in the information age.* New York: Cambridge University Press.

National Telecommunications and Information Administration (NTIA). 1999. *Falling through the Net: Defining the digital divide.* http://www.ntia.doc.gov/ntiahome/fttn99 (28 July 1999).

Negt, Oskar, and Alexander Kluge. 1993. *Public sphere and experience: Toward an analysis of the bourgeois and proletarian public sphere.* Translated by Peter Labanyi, Jamie Owen Daniel, and Assenka Oksiloff. Minneapolis: University of Minnesota Press.

Offe, Claus. 1985. New social movements: Challenging the boundaries of institutional politics. *Social Research* 52:817–868.

Pateman, Carole. 1988. The fraternal social contract. In *Civil society and the state: New European perspectives*, edited by John Keane. London: Verso.

Phillips, Kendall. 1996. The spaces of public dissension: Reconsidering the public sphere. *Communication Monographs* 63:231–247.

Robbins, Bruce. 1993. Introduction: The public as phantom. In *The Phantom Public Sphere*, edited by Bruce Robbins. Minneapolis: University of Minnesota Press.

Ryan, Mary P. 1990. *Women in public: Between banners and ballots, 1825–1880.* Baltimore: Johns Hopkins University Press.

Sassen, Saskia. 1996. *Losing control? Sovereignty in an age of globalization.* New York: Columbia University Press.

Schudson, Michael. 1992. Was there ever a public sphere? If so, when? Reflections on the American case. In *Habermas and the public sphere*, edited by Craig Calhoun. Cambridge: Massachusetts Institute of Technology Press.

———. 1994. The 'public sphere' and its problems: Bringing the state (back) in. *Notre Dame Journal of Law, Ethics, & Public Policy* 8:529–546.

Scott, James C. 1985. *Weapons of the weak: Everyday forms of peasant resistance*. New Haven, CT: Yale University Press.

——. 1990. *Domination and the arts of resistance: Hidden transcripts*. New Haven, CT: Yale University Press.

Sennett, Richard. 1976. The fall of public man. New York: Alfred A. Knopf.

Smith, Anthony D. 1995. *Nations and nationalism in a global era*. Cambridge, UK: Polity Press.

Taylor, Charles. 1995. *Philosophical arguments*. Cambridge, MA: Harvard University Press.

Tsagarousianou, Roza. 1998. Electronic democracy and the public sphere: Opportunities and challenges. In *Cyberdemocracy: Technology, cities, and civic networks*, edited by Roza Tsagarousianou, Damian Tambini, and Cathy Bryan. London: Routledge.

Tsing, Anna Lowenhaupt. 1993. *In the realm of the diamond queen: Marginality in an out-of-the-way place*. Princeton, NJ: Princeton University Press.

United Nations Development Programme (UNDP). 1999. *Human development report*. http://www.undp.org/hdro/99.htm (23 July 1999).

Willard, Charles Arthur. 1996. *Liberalism and the problem of knowledge: A new rhetoric for a modern democracy*. Chicago: University of Chicago Press.

Williams, Raymond. 1985. *Keywords: A vocabulary of culture and society*, rev. ed. New York: Oxford University Press.

Young, Iris Marion. 1996. Communication and the other: Beyond deliberative democracy. In *Democracy and difference: Contesting the boundaries of the political*, edited by Seyla Benhabib. Princeton, NJ: Princeton University Press.

——. 1997. Difference as a resource for democratic communication. In *Deliberative democracy: Essays on reason and politics*, edited by James Bohman and William Rehg. Cambridge: Massachusetts Institute of Technology Press.

Part I

Conflicted Encounters

1 Prisoners of Conscience and the Counterpublic Sphere of Prison Writing

The Stones that Start the Avalanche

GERARD A. HAUSER

The idea that the people reign has been a staple of Western political systems since Greek antiquity and is firmly embedded in Western political discourse. Appeals to "the people" (McGee 1975) undeniably carry political cachet, but they also reflect acknowledgment by lawmakers and leaders that their acts require authorization (Bitzer 1978). Democratic leaders especially rely on public discussion of the people's business to solicit and solidify public support. In this light the ancient Athenian experience that linked the people to rhetorical discourse becomes more than a vestige of democracy's origin. Historically, Western politics has sustained the connection between discourse on civic issues and setting public policy. It has regarded the people's interests as its rhetorical, if not theoretical, foundation and has narrated advancing their interests as a primary virtue of good governance. For this reason, the principle of the public sphere is basic to the possibility of a liberal democracy. It theorizes the arenas in which a liberal democracy protects the rights and advances the interests of the governed insofar as they may constitute themselves as a public—an interdependent and active body of society's nonvested members who exist outside of power (such as the state), whose rights and interests are at stake, and who attempt, through expressions of opinion, to influence how power will address these interests.

A public's power rests on its capacity to express its opinion. The *sine qua non* for this activity is the public sphere. As Habermas (1974, 1989)

35

has argued, and numerous other scholars have agreed (Barber 1984; Dryzek 1990; Farrell 1993; Fishkin 1995; Fraser 1992; Goodnight 1982; Hauser 1999; Rodger 1985; Yankelovich 1991), the rational basis of public opinion requires the existence of a discursive space of open arenas in which individuals and groups can associate and discuss matters of mutual interest and, where possible, reach a common judgment about them. In its absence, public opinion would be reduced to a volatile expression of mood, as is often reflected in the spikes and dips of opinion polls (Hauser 1998). The concept of the public sphere projects a civil society's agency for its ongoing negotiation of how its members shall act and interact. It is the locus of emergence for a civil society's rhetorically salient meanings. Consequently, the existence and defining conditions of the public sphere open to us bear directly on the character and quality of our civic and civil existence.

The claim that a public sphere is a discursive space has important theoretical implications. Among them, and relevant to this discussion, it implies that specific public spheres are defined by the conditions for communication and the character of the communication that transpires there. In this respect, public spheres are definitively rhetorical. A public sphere's discursive character implies that although institutional guarantees are essential for a free society to engage in the democratic practices of public deliberation, we can conceive of public spheres emerging in the absence of such guarantees, provided certain antecedent rhetorical conditions are met. It implies a relationship between the character of discourse and the quality of judgments it produces. Insofar as a public sphere excludes ideas and speakers through impermeable boundaries, privileges public relations over deliberation, enforces the technical jargon of elites over contextualized language specific to issues and their consequences, limits believable appearance before an audience of strangers on the basis of class and identity, presupposes conformity of values and ends, and imposes a preordained orientation, its discursive features compromise the rational integrity of its outcomes and undermine its status as a *public* sphere. These requirements make the public sphere a normative rather than descriptive concept. Finally, when official public spheres repress the emergence of rhetorically salient meanings, those meanings are likely to emerge elsewhere in oppositional sites, or counterpublic spheres.

A counterpublic sphere is, by definition, a site of resistance. Its impetus may arise from myriad causes, but its rhetorical identity is as an arena for hearing proscribed voices, expressing proscribed ideas, and entertaining the alternative reality they advance to the existing order. Sometimes this resistance is militant, as in an underground movement, and sometimes it is apparently benign, as in the counterpublic sphere of a minority community enacting its own internal business. But even in benign cases, their discourse speaks, if ever so subtly, of an alternative reality to that of the majority culture and their exclusion from its processes of decision making that bear on their lives. Equally, when the excluded group gains inclusion in the public spheres of influence, the raison d'être for its counterpublic sphere diminishes and may even disappear, as Susan Herbst's (1994) study of Chicago's black community from the 1930s to the 1960s shows. There, once leaders of Chicago's excluded black community gained access to the city's official public sphere, that community's counterpublic sphere was no longer needed to provide political and social organization. Although there are instances of such spheres with longevity, their opposition invariably grows from a power differential that excludes their issues and/or voices from general consideration and weight in official judgment. Were they acknowledged the need for resistance would disappear and with it the counterpublic sphere. That, of course, also would usher in a utopian era. In actually existing democracies, where power differentials and resistance are real, counterpublic spheres remain important sources of political activity.

As a site of resistance, a counterpublic sphere contains valuable evidence of the ongoing struggle over society's self-production. Society's struggle to appropriate and reappropriate resources includes conflict over symbolic resources, as social actors seek control of rhetorically salient meanings that may claim political allegiance and inspire coordinated action. As a significant segment of society finds its aspirations cannot be expressed in the language of public spheres that matter to the state or the language of relevant decision-making bodies for nonpolitical public spheres, the currency grows for alternative arenas in which a more congenial language prevails. This growth increases the chance of coordinated resistance. The ability of a counterpublic sphere to foster resistance and the level of that resistance are functions of its reach across society. As we learned from the fall of the Soviet bloc, rhetorical resistance in a subterranean arena can foster a level of consensus so great that this counterpublic sphere may eventually displace the official arena as the locus of legitimation. This potential to inspire effective resistance and change is especially evident in the writings of prisoners of conscience.

Prisoners of conscience are unlike ordinary felons in that their incarceration grows from the threat of their ideas. Often they have not broken laws, other than the unspoken one prohibiting disagreement with a totalitarian power. Removing them from society takes the calculated risk that the fragility of political memory will facilitate airbrushing the dissident from her own political archive.

As recent history has demonstrated, the threat of being airbrushed from one's own political archive is both real and pervasive. In both hemispheres repressive regimes have shown their willingness to liquidate leading dissidents and even entire ethnic groups with genocidal fervor. However, the impulse toward a pogrom may be checked in cases where the opposition has been highly publicized and the enemy defined less on group identity than ideological differences. There prudence dictates that mere incarceration will suffice. Against the risk that the prisoner of conscience will find his or her way into the public imagination as a symbol of the state's alien ethos, the regime calculates that removal from public view will toll the dissident's political death knell. It banks on intimidation forcing oppositional politics underground where, if politics continues at all, it is convoluted to accommodate an inverted domain in which discourses and actions intended to influence public life are transacted in tenebrous enclaves that carry the risk of political and even physical extermination if discovered. This may be an environment breeding disaffection, but without the yeast of leading dissident voices disaffection often succumbs to the toxicity of cynicism. The aspirations alive in a counterpublic sphere are unlikely to penetrate public imagination and overpower the existing order's claim to legitimacy without rhetorical champions. By the same token, the prisoner of conscience remains alive as a viable political being only through the channels of the political counterpublic sphere.

The prisoner of conscience with clandestine means to communicate not only survives but often leads. The political prisoner may be exiled from public life, but this exile contains a political paradox. Impounded in environs intended for civic eunuchs, imprisonment removes the activist's voice from the epicenter of evolving events. At the same time, political imprisonment bestows a perverse imprimatur, since one presumes the state would feel no need to remove the political prisoner from society were he or she unimportant. Through incarceration, the prisoner's messages acquire an aura of authority to direct thought and action against the existing order, as Martin Luther King, Jr.'s, "Letter from Birmingham Jail" eloquently testifies (see Baker 1995, 18–19). Consequently, prison writings form a valuable source of information and insight into the ways by which movements are shaped and community sustained in discourses that are banished from official public life, though not necessarily from the general public's view. They offer insight into the power of the counterpublic sphere as a locus of resistance with the potential to invert society's ostensible power vectors.

In this chapter I consider how Adam Michnik's letter from Bialoleka prison, "Why You Are Not Signing," contributed to sustaining a definition of social identity essential for a social movement to survive. I will examine it as a source of strategic guidance for the members of the Polish trade union Solidarity during the early stages of martial law imposed by the regime of General Wojciech Jaruzelski. I will argue that Michnik valorized his counterpublic sphere of political dissidence and resistance as a lifeworld of unsentimental cultural commitments that formed an alternative to the official public sphere and hastened the migration of Poland's political center of gravity from the state to civil society.

COPING WITH TERROR

The realities of prison are somewhat different for prisoners of conscience than for convicted felons in that political prisoners represent a source of power to the authorities who have jailed them and the warders now responsible for their bodies. When a Václav Havel or Stefan Cardinal Wyszynski is imprisoned or detained, his incarceration becomes a source of rhetorical invention. His removal enters public imagination as a synecdochic representation of the struggle against political ills. Partisan appeals memorialize him as a model of political principle. When such celebrated opponents of repressive regimes as Nelson Mandela or Aung San Suu Kyi refused to cave, dissident rhetoric transformed their confrontation with authorities into the state's tacit acknowledgment of their cause's superiority. Without rhetoric capable of commanding its citizens' minds and hearts, the state is reduced to using force.

Within prison, the external world's war of words often migrates to the prisoner's body. A confession of guilt, recantation, or renunciation of the dissident movement itself can be publicized to reap the dissident's political demise. Often the means to this end is torture. Accounts of prison life such as Elaine Scarry's (1985) meditation on pain, Havel's (1989) detailed letters to his spouse, or Irina Ratushinskaya's (1989) account of confrontations with her warders chronicle how the prisoner's body comes under assault. As Jacobo Timerman (1981) details in *Prisoner without a Name, Cell without a Number*, the cruelties of prison come not only from beatings and torture but from insulting treatment, isolation, physically exhausting and degrading conditions of internment, and psychological abuse. Not the least of these is the captor's insistence that one's pain and degradation are self-imposed. The prisoner need only recant to gain release from this nightmare of horror. But to choose one's physical life by such means is also to choose political euthanasia.

The prison writer has already resolved this dilemma by electing to remain a political prisoner. The more salient problem is the rhetorical

method for confronting terror within the prevailing constraints of communication. Through letters smuggled to the outside the prisoner of conscience offers testimony to the value of resistance and keeps the call to
identity alive. Her rhetorical practice speaks an alternative language
advancing an alternative political aspiration to the existing power, and its
currency serves as a further indictment of the state's alien status in the eyes
of the governed.

James Boyd White (1984) offers us guidance here. In *When Words
Lose Their Meaning*, White is concerned with the problem caused by confrontation with reality that can no longer be explained and acted on with
the language we use to represent it. In such a context rhetorical invention
opens the possibility of forging a new relationship with a public in need of a
language able to explain its world and offer guidance for acting in it. This
inventional possibility, in White's view, grows from the relationship with
readers constituted by the writer's language. Speaking of the reader, he says:

> This is reading of a reconstructive and participatory kind, an
> active engagement with the materials of the text in order to
> learn about the real or imagined world of which they are a
> part. The hope is that we can establish some sense of the rela-
> tionship that exists between the speaker and the materials of
> his culture; that we can experience from the inside, with the
> intimacy of the artisan, if only in a tentative and momentary
> way, the life of the language that makes a world. (9)

White's concern with how the writer constitutes a textual community is apropos of the prison writer. Imprisonment institutionalizes the
political dissident's already marginalized condition by isolating him from
society as a public menace. But isolation makes the prisoner's writings a
form of interpretive marginalia: notes, criticism, questions, interpretations, reading rules that bring the text of society within our power by
telling us how to come to terms with it. How the prison writer deals with
being isolated—how he imagines each audience, how she constructs her
language—constitutes a textual community that the dissident hopes will
reconstitute society. The political prisoner finds herself like a stone in the
avalanche of events.[1] Her writings, inadvertently inscribed by the established order as threatening to its existence, stake a unique claim to influence, sustain and even redirect social momentum already in process. Her
rhetorical choices are, in that sense, sources of opportunity to shape the
political future. This was the opportunity seized by Adam Michnik, a Solidarity leader arrested and imprisoned following the imposition of martial
law in Poland on 13 December 1981.

DISSIDENCE REPRESSED

The Gdansk Agreement of 1980 had given Solidarity institutional status as a trade union. As such it had legitimacy as a representative of Polish workers' interests apart from the Communist Party. But it created more than a trade union, since the twenty-one worker demands conceded in the agreement itself were not narrowly focused on the broad economic concerns that had precipitated the national wave of strikes in Poland during the summer of 1980. For this discussion the first six concessions are especially noteworthy: the right to representation, the right to strike, the right to open expression, the right to religious expression, the right to disagree, and the right to information. Each of these points is a demand related to discourse: to speak, to be heard, and to have one's words taken seriously.

These demands echoed those in Jacek Kuron and Karol Modzelewski's "Open Letter to the Party" (1968), an underground document calling on the Party to reform itself and make Poland into a true Marxist state, and views that evolved independently among Polish intellectuals between 1976 and 1980 (Curry 1983, 156). During the sixteen months between its legalization and official decertification after General Jaruzelski imposed martial law, Solidarity was a paradigm of social actors attempting to define society. The strike actions and subsequent deliberations in the Gdansk shipyard at Solidarity's inception and the movement's subsequent congresses were observed and reported as politics and rhetoric at work. Each dialogizing[2] episode problematized the assumptions of participants as well as the state, located common concerns, discovered the possibilities for a new, more desirable social order, and exercised their members' freedom to develop shared opinion about the shape it should take. The union's organizational independence from the Party meant that formal and informal interactions among its members were, by definition, discursive acts of resistance. Members operationally defined Solidarity as a realm for deliberative discourse on public issues. Its independence from the state and insistence that its emerging opinions should influence parliamentary action transformed the counterpublic sphere of Polish dissidence into an arena that encroached on the official public sphere of Polish politics.

Early in December 1981, the leaders of Solidarity were engaged in heated debate over the future course of the union's activities. Lech Walesa believed the time was not right to press hard choices on the regime. He advocated negotiating in order to secure more firmly the legitimate place of Solidarity in the economic decision making of the state. More militant members were urging an increasingly aggressive pursuit of political power-sharing with the Party. In protest of Walesa's apparent willingness to be conciliatory, Andrzej Gwiadzda and fourteen members of the Gdansk Solidarity commission resigned three weeks before the military coup.

In addition to disputes among the leadership, a cleavage was developing among the rank-and-file concerning Solidarity's objectives. In his study of Solidarity, Alain Touraine (1983) found that various regions in Poland were attributing different meanings to the union and the movement and that these differences seemed to place its membership at odds over the nature of their shared enterprise. By October 1981, workers in Gdansk were still defining the union's meaning in terms of the Gdansk Agreements. They considered Solidarity to be a free trade union and judged its activities in this light. They were concerned that the rest of the membership seemed to be losing sight of the union's objectives. In the mining regions of Katowice, workers were defining their activities in terms of economic gains. They were beginning to express discouragement that resistance had not improved their economic condition. In Warsaw, discussion of Solidarity had acquired more theoretical overtones, as members speculated about the union moving Polish society toward a system of self-management such as Yugoslavia's. These differences suggested to Touraine's team of sociologists that the movement was showing signs of fragmentation, as the initial enthusiasm from forcing the government to recognize their legitimacy gave way to the realities of Poland's desperate economy.

Against this backdrop, Solidarity leaders were occupied with strategies to keep the union united and to keep pressure on the government and the Party for cooperation. The government's military action that cordoned the country and subsequent declaration of a state of war caught Solidarity's leadership, along with the Polish people, by surprise. The outlawing of Solidarity and the detention of 10,000 of its leaders, accompanied by the imposition of martial law, threatened the continued existence of the union as a source of opposition to the regime and hope for participation in the political life of the nation. The writings of Adam Michnik were important in this context to sustain and direct Poland's future course.

Since his undergraduate days, Michnik was among Poland's leading dissidents. He was a frequent critic of the Communist Party and was among the drafters of a blueprint for reestablishing Polish civil society. Among the tenets of this plan was an insistence on open communication. This meant that, as a newspaper editor and also as a leader in the Solidarity movement, Michnik had national visibility both for his dissident opinion and his confrontations with the state.

Michnik's letters are an intervention in the juggernaut of intimidation following the state of martial law. Their inspiration lies in the dissident blueprint for a democratic Polish society capable of existing within the sphere of Soviet influence. Referring to that blueprint in another place, Michnik (1985, xxvi) wrote: "I believe that what sets today's opposition apart from the proponents of those ideas of reform in the past is the belief that a program for evolution ought to be addressed to independent public opinion, and not totalitarian power. Such a program would offer advice to the people regarding how to behave, not to the government regarding how to reform itself." His letters reflect a conscious choice, therefore, not to direct his remarks to or against the government. Although his writings drip with sarcasm in their references to the state and Party leaders, they focus on the possibilities for creating a free society and for the choices that must be made to accomplish this end. Illustrative is the letter "Why You Are Not Signing" (Michnik 1985).

THE RETURN OF THE ACTOR

Dated 25 March 1982, from Bialoleka Internment Camp, "Why You Are Not Signing" confronts the issue of whether to sign a loyalty declaration to the government.[3] The state had offered to release imprisoned Solidarity members who agreed to do this. The letter offers compelling reasons to resist. The integrity of its argument depends less on its logical structure than on its powers of depiction. Michnik recounts experiences with police brutality and duplicity through a narrative that seeks to demonstrate the very principles on which the Polish people may be energized to continued activism.

Michnik's main interest in "Why You Are Not Signing" is to bring a sense of orderliness to the public disorder instigated by the imposition of martial law. Certainly for the members of Solidarity, now outlawed, declared irrelevant to Polish civic life, and transformed against their wishes into an underground movement, there were seeds both for despondency and capitulation and for reckless acts of resistance.

Following the declaration of war, Polish society was subjected to a massive propaganda effort to discredit Solidarity. The official public sphere, dominated by the state-controlled press and the Party, portrayed Solidarity as instrumental in forcing the imposition of martial law. It alleged that Solidarity wished to challenge the state's authority in Polish public life. By discrediting the union, the Party hoped the absence of active dissident leadership might induce political lassitude among a people grown weary of resistance without apparent results. Outlawing the union and jailing its leaders created a political vacuum that the Party sought to fill by asserting itself as the leading edge of Polish public life.

For Solidarity leaders, of greater concern than lassitude was the possibility that frustration and anger over a coup by the ruling government would lead to violence. Michnik's objectives unmistakably are to lead the now incarcerated and underground Solidarity members in another direction. "Let me make myself clear," he writes, "this is not a program of romantic intransigence but rather a strategy for social resistance" (11).

If a political prisoner's reality includes the constant threat of terror, then the reality of martial law generalizes this threat. Under martial law, orderliness is not synonymous with calm, and the prevailing circumstances in Poland following Jaruzelski's declaration of a state of war made calm unlikely in public life. Michnik seeks the orderliness that comes from holding a defined objective and a plan to reach it. It is the antidote to spasms of public outrage that provoke violence but leave the essential problem unresolved.

Solidarity is a step on Michnik's journey to democratize Polish society. From his perspective, Solidarity's transformation from a legitimate voice in Poland's political process to a disenfranchised dissident movement scrambling to reassemble a viable discursive domain as a counterpublic sphere of resistance is a temporary setback. In past setbacks the historical struggle has always continued. Solidarity represents a force for institutional change only if there is solidarity among its rank and file. More fundamental than institutional forms of opposition are individual commitments of those striving to reform Polish society. In practical terms, democratization begins with individual acts of responsibility.

"Why You Are Not Signing" is a plea for maintaining a sense of social direction among Poles. Polish dissidents had not advocated overthrowing the state nor removing Poland from the Soviet sphere of influence. The goal of democratization implied a state with alternatives to the Party and institutional practices that guaranteed dissident voices would have a greater say in matters of governance. Solidarity sought entry to the official public sphere of political deliberation. Signing a loyalty oath would undermine this goal. It would commit one to the final step of supporting the existing order in whatever measures it enacted. Clearly this would put an end to Solidarity as an arena for political opinion formation. It also would end the political viability of its leaders. More important, it would terminate the process of Poles seeking to legitimize a *national* voice distinct from the state's in Polish society and governance. The letter finds its rationale for continued refusal by enmeshing its reader in claims of personal responsibility that make signing an act of betrayal.

Michnik addresses his letter to "My dear friend," a subject whose identity is kept fluid throughout the text through references to an ambiguous *you*. Could *you* be the Polish people? or the reader? or Michnik himself? By not specifying the subject he situates his reader inside incidents and personal experiences that transpired during the military takeover and its aftermath. He engages his reader in an active interpretation of a narrative that not only tells another's story but serves as a mirror reflecting the self as the social actor who chooses democracy. The reader is clear that in many of these passages Michnik is talking about himself, but he also uses a tone of address that suggests familiarity with his reader. *You* have shared common experiences with this writer. These specific events may be from Michnik's life, but they could have happened to *you*. And the responses reported might be the ones Michnik made, but the ambiguity of *you* allows them to be read as the assessments of a confidante and friend who knows your commitments. Surely these responses are the ones *you* made in your own confrontation with the authorities, or would have made if confronted with these choices. In this way the text creates a profound identification with its readers, implicating them in a community of commitments and values populated by others on whom *you* can rely.

The basis for this community, Michnik insists, is moral action. He equates "moral" with conduct that is self-evidently right. The banality of such truths, Michnik observes (10–11), "if they are to remain banal, must be remembered, especially at times when banal behavior requires some courage, whereas relativism—which incidentally does serve a purpose in intellectual activity—can lead people to dilute moral standards and question what should be morally self-evident." Among the most basic of these truths is the primacy of human dignity. Nothing that compromises human dignity can ever be other than evil. Honoring the dignity of every human is necessary for the individual responsibility that lies at the core of Michnik's vision for a moral actor and for constituting a moral community.

Michnik restrains his reader from theoretical speculations on the nature of social relations with rhetoric not easily transformed into a social theory. Instead he reminds *you* of experiences that are close to the terror and brutality of the times. Expedient choices may appear to produce political advantage, but personal experience tells *you* that principle alone can sustain *you* against the authorities' duplicity. He writes:

> Impotence in the face of armed evil is probably the worst of human humiliations. When six hulks pin you to the ground, you are helpless. But you do not want to give up your natural right to dignity: you are not going to reach any agreements with the ruffians, you are not going to make any commitments. When they take you from your house, beat you with all their might, burn your eyes with tear gas, break open your front door with a crowbar and wreck your furniture right in front of your family, when in the middle of the night they

drive you to the police station in handcuffs and order you to
sign statements, then your ordinary instinct for self-preservation and your basic sense of human dignity will make you say
NO. (5)

The narrative's drumbeat of abuses signifies failure by a regime unworthy
of personal allegiance. How could *you* pledge loyalty to such authorities
without your oath contracting a Faustian bargain? The particularity of
these brutalities confronts the principle of "your natural right to human
dignity," and that principle makes these assaults meaningful in a way that
diminishes their effectiveness as coercion to complicity. Signing would be
an act of self-betrayal.

The principle of human dignity that leads *you* to resist in the face of
beatings also fortifies *you* in prison. Friends ask him why he does not sign.
This would give him his freedom. Michnik's response defines the value of
physical freedom through the lens of Poland's corrupted public life that
makes a public sphere impossible and shifts self-interest to the side of not
signing. If *you* sign:

The steel gates of Bialoleka will open before you, and instead
of the prison yards you will see the streets of your hometown,
filled with strolling army patrols and rolling tanks. You will see
people being asked for identification cards, cars being stopped
to have their trunks inspected, the security agent, with his keen
eye, fishing out of the crowds individuals suspected of "violat-
ing the state of war legislation." You will hear World War II
terms that until now you knew only from history books:
"roundup," "Volksliste"—words cleansed of the dignifying
patina of time and pulsing with new menace. You will hear
about new arrests, about people sought by the police or in
hiding, about Draconian sentences.
And if you are capable of making self-interested decisions,
then the first reason for not signing is: it isn't worth it. (3–4)

Remaining in prison is no worse than being on the streets, and it has certain advantages. In prison, the authorities take *you* seriously and, whereas
the streets are filled with cynics and stool pigeons, here *you* know the
character of those you meet. Compared to the streets, "Bialoleka is a
moral luxury and an oasis of dignity" (4).

By defining moral action in experiential terms Michnik heightens the
individual's importance. Each individual is the prime determiner of personal choice. Consequently, even those who have decided to sign the loy-

alty oath are not condemned. Michnik recognizes that there may be extenuating circumstances, that incomprehensible pressures or uncompromising torture may lead one to sign.

> The choice is always up to the individual—to the voice of his or her conscience and reason: no one can condemn anyone else's choice. Ostracism would play into the hands of the people in power, since this is precisely what they want—to break society's resistance and the solidarity of the people by creating divisions. To tolerate and understand, however, is not to decide the act of signing the declaration is in itself morally indifferent. It is not. Every loyalty declaration is an evil; and a declaration that was forced out of you was an evil that you were forced to commit, although it may, at times, be a lesser evil. So this act sometimes deserves understanding, always compassion, but never praise. (5)

Michnik accomplishes the hard work of keeping his audience unified by playing off the expectations of the other side. The authorities expect society to turn against those who sign the oath, to regard signers as traitors to the cause of Polish resistance. But through dissociation—"techniques of separation which have the purpose of dissociating, separating, disuniting elements which [*sic*] are regarded as forming a whole" (Perelman and Olbrechts-Tyteca 1969, 190)—Michnik segregates even those who have signed from the evil of those in power.

Still, as much as specific cases may elicit our sympathy and as much as judgment of others' motives may be inappropriate, Michnik is uncompromising in holding that individual acts do not alter the self-evidence of moral truths and that a society can survive only if it is based on moral foundations. In the absence of institutional guarantees, morality secures the possibility of civil society and a vibrant public sphere. Political circumstances that obliterate a viable civil society of open exchange force the principle of publicity into a counterpublic sphere of underground discourse. In that environment personal responsibility alone protects the possibility of a discourse freed from hypocrisy and possessed of sufficient moral weight to alter the course of events.

In a formulation that mirrors the three levels of community found in classical rhetoric—the absolute, prudence, and patriotism—Michnik advances three reasons for not signing: human dignity does not allow it, common sense tells you signing will actually forfeit your freedom, and national memory dictates that resistance honors Poland's political heritage. Through a succession of contrasts between the acts of the authorities and the choices *you* make in response, Michnik provides the reader with the experiential bases for choosing to remain a political prisoner, and he provides the ethos for a community grounded in human dignity. The cascade of oppression unleashed by the state may have seemed overwhelming to most Poles, but Michnik finds strength in reaffirming personal subjectivity. His argument foreshadows the dramatic ending to his letter by depicting subjective choice as influencing the eventual course of whatever passes over *you*. In this sense, his readers, as subjects, are constituted into a textual community of stones influencing the course of an avalanche.

He recounts the night of the military coup and the rush of thoughts *you* try to control amid your lack of information. *You* try to make sense of why *you* have been arrested.

> Only when, a few hours later, they drive you in the direction of Bialoleka . . . will you hear on the prison van's radio, as your teeth chatter from the cold (these circumstances will later be called "humane conditions"), that war has been declared on your nation. It was declared by people who on behalf of this nation govern, proclaim, sign international agreements—the same people who publicly held out a conciliatory hand while secretly issuing orders to hunt us in the night. (5)

The government's duplicity in hunting "us"—perhaps a collective *you*—contrasts with the, yet unknown to *you*, collective brave acts of others—the massacre of miners who will resist the government in the Wujek mine, the soon-to-follow images of friends forced into exile or already sentenced. But *you* know that "you will not make a gift of your loyalty declaration to these people, for they are incapable of any loyalty whatsoever"; that "to sign this declaration would be to negate yourself, to wipe out the meaning of your life; to betray the people who have faith in you" (6). The competing ethical valences in these depictions constitute a polarity between the authorities of the state and the nation of Polish people they govern and argue through implication for your refusal to sign.

The contrast of worlds continues as he explores further the psychology of the police who are seeking your complicity. Michnik invites the reader to consider that, quite apart from the absence of common sense in striking an agreement with people given to arbitrary behavior, the police live in a world where life has no intrinsic meaning. That is why *you* can think of no one who has entered an agreement with them and not felt cheated.

> To these people with their lifeless but shifting eyes, with their minds that are dull but skilled in torture, with their defiled

souls that yearn for social approval, you are only raw material to work with. They have their own particular psychology: they believe that anyone can be talked into anything (in other words, everyone can be either bought or intimidated). To them it is only a matter of price to pay or pain to inflict. Although they act according to routine, your every stumble, your every fall gives meaning to their lives. Your capitulation is no mere professional achievement for them—it is their *raison d'être.* (6–7)

This is not a rational world where intelligent discourse may lead somewhere, but the twisted regime of imposed fear; and Michnik provides his readers with a hermeneutics of its incorrigibility. The dialectic of this world is quite unlike any *you* have previously encountered. Here the existence of captors and inquisitors has no meaning except in their ability to impose themselves on their captives. They embody the eternal and demented debate between parasites of fear and the victim who knows, as the Polish philosopher Henryk Elzberg had observed, that "your participation cannot be gauged in terms of your chances for victory but rather by the value of your idea" (7). In this dreadful dialectic, *you* win not by gaining power "but when you remain faithful to yourself" (7).

In the face of incorrigibility, the choice of moral rectitude thus becomes an act of war. Without making unrealistic claims that the state will fall, Michnik places police brutality and intimidation in a context of obeying one's conscience. Refusal to sign the oath as an act of conscience, and therefore, as a morally self-evident choice, frames the beatings and humiliations in a way that dissipates their power. They have no more authority over the individual than the individual is willing to grant. Michnik's narrative of dissociation projects a bipolar choice between moral integrity and corruption. In this bipolar universe, fidelity to one's own conscience is a more effective means for laying siege to the fortress of evil than reciprocal violence. By refusing to cooperate, the victim of brutality reverses the power equation, as in Hegel's master-slave relationship, and triumphs through moral superiority. *You* will starve your victim to death. That is why *you* do not hate the policeman; he is the object of your pity. "You know that every one of them is ashamed in front of his children" (7).

Unlike the police, who have as their heritage the entirely forgettable names of executioners and informers cursed to pass into national oblivion, *you* have the legacy of Polish history—its heroes and its national life. Your memory tells you that the community of moral commitments is part of your tradition. *You* know that your country has been through this before—the partition, the German occupation, the betrayal at Yalta. But there has always been resistance to atomizing your national identity, and with resistance comes hope. The *true* Poland is memorialized in this collective memory; it lives in the counterpublic sphere of nonsigners who sustain it through dissociation from the *apparent* Poland of the state. "You know that in its [Poland's] history a loyalty declaration signed in jail has always been a disgrace, loyalty to oneself and to the national tradition a virtue" (8).

Michnik argues through another series of specific references to police brutality and to real events still unknown to *you* that the only way the police gain victory is if *you* deny your tradition and surrender hope. *You* still don't know that others have signed, but *you* do know that "no one is born an informer" (8). *You* know that you choose your own future; your history whispers that *you* can be like resisters of the past. By choosing to remain in prison *you* intensify the policeman's fear that he cannot control you. From his fear *you* know there is still hope. Michnik offers this as the sign of victory.

> So by refusing to talk with the policeman, by refusing to collaborate, by rejecting the status of informant, and by choosing to be a political prisoner you are defending hope. Not just hope within yourself and for yourself but also in others and for others. You are casting your declaration of hope out of your prison cell into the world, like a sealed bottle into the ocean. If even one single person finds it, you will have scored a victory. (10)

Michnik's summation projects the individual's act into a counterpublic sphere of resistance. But he also envisions the transformation of that sphere from a narrow resistance community, which knows only what it opposes, to a community of hope, defined by a vision of civic life to which it aspires. The conscious choice to remain a political prisoner rises beyond cynicism, in which political reality and possibility are defined by the authorities, to a course of action that bears allegiance to public memory. The dissociation between a true and apparent Poland that requires *you* not to sign sustains this memory in the public imagination. Individual victories will reform Polish society, at the very least, into a community that honors the principles he has used to delineate a universe of moral incorrigibility from one of individual responsibility, and ideally into one that practices a politics of moral action. Michnik's community of hope represents a self-limiting revolution that seeks to open Polish society to freedom of choice.

In detailing why *you* are not signing he follows his own prescription to "offer advice to the people regarding how to behave, not to the government regarding how to reform itself" (11). He offers his reader advice through appeals that shy away from analysis of underlying presuppositions to draw, instead, on sadly typical events in Poland during the 1970s and earlier and likely to have touched readers' lives. Although the abuses of the state are committed against each as an individual *you*, the transcendent issue is not the personal welfare of any given individual; it is the welfare of society. Signing only prolongs and clouds the issue by allowing the state to divert attention from its failures by questioning the sincerity of those who have asked society to sacrifice but themselves are willing to endorse the state. The real failure is the incompetence of the state. Refusing to cooperate forces this issue. Refusing to sign is, in Michnik's words, "not a program of romantic intransigence but rather a strategy of social resistance" (11).

Michnik's text is an example of the resistance he advocates. Its argument developed in terms of an ambiguous *you* makes no pretense to conceptual sophistication. It is organized and articulated in terms of the ordinary experiences that give meaning to life and that provide hope for a future. It affirms what *you* know to be true by citing examples and relations with a knowing but familiar voice that recites what everyone knows to be true. His concrete affirmations do not specify what type of community his reconstituted Poland will have but more generally they demonstrate the attitudes and actions required for Poles to proceed with its development.

Michnik develops this case in a voice that is rhetorically trustworthy. He abstains from a rhetoric of abstractions and ideological commitments. He talks in the voice of one who has endured what he asks his reader to endure. The reader knows that the *you* who has suffered these specific beatings and interrogations has chosen to talk about his own experience without attempting to draw attention to himself. He has chosen a literary convention that exemplifies what it means to be like a stone without claiming to be self-righteous.

Moreover, he writes in a narrative voice that establishes a relationship with his reader. He does not resort to clichés or polemics. He enters into conversation that reflects an assumed background of factual knowledge and common experiences. He shares observations that treat his reader as capable of making distinctions and of appreciating irony. Describing the soldiers imposing martial law as "strolling" on hometown streets, or Bialoleka prison as "an oasis of dignity," or the language of military rule as "words cleansed of the dignifying patina of time and pulsing with new menace," or the police as "defiled souls that yearn for social approval," as "ashamed in front of [their] children" reflects a mind that has thought about what it has observed. He seems capable of occupying the shoes of everyone, even the police. That sense of shared humanity rises above mere ideology and lends ethos to his voice.

Accounts like these do not argue in terms of propositions. They make points enthymematically as one does with a friend; one mentions and depicts in ways that leave the rest to be completed. Their mode of delivery is more a reminder of what is shared together and offers in it an interpretive mood that says, "Things are settled, we share the same world. We know its constituting events and moral code, as the opposition may never hope to know."

The familiar tone of such appeals suggests a respect for the reader as a thinking and feeling person. The moral, rational, and emotional orbit in which this letter is cast recognizes the complexity of human responses to the terror of prison and to the uncompromising moral stand he is taking. The reader is capable of responding (as does *you* throughout the letter) in ways that the police are not. Michnik writes with confidence that the reader can feel his argument and can make choices to inhabit a world of amity and hope.

At the end of his letter, after a brief excursus in which he critiques the strategic alternatives posed by other dissidents (so familiar that first name and last initial are all "dear friend" needs to identify them), Michnik expresses this hope most dramatically by returning to a second-person narrative to recount the emotional uncertainty at the time of arrest. *You* feel isolated and powerless. *You* don't know your fate. *You* don't know that months later there will be an underground structure, an underground press, and illegal union structures. In a community of hope, the overwhelming force of the state provides no excuse. Moral purpose requires that you stand your ground.

> You still don't know that the generals' vehicle is sinking in sand, its wheels spinning in place, that the avalanche of repression and calumnies is missing its aim.
>
> But you do know, as you stand alone, handcuffed, with your eyes filled with tear gas, in front of policemen who are shaking their guns at you—you can see it clearly in the dark and starless night, thanks to your favorite poet [Milosz]—that the course of the avalanche depends on the stones over which it rolls.
>
> And you want to be the stone that will reverse the course of events. (15)

The letter's ending transforms a seemingly exceptional heroic act into a fundamental one for self-preservation. Michnik insinuates the backdrop of terror without dwelling on it, allowing the choices *you* make to serve as a beacon of social conduct. Even if *you* had never encountered the police except as they are rhetorically constructed in this letter, its specificity provides each narrated scene with a moral compass in which there is a self-evident truth. Members of his textual community may wonder in the abstract whether or not they could withstand such terror, but there can be no doubt that to falter, to be anything but a "stone," would carry no honor.

Michnik's portrayal of Polish political life has a force that, finally, leaves his reader with no real choice but Michnik's own. His uncompromising stand against signing, his summoning of moral virtue in the service of a single choice, his steadfast emphasis on personal responsibility, his dismissal of the opposition as morally incorrigible invite the reader to live in a world where political relations go beyond partisan endorsement of one side and vilification of the other. Michnik's ideal reader turned conversant must become a social actor adhering to a rational plan and a common sense language to express it. His reader must endorse his world and its sentiments or be his enemy.

CONCLUSION

On 27 September 1983, Colonel Wlodzimierz Kubala, Prosecutor of the Chief Military Prosecutor's Office, brought an indictment against Adam Michnik and three others for attempting "to overthrow by force the (political) system and to weaken the defensive power of the Polish People's Republic by breaking the alliance with the Soviet Union" by undertaking acts prepatory to this end (Kubala 1983, box 43, file 1). The specific "treasonous acts" consisted of forming an association that provided information, advice, and support for disaffected workers (KOR, or Workers' Defense Committee); free university courses that offered an alternative literature and historical interpretation to the state-controlled curriculum; and student committees that discussed social issues, free trade unions, and the like. In these venues they had committed the crimes of offering instruction on Polish history, disagreeing with state policies, questioning the efficacy of Poland's relations with the USSR, listening to Radio Free Europe and supplying information to such outlets about conditions in Poland, and committing their disagreements with the government to writing and sharing them.

When Colonel Kubala came to Michnik, he listed his "crimes" as acting precisely *as if* he were a free citizen. Against the state's claim that Poland was a People's Republic, Michnik's offense was, ironically, to act *as if*, as one of the people, he had the right to speak his mind in public. He had committed a treason that undermined Polish freedom when, in Kubala's (1983, 12) words, he "pointed out that the 'blood spilled' was a lesson on what kind of language should be spoken with the government, if anything is to be attained; one must oppose 'authorities relying on bayonets, informants, and gendarmes'; resistance is a way out, but cooperation with, or obeying, the authorities—is collaboration, resistance is what Polish honor demands, and it is common sense." Kubala displaces the common-sense assumption that voicing disagreement with the state is not sedition. In his Orwellean world, we make sense of these charges only by inverting the shared meaning of everyday language, so that a People's Republic does not represent the will of the people and it is treason to speak freely about principles of self-interest. Michnik's crime against the people was to suggest that in a People's Republic the people's interests should inform the state. But in an Orwellean world, the normal horizon of self-interest takes rapid flight.

Kubala's indictment assumes that political relations are based on the formal structures of institutional power, not on negotiated understanding. The contrast between his indictment and Michnik's letter provides a microcosm of the disparity between the Communist Polish state's centrist power and its citizens' aspiration for civil society. The efficacy of Poland's counterpublic sphere as more than a place for resistance was nourished by this distance that made it the arena for forming national aspirations and guiding social action.

"Why You Are Not Signing" is illustrative of Michnik's indictable mode of communication. It addressed Poles as if the civil society Michnik sought were a reality: a society marked by openness in expressing opinions, truthfulness in making claims, commitment to the autonomy of each person to act freely, but unwillingness to sit in judgment of others for their shortcomings, and, within the bounds of common sense, treatment of others with trust (Schell 1985, xxviii). Unlike Kubala's indictment, Michnik's letter projects a public sphere in which allegiance comes from the bona fides of cultural memory. His rhetorical frame for public memory inverts Poland's ostensible power vectors. He constitutes a lifeworld with dissociative patterns that give direction to the counterpublic sphere of political dissidence and resistance through their valorizing of unsentimental cultural commitments. This lifeworld shifts the focus of dissident discourse from the official public sphere of the state to a second source of power, public opinion.

Habermas (1974) has written that the principle of the public sphere is enacted whenever two or more gather to discuss matters of general concern. Michnik's writing locates this individual enactment at the center

of public life. The oppressive weight of the totalitarian state—its administrative reach and military might—makes this type of discourse risky at
best. Even in the counterpublic sphere of the underground, danger of
detection carries consequences of imprisonment and its threat of physical
and psychological abuse. Under totalitarian conditions, the challenge to
the counterpublic sphere lies in overcoming a seemingly insurmountable
power differential. Yet there are successes: Michnik in Poland, Havel in
Czechoslovakia, Suu Kyi in Burma, Anatoly Shransky in the former
Soviet Union, and Mandela in South Africa are among the most celebrated. In each case they have leveraged their position as a prisoner of
conscience to reach the minds of their countrymen and women, to mold a
body of shared meanings with salience unavailable for the government to
use, much less command. They have shared a genius for carving a counterpublic sphere in which public opinion might form. They have shared a
sense of the cultural and social commitments that may hasten the political center of gravity's migration from the state to a national civil society
whose political relations emerge from the choices of freely associating
individuals and groups. Their shared lifeworld delegitimates the state as a
political power and marginalizes it as irrelevant to the types of decision-
making necessary to build an open society and a free nation. Certainly
there are complex webs of organized action necessary for the rhetorical
forcefulness of a counterpublic sphere of resistance to prevail. But
equally, the unusual rhetorical force that accompanies the writing of the
prisoner of conscience must be considered in charting the course of resistance from the margins to the center.

NOTES

1. Michnik regards the image of the stone that alters the course of
the avalanche, which he takes from the Polish poet Czeslaw Milosz, as
descriptive of the dissident's role. This image returns at the end of "Why
You Are Not Signing."

2. In *The Dialogical Imagination* (1981), Russian literary theorist
Mikhail Bakhtin advances the thesis that meanings are always unfolding
through *dialogizing of the word*. The internal structure of dialogue entails
interaction among the meanings of interlocutors' language. By interacting
with each other's meanings we also interrogate them and challenge their
self-contained meanings by bringing each into the space between them.
Bakhtin (1981, 324) tells us, "The struggle and dialogical interrelation-
ships of these categories of ideological discourse are what usually determine the history of an individual ideological consciousness." Each context

of interaction thus provides a space in which the confluence of history, society, psychology, and culture create a turbulence unlike any that has existed before or any that will follow. He calls this dialogic agitation "an intense struggle within us for hegemony among various available verbal and ideological points of view, approaches, directions and values. The semantic structure of an internally persuasive discourse is *not finite*, it is *open*; in each of the new contexts that dialogize it, this discourse is able to reveal ever newer *ways to mean*" (345, emphasis his).

3. I have been unable to locate an account of how Michnik smuggled his letter from the Bialoleka internment camp. A common practice among political prison writers, however, is to compose their letters on cigarette paper, seal it in plastic wrap, and hide it on their body when they go to meet visitors who are their confederates, to whom they transfer the message with a handshake or a kiss. Once on the outside, these letters entered the underground's uncensored media, where they were printed, copied, and widely circulated. See Curry (1984).

REFERENCES

Baker, Houston A., Jr. 1995. Critical memory and the black public sphere. In *The black public sphere*, edited by The Black Public Sphere Collective. Chicago: University of Chicago Press.

Bakhtin, Mikhail M. 1981. *The dialogic imagination: Four essays*. Edited by Michael Holquist. Translated by Caryl Emerson and Michael Holquist. Austin: University of Texas Press.

Barber, Benjamin. 1984. *Strong democracy: Participatory politics for a new age*. Berkeley: University of California Press.

Bitzer, Lloyd F. 1978. Rhetoric and public knowledge. In *Rhetoric, philosophy and literature: An exploration*, edited by Don M. Burks. West Lafayette, IN: Purdue University Press.

Curry, Jane Leftwich. 1983. Polish dissent and establishment criticism: The new evolutionism. In *Dissent in Eastern Europe*. New York: Praeger.

———, ed. and trans. 1984. *The black book of Polish censorship*. New York: Vintage.

Dryzek, John S. 1990. *Discursive democracy: Politics, policy, and political science*. New York: Cambridge University Press.

Farrell, Thomas B. 1993. *Norms of rhetorical culture*. New Haven, CT: Yale University Press.

Fishkin, James S. 1995. *The voice of the people*. New Haven, CT: Yale University Press.

Fraser, Nancy. 1992. Rethinking the public sphere: A contribution to the critique of actually existing democracy. In *Habermas and the public sphere*, edited by Craig Calhoun. Cambridge: Massachusetts Institute of Technology Press.

Goodnight, G. Thomas. 1982. The personal, technical, and public spheres of argument: A speculative inquiry into the art of public deliberation. *Journal of the American Forensic Association* 18:214–227.

Habermas, Jürgen. 1974. The public sphere: An encyclopedia article (1964). *New German Critique* 3:49–55.

———. 1989. *The structural transformation of the public sphere: An inquiry into a category of bourgeois society*. Translated by Thomas Burger and Frederick Lawrence. Cambridge: Massachusetts Institute of Technology Press.

Hauser, Gerard. A. 1998. Vernacular dialogue and the rhetoricality of public opinion. *Communication Monographs* 65:83–107.

———. 1999. *Vernacular voices: The rhetoric of publics and public spheres*. Columbia: University of South Carolina Press.

Havel, Václav. 1989. *Letters to Olga*. Translated by Paul Wilson. New York: Henry Holt.

Herbst, Susan. 1994. Race discrimination, mass media, and public expression: Chicago, 1934–1960. In *Politics at the margins: Historical studies of public expression outside the mainstream*. New York: Cambridge University Press.

Kubala, Wlodzimierz. 1983. Act of indictment. In Amnesty International USA Papers, Yadja Zeltman Collection. University of Colorado Library, Boulder, Colorado.

Kuron, Jacek, and Karol Modzelewski. 1968. An open letter to Communist Party members. In *Revolutionary Marxist students in Poland speak out*, edited by George L. Weissman. New York: Merit Publishers.

McGee, Michael Calvin. 1975. In search of "The People": A rhetorical alternative. *Quarterly Journal of Speech* 65:235–249.

Michnik, Adam. 1985. *Letters from prison*. Translated by Maya Latynski. Berkeley: University of California Press.

Perelman, Chaïm, and Lucie Olbrechts-Tyteca. 1969. *The new rhetoric*. Translated by John Wilkinson and Purcell Weaver. Notre Dame, IN: Notre Dame University Press.

Ratushinskaya, Irina. 1989. *Grey is the color of hope*. Translated by Alonya Kojevnikov. New York: Vintage.

Rodger, John J. 1985. On the degeneration of the public sphere. *Political Studies* 33:203–217.

Scarry, Elaine. 1985. *The body in pain: The making and unmaking of the world*. New York: Oxford University Press.

Schell, Jonathan. 1985. Introduction to *Letters from prison*, by Adam Michnik. Berkeley: University of California Press.

Timerman, Jacobo. 1981. *Prisoner without a name, cell without a number*. Translated by Toby Talbot. New York: Knopf.

Touraine, Alain. 1983. *Solidarity*. Translated by David Denby. New York: Cambridge University Press.

White, James Boyd. 1984. *When words lose their meaning*. Chicago: University of Chicago Press.

Yankelovich, Daniel. 1991. *Coming to public judgment: Making democracy work in a complex world*. Syracuse, NY: Syracuse University Press.

2   In the Name of Reconciliation

The Faith and Works of Counterpublicity

ERIK DOXTADER

The faith of counterpublic theory is that difference contains the potential (*dynamis*) for unity. The work of counterpublic theory is to explain this potential without mediating one—difference *or* unity—into the other. Whether by faith or works, however, the justification of counterpublic theory remains open to question. Where do we find counterpublics? As there seem to be few groups that self-identify as (subaltern) counterpublic, it is not clear whether these associations are an actually existing feature of democracy, a normative benchmark, or a metaphor for certain kinds of activity.[1] More important, how do counterpublics operate? With the promise to expand the *topoi* and form of public life, they may challenge the conventions of deliberation, creating alternative conduits of discussion. Or they may use opposition to create the basis for consensus. An apparent challenge to the law of noncontradiction, this latter transformation appears frequently in counterpublic theory as "word magic." What might allow us to plot the dynamics of such communication and represent its political value?

Counterpublics are not counterfactual. By one account, they are actual features of democracy (Fraser 1992). The claimed benefit of counterpublic theory, however, is a normative model of political participation and representation. Slippery, critique moves between the local and the general, playing the concept of the public off of heterogeneous discourse practices that are then (re)conceptualized in the name of the collective good. Thus, if it is to be less than the expansion of the public to the point where the idea accommodates everyone but means nothing and more than a hedged reenactment of the ideal-ideological public, counterpublic theory has some obligation to explain the (communicative) action it names. This work may entail a kind of reconciliation, a unity in difference in which examples of counterpublic speech are related to its theory. To keep its good faith and to do its work, counterpublic theory may require something that philosophy has long avoided—a rhetorical sensibility.

This essay contends that the critical study of *counterpublics* benefits from the rhetorical investigation of *counterpublicity*. By this, I mean that the formation, development, and politics of a counterpublic may be clarified by inquiry into *how* particular situations lead groups to devise and employ forms of speech that turn between moments of opposition and moments of consensus in the name of remaking the collective good. The first portion of the essay derives the need for such an approach. I contend that Nancy Fraser's important counterpublic theory rests on a normative stipulation that unduly relieves critique from investigating how counterpublic opposition and contestation cultivate the grounds of dialogue and agreement. This claim is both sympathetic and critical, committed to deliberative democracy but concerned to develop vocabularies that plot its development. In the second section of the essay, I look to one moment in South Africa's turn from apartheid to constitutional democracy in order to illustrate the rhetorical potential of counterpublicity. More precisely, I examine the mid-1980s civil-theological debate over whether and how reconciliation is a valuable means of political resistance. In a key part of this exchange, reconciliation entails opposition that names injustice in order to open spaces for dialogue. In a time of choice, reconciliation discerns the grounds of collective political action from the midst of violence.

This essay investigates two grammars of faith. In their interplay, between the rhetorical assumption and invention of democratic politics, each engages a very old discourse of globalism. Whether we follow Burke's dictum—words about words are like words about god—or Derrida's recent deconstruction of "globalatinization," political appeals for globalism frequently depend on the form of religious discourse (Derrida 1998, 29). Counterpublic theory may both enact and critique this appetite. Against the monovocal "good news" of democracy, the dream to end history in a sort of liberal apocalypse, counterpublic theory constitutes a messianic faith that challenges the sacred (universal) hope of public life. It may contest idealism by sublimating the name (of God) in order to divine the words (history) that relate reason and politics. In South Africa, reconciliation has been defended as one means of constructing this present time (*jetztzeit*) of democratization, a way of delineating the theological difference between the violent dis/unification of apartheid and the "constitution" of unity. Before the beginning of a transition that captured the world's attention, debates in the mid-1980s over reconciliation saw citizens and civic leaders invoke the word of God in order to name the reasons for politics. The (globalist) potential for unity in difference was wed to an "interruptive unraveling" of the divine-sociopolitical bond, a challenge that both disclosed and reconstituted the grounds of faith (Derrida 1998, 64). In these terms, counterpublicity appeared within a history of conflict that rendered its potential contingent on its risk.

COUNTERPUBLIC TROPOLOGY

Our faith in the public sphere has been shaken by an inability to discern how it works. While it is perhaps the burden of each generation to question the common good, the present crisis is quite severe. The complexity of modern democracy obscures many *topoi* of public life. Amid the institutionally directed and increasingly virtual crowd, the public is difficult to find. As either quantity or quality, it appears to have no discernable place in the monetarily mediatized forums of sound bite society. This practical problem is compounded by a contemporary theoretical *pathos* that finds ideal models of public deliberation both naïve and exclusive. As there is no standard citizen, it seems unlikely there is a single form of public communication. Counterpublic theory addresses both of these dilemmas. Unwilling to forgo the public in favor of a postmodern "we know not what," it aspires to discover unrecognized sites of deliberation and reveal that the invention of collective interest entails several modes of communication.

Counterpublic theory seeks to unveil the productive heterogeneity of public deliberation without dissolving its form. This promise rests explicitly on an explanation of the ways in which nontraditional and oppositional forms of communication have the potential to open and expand channels of public dialogue. Thus, to no small degree, counterpublic theory is obliged to discern and detail the "how" of deliberation. In this section, I question whether counterpublic theory is fully equipped to undertake such an investigation into the communicative "mechanics" of public speech. My contention is that it is not. Specifically, the announced double *telos* of counterpublic theory, the desire to introduce oppositional argumentation into the public sphere but to do so in a manner that preserves the consensual nature of deliberative democracy, is underwritten by a "weak idealism" that leads critique to assume precisely that which it sets out to explain.[2] In the simplest terms, theory has incentives to mistake the existence of counterpublics for an explanation of counterpublicity, the rhetorical processes by which the grounds of agreement are cultivated from within expressions of opposition. In this light, the task at hand is to explain why counterpublics employ modes of rhetorical invention and whether the investigation of these generative moments can clarify the relationship between public deliberation and democratic representation.

In a multicultural society, the public is charged with representing diverse interests, bridging different forms of life, and defining a coherent definition of collective interest (Taylor 1995). This means that the public is a creature of controversy. It is neither singular nor immune from "deep" conflicts that threaten to undermine the ability of individuals to reach consensus (Benhabib 1986; Goodnight 1991; Bohman 1996; Young 1987, 1997). This insight has been central to the development of (subaltern) counterpublic theory. In her groundbreaking work, Nancy Fraser argued that democratic pluralism is best served when public discourse is not reduced to the procedures of consensus-building. Against the well-known position of Jürgen Habermas, Fraser holds that the bourgeois public sphere (Öffentlichkeit) is a utopic rationalization that reinforces masculine and institutional power. A means to "mask domination," rational-critical debate represents neither the material nor the moral-ethical exigencies of "actually-existing democracy" (1992, 119). The traditional-liberal procedures of public deliberation give rise to definitions of collective interest that both silence the expression of "marginal" interests and obscure the generative value of strident disagreement (1992, 116).

If the "narrative" of public life stages a "gap in participatory parity between dominant and subordinate groups," stratified societies with a historical commitment to pluralism benefit from "arrangements that accommodate contestation among a plurality of competing publics" (1992, 122). This means, according to Fraser, that there are "subaltern counterpublics" that appear outside, within, and beneath the "dominant" public. In opposition to the form and substance of established collective interest, these groups "invent and circulate counterdiscourses to formulate oppositional interpretations of their identities, interests, and needs" (1992, 123). They use communication to challenge given forms of deliberation and train for "agitational activities" that can remake the dominant public's construction of consent.

In these terms, Fraser's position is both historical and critical. Subaltern counterpublics actually exist and they should exist. Viewed over time, she contends, subordinated groups—"women, workers, persons of color, and gays and lesbians"—have founded alternative publics in order to contest their disadvantage in the "official" public sphere. Normatively, these organizations enhance the project of democracy. They afford interested individuals spaces to find their voice outside the censoring procedures of mainstream deliberation and the means by which to express interests that deserve recognition and representation. Counterpublics are both safe-spaces and launching pads for constructive engagement. Walking a very fine line, they challenge the dominant conventions of public deliberation but do not necessarily contest the value of deliberation per se. In a key turn, Fraser theorizes the means by which this difference is split:

> In my view, the conception of a counterpublic militates in the long run against separatism because it assumes a *publicist* orientation. Insofar as these arenas are *publics*, they are by definition not enclaves, which is not to deny that they are often involuntarily enclav*ed*. After all, to interact discursively as a member of a public, subaltern or otherwise, is to aspire to disseminate one's discourse to ever widening arenas. (1992, 124) [emphases in original]

While an apparent attempt to distinguish the aims of a counterpublic from a politics of authenticity, this position makes a historical-practical claim—counterpublics are a kind of public—and introduces a theoretical-critical stipulation—the concept of a counterpublic *assumes* a "publicist orientation." Read against Fraser's critique of the public sphere, a critique in which the existence and need for counterpublics is set against the (ideological) procedures of rational-critical debate, these arguments confirm that the "public sphere is indispensable to critical theory" (1992, 111) but run perilously close to either enacting a performative contradiction or mediating the public sphere and counterpublics to the point where the difference fades. More precisely, Fraser's attribution of a "publicist orientation" to subaltern counterpublics appears to tame discursive contestation and obscure inquiry into the ways in which opposition actually engages and remakes norms of public deliberation.

In her essay, "Can the Subaltern Speak," the very work which Fraser cites as the inspiration for her use of the term *subaltern*, Gayatri Spivak finds that appeals to the subaltern sometimes (re)inscribe the very sovereign subject which they claim to displace. Presupposing what must be created, the impulse to represent the subaltern as a "transparent" domain—a population endowed with the creativity needed to enact "real" change—trades ideology critique for an "essentialist, utopian politics" (1988, 275–276). Arguably, this problem recedes when counterpublics work from a "publicist orientation." Counterpublics are not isolated formations. They reflect, engage, and represent the (procedural and material) terms of public deliberation. However, as Spivak points out, this kind of definitional move carries a risk of its own. As a theoretical conception, the publicist orientation of a counterpublic seems, at the very least, to mark a procedural commitment to the achievement of understanding.[3] If so, which procedures of public deliberation should we accept and how do we assess the risk that they may depreciate precisely those "constitutive contradictions" (oppositional arguments) which energize subaltern history-making?[4] At some unspecified level, it appears that counterpublic theory may be conditioned by the very (ideological) idealism that it claims to oppose. Alternatively, defined as a natural inclination, this same orientation appears to set counterpublic activity on teleological grounds; counterpublic theory presupposes that individuals will "choose" to adopt particular forms or modes of communication. What's more, hermeneutic analysis of counterpublic activity would not necessarily alleviate this risk of deliberative standardization. As Linda Hart points out in her reading of second-wave feminism, a movement to which Fraser repeatedly refers, it has frequently been difficult to separate out those cases where the designation "counterpublic" collectivized opposition in order to legitimize the power of a dominant public from those instances in which opposition changed the form and content of public deliberation (Hart 1998, 38).

To the degree that it blesses counterpublics with a proper orientation, counterpublic theory may sublimate some of its most interesting practical questions: How do counterpublics actually speak? Under what circumstances do *oppositional* arguments (re)invent *shared* norms of deliberation? Can we plot the difference between disseminating "one's discourse to ever widening arenas" and having it heard? Fraser holds that counterpublics are "parallel discursive arenas" that use counterdiscourses to transgress norms of deliberation, generate debate, and remake shared meaning. However, the metaphor's confusing geometry obscures the problem at hand. While parallel objects stand in a kind of opposition, they do not meet (except in those cases where an object is found to be parallel with *itself*). However, Fraser's claim is that counterpublics stand apart from, cross into, and engage their dominant counterparts. They employ oppositional argumentation to delegitimize and (re)form the procedures of collective deliberation. Citing Eley, Fraser notes that counterpublics can be structured settings for "cultural and ideological contest or negotiation" (1992, 125). But, read with the anecdotal-historical claim that subaltern counterpublics *have* invented new languages which altered the terrain of public life, this finding does not delineate the *kinds* of opposition that are productive of dialogue and change. It does not speak to the question of *how* oppositional communication works. Instead, the issue is resolved by appealing to a "publicist orientation" in which interlocutors seem predisposed to resolve conflicts through procedural appeals to the "force of the better argument."

The critique of idealism implicit in counterpublic theory raises the question of why counterpublics do not burst the possibility of collective deliberation. In response, theory has shown a tendency to define counterpublics through background norms that subtly attribute a communicative interest to those who would choose to transgress or oppose the taken-for-granted procedures and topics of collective interest formation. However, for the same reasons that this attribution deters the enclave, it may also assimilate subaltern populations into an "orientation" that fixes their identity and narrows the range of their voice. Theory resolves the question of how difference contains the potential for unity by pressing unity *onto* difference. One potential cost of this attribution is that it allows critique to abdicate the explicitly political questions of whether counterpublics *actually* exist and how they *actually* devise and employ oppositional forms of communication. If so, and to the degree that we wish to resist a (postmodern) antipolitics of "unity *as* difference," the task at hand is to consider how critique speaks of counterpublics and whether this language can sustain inquiry into how counterpublics speak.

When we refer to a counterpublic our usual assumption is that we are speaking about a body that is somehow distinct from, outside, or opposed to the public. A counterpublic *is not* the public. While accurate, this perspective obscures an important paradox that has much to do with our ability to hear and understand how counterpublics speak. Although relevant, the paradox is not that a counterpublic might be related to the public, joined to it through opposition that does not aspire to negation. Rather, the paradox is that a counterpublic may be public as the public is not. In positive terms, a counterpublic may be more public than the public it opposes. Why? In an important *ontological* argument, Hannah Arendt claimed that "our feeling for reality depends utterly upon appearance and therefore upon the existence of a public realm in which things can appear out of the darkness of sheltered existence" (1958, 51). In public, a common world that promises permanence and meaning, humans are gathered, related, and separated (1958, 53–54). The difficulty, however, is that this promise takes shape in the transitory, unpredictable, and anonymous processes of speech and action. Addressed to the "in-between" of human affairs, the times and spaces in which we forge relations and divisions, word and deed wed the power of beginning to the fate of unexpected consequence, exclusion, and guilt (1958, 233). It is this dynamic process that contains a tentative explanation of our riddle. Against rigidified norms of public deliberation, the reification of creativity into labor, counterpublics may use speech and action to recover the public's capacity for speech and action. Opposed less to what the public *is* than to what it *is not*, a counterpublic is more public than the public.

Counterpublic is a verb. Made evident by Arendt, the term connotes a series or process of speech-actions that (aim to) replace (public) violence with speech and action. Counterpublicity would seem to be the proper name for this work. Moreover, its study may reveal clues as to how individuals and groups find the potential for shared understanding or consensus from within expressions of opposition and difference. Against philosophy that has long been "allergic to expression," loathe to admit its dependence on texts, and quick to contain the particularity of speech with its prototype, such inquiry entails a rhetorical turn (Adorno 1973). Most simply, this means that the study of counterpublicity does not ascribe an interest in consensus to counterpublics but endeavors to observe whether and how local speech acts invent the basis for dialogue and agreement. While slight, this distinction means that the rhetorical study of counterpublicity is concerned to plot the (tropological) turns by which counterpublics identify themselves, challenge the conventions of dominant discourse, and recover the productive contingency of speech and action.[5] It thus addresses the double problem of relationality built into counterpublic theory. On the one hand, the rhetorical investigation of counterpublicity is concerned to plot the "middle voice" of human relations, the bonds of the "in-between" that are occasioned by controversy, invented in speech, and that establish the basis for collective action (Arendt 1958, 182–183; White 1992; Jay 1993). On the other hand, it strives to make good on critique's explicit claim that counterpublic theory has a reflexive relation to counterpublic practice. Moving between the general and particular, a rhetorical view endeavors to uncover the occasion, tropology, and representational functions of a counterpublic.[6]

TROPES OF COUNTERPUBLICITY

The faith of a negotiated revolution is that communication works. In 1994, South Africa accomplished what many deemed impossible. Averting civil war, it replaced the institutions of apartheid with a multiracial democracy. Ongoing, this transition was carried out in the midst of horrific violence and through negotiations that rested heavily on the assumption that South Africans could reconcile their interests and differences. Written in the last days of the 1993 constitutional convention, the postamble of the interim South African constitution rendered this premise explicit: "The pursuit of national unity, the well-being of all South African citizens and peace require reconciliation between the people of South Africa and the reconstruction of society" (quoted in De Villiers 1994, 401). The basis for legislation that created the well-known Truth and Reconciliation Commission, this mandate has provoked substantial controversy. What is reconciliation? How can the animosity and hatred of the past serve as a basis for political change? Does reconciliation represent the needs of citizens and serve the ends of justice?

South Africa's turn to reconciliation did not begin with the formation of the Truth and Reconciliation Commission (TRC). In the mid-1980s, at a crucial moment in the struggle, theologians and church leaders debated whether reconciliation was an appropriate and effective means of undermining apartheid. Frequently ignored, this controversy sheds light on the dynamics of (subaltern) counterpublicity. Here, I argue that the history of theo-religious opposition to apartheid is an example of how groups in a civil society have used rhetorical arguments to create the time and space needed to contest sociopolitical injustice and violent oppression. More precisely, many prominent figures in the South African religious community argued that reconciliation was a politically efficacious process of communication, a mode of speech that used histories of oppression and violence to fund collective action and democratic reform. This view did not enjoy universal support, however. In 1985, a group of theologians issued the *Kairos Document*. This influential tract argued that traditional definitions of reconciliation were reinforcing the state's power and undermining the church's role in the resistance movement. A moment of dissent, directed against *both* the state and the (already) oppositional aims of the church organizations, the *Kairos Document* redefined reconciliation as a moment of history-making, a means of oppositional identity formation, and a potential for political representation. Set into the larger struggle against apartheid, the precise movement of these claims performs and advocates a kind of counterpublicity. In it, the power to name constitutes a critique of state legitimacy and delineates one way that citizens can derive unity from difference.

In the history of South Africa's transition to democracy, theological controversy over the nature of reconciliation offers insight into the occasion, dynamics, and potential value of counterpublicity. This thesis does not aspire to the typological. An example that raises questions about the nature of counterpublicity, reconciliation is not *the* norm of counterpublicity. Similarly, the study of reconciliation may enhance our understanding of the complex relationship between the forces that ended apartheid and the publicity that energizes South African civil society. This does not mean, however, that the theological debates over reconciliation fated the form of the South African transition or that the transition was no more than a process of counterpublicity. In addition, the transition has not produced a *state* of reconciliation. Rather, it involves an ongoing rhetorical argument in which advocates of reconciliation call on citizens to adopt modes of communication that discover the grounds of understanding from within histories of opposition (Doxtader 2001).

The form of South Africa's transition to democracy took shape in a complex set of historical dynamics. Rooted in a theo-colonial logic that called for "a self-governing white community, supported by well-treated and justly-governed black labour from Cape Town to Zambesi," apartheid was maintained by excluding blacks from the halls of government, "relocating" vast populations to barren "homelands," enforcing material inequality, and legislating the practice of state terrorism (Thompson 1995, 144). By the mid-1970s, however, the facade of this racist regime could no longer cover its own instability. War-weary, confronted with international calls for reform, and unable to bridge the political and economic tenets of apartheid, the state appeared increasingly vulnerable (Waldmeir 1997, 24–27). More important, domestic opposition to apartheid was escalating its campaign to render the country "ungovernable" (African National Congress 1985).

The African National Congress (ANC) was at the center of this effort. Backed by its well-known *Freedom Charter*, the ANC's declared aim was to replace "all bodies of minority rule, advisory boards, councils and authorities" with "democratic organs of self-government" (African National Congress 1955). With its ambivalence about the necessity of revolution, this position provoked controversy (Asmal 1997, 113; Marais 1998, 25). While the ANC argued that it was committed to the (negotiated) formation of a multiracial democracy that served the will of *all* people, it also held that violence was an appropriate and necessary means of ending apartheid (Johns 1991). By the late 1970s, this double agenda had created a complex situation. While mass action and violence had weakened the state substantially, it was not clear that armed opposition could carry the day. Against the state's enormous military power, a full escalation of the struggle risked a protracted civil war that the ANC was unlikely to win (Sparks 1996; De Klerk 1994, 4).

Set between the unacceptable pace of incremental change and the risk of perpetual violence, civil society played a key role in the struggle against apartheid during the 1980s (Borer 1998). Situated outside the state, South African civil society was composed of "organisations of survival" and "organisations of resistance" (Rietzes 1995).[7] An "organic" by-product of collective struggle, according to Sue Rubenstein (1995), these groups mobilized citizens and played a key role in coordinating mass action, national strikes, and demonstrations. They also contested the ANC's vision of postapartheid democracy. Beneath the shared goal of "national liberation," many organizations, including some in the powerful South African Communist Party, argued that the ANC was not representing the economic and political interests of those it claimed as constituents (Friedman 1991). Bitterly, critics charged that the organization undervalued "popular power" and ignored the needs of citizens who lived in rural areas (Marais 1998, 14–28). Unified, South African civil society stood against apartheid. Fragmented, an expression of the different and sometimes competing inequalities imposed by apartheid, it could not agree on the nature of state power, the means by which it was best opposed, or the terms of postapartheid political representation (Friedman 1991; Reitzes 1995, 99; Kotze 1998).

Religion has long been central to the purpose, operation, and "contested terrain" of South African civil society (Klaaren 1987, 382). Apartheid had deep theological roots. Influential in the halls of government, the powerful Dutch Reformed Church (NGK) helped build and legitimize the regime. Tied to Dutch and German Calvinism, its doctrines of "sovereignty" and "white guardianship" underwrote legislation designed to "insulate" the Afrikaner *volk* and cultivate the "potential" of blacks (von Tonder 1996; Gastrow 1995; Lotter 1991). Opposition to this faith evolved slowly. Early in the century, the English church attempted to forge ties with the ANC by voicing objections to the NGK's racist theology. In practice, however, it both appeased and practiced segregation. In 1949, during the National Party's rise to power, the Christian Council of South Africa (later renamed to the South African Council of Churches—SACC) declared its explicit opposition to apartheid but declined to integrate its houses of worship. Convened after the 1960 Sharpeville massacre, the Cottesloe Consultation left the NGK as the last mainstream supporter of apartheid and constituted an open challenge to the state. Later, the black consciousness movement and black theology fueled organized religion's role in the struggle for liberation (Borer 1998). By the early 1980s, this shift from thought to consciousness to action was readily apparent (Borer 1998, 99; Walshe 1997, 390).

Backed by its declaration that apartheid was heresy and a campaign against theologies of "accommodation and acquiescence," SACC called for international sanctions, protested the reentrenchment of apartheid in the "new" 1983 constitution, and strongly hinted that civil disobedience was justified in the name of protecting human rights (Borer 1998, 55–57). This activist commitment was strengthened further when the state's attempt to ban all opposition movements created a leadership vacuum in which the "only space that existed where some form of resistance could take place was within religious organizations" (Borer 1998, 208). At the center of civil society, churches were transformed into "intense sites of struggle." They directly challenged the theological justifications for apartheid in order to undermine the state's moral and legal legitimacy. With appeals to scripture and the tenants of prophetic theology, many church leaders argued that the regime had betrayed God, replacing its expressed commitment to the common good with violence (Borer 1998, 66–68).

Reconciliation was a central and controversial element of the religious fight against apartheid. In 1982, led by Allan Boesak, the Dutch Reformed Missionary Church (NGSK) made an important appeal to reconciliation in its *Belhar Confession*:

> Because the secular gospel of apartheid fundamentally threatens the reconciliation in Christ as well as the unity of the church of Jesus Christ, the NGSK in South Africa declares that for the church of Jesus Christ a *status confessionis* exists. (quoted in Kinghorn 1997, 153)

In this call, reconciliation addressed two problems. On the one hand, it marked a need for the churches of South Africa to bolster their activist credentials by confessing their complicity in the formation and practice of apartheid. On the other hand, reconciliation expressed the injustice of apartheid and a means by which it could be overcome.

In the 1980s, many churches were caught between the need to oppose the state and their long-standing opposition to violence. In many quarters, reconciliation was seen as a solution to this dilemma, a means of resistance that could produce reform and avert the growing risk of civil war. The mechanics of such a transformation were explained in very different ways.[8] Evident in the *National Initiative for Reconciliation*, for instance, reconciliation buttressed a "third way theology." Here, the church was a mediator, a neutral party that could guide the country through a negotiated transition (Borer 1998, 244). While dedicated to this end, Desmond Tutu offered a different interpretation when he argued that reconciliation is less a mediation than a process of human interaction in which individuals recognize and concede their interdependence. Based on a powerful critique of identity politics, Tutu's *ubuntu* theology holds that reconciliation contains the potential for peace and justice.[9]

Theo-religious appeals to reconciliation did not go unchallenged. For one, critics charged that reconciliation sold the opposition short. Concerned more with averting violence than achieving justice, they argued that reconciliation was a tactic of accommodation which ensured the continuation of white power (Balcomb 1993). In 1985, this controversy came to a head. Amid rapidly escalating violence, a small group of loosely affiliated theologians gathered in Soweto to discuss the church's role in antiapartheid activism and the value of reconciliation. Sponsored by the Institute of Contextual Theology, the group deliberated and wrote. They considered the needs and standing of Christians in South Africa and whether the church was contributing to the demise of apartheid.

Set out in the *Kairos Document,* a short tract that received considerable attention after its release, their conclusion was that South Africa faced a time of choice, a moment of *kairos* or a "favorable time in which God issues a challenge to decisive action" (1986, 1). A "situation of death" had enveloped the country. Alike, politics and religion had brought only violence and appeasement. At the center of the storm was the long history of apartheid theology and its liberationist counterpart:

> Both oppressor and oppressed claim loyalty to the same Church. They are both baptised in the same baptism and participate together in the breaking of the same bread, the same body and blood of Christ. There we sit in the same Church while outside Christian policemen and soldiers are beating up and killing Christian prisoners to death while yet other Christians stand by weakly and plead for peace. The Church is divided against itself and its day of judgment has come. (2)

In this moment of truth, the *Kairos* theologians called for critique that could reenergize efforts to end apartheid. They initiated this "social analysis" by delineating why "state theology" was guilty of "misusing theological concepts and biblical texts." In the name of security, the regime was accused of converting the contextual meaning of God's word into an "absolute and universal principle" (4). Against the Church's "right" to interpret revelation, its biblical appeals supported a demand for obedience that was "reserved for God alone" (6). Coupled with a "myth of law and order" that used the specter of communism to justify oppression, this "blasphemous use of God's name and God's word" led the theologians to conclude that the state was the "antichrist" (8).

In its second line of argument, the *Kairos Document* claimed that the doctrinal pronouncements of "English-speaking Churches" offered no more than a "superficial and counterproductive" criticism of apartheid (1986, 9). Largely, this shortfall-*cum*-complicity was attributed to how the church had cast the nature and practice of reconciliation. Defined as an "absolute principle that must be applied in all cases of conflict or dissension," reconciliation was condemned as a betrayal of the Christian faith and a cause of injustice (10). "In our situations in South Africa today," the theologians contended, "it would be totally unChristian to plead for reconciliation and peace before the present injustices have been removed. Any such plea plays into the hands of the oppressor by trying to persuade those of us who are oppressed to accept our oppression and to become reconciled to the intolerable crimes that are committed against us. This is not Christian reconciliation, it is sin" (10). Thus, reconciliation was problematic at three levels. It erased the crucial distinction between right and wrong, reduced Christian theology to a private expression of contrition, and allowed the Church to remain "neutral" in the justifiably violent fight against an unjust regime.

Caught in its accusations, some critics charged that the *Kairos Document* was a crude manifesto of revolution, a dangerous attempt to justify violence through an appeal to divine will (Beyerhaus 1987). However intuitive, this rebuttal was not the product of a close reading. While radical, the *Kairos Document* was underwritten by a subtle concern for how South African citizens could recover the capacity for speech and action. The tract performed an immanent critique of the "universal principles" that supported apartheid and exposed how they deterred the formation of politically efficacious communities. It found that apartheid was a "tyrannical regime" legitimized by a (theological) norm of silence. To trump justice with "security," the state had appropriated the Word of God. For its part, the religious community opposed apartheid with concepts that conceded the "legitimate authority" of the state (1986, 14). Wed to a passive vision of reconciliation, it had undermined political-public action with an unheard faith that could not break the censoring effects of state theology. Read together, these claims did much more than challenge the theological roots of apartheid. They held that the state's supporters had compromised their relationship with God. Institutional violence had broken the covenant of divine justice. Simultaneously, the document opposed itself to those organs of civil society that had advocated reconciliation as a way of affecting political change. By preaching private and politically neutral interpretations of reconciliation, committed to the idea that it could mediate between oppressed and oppressor, organized religion was complicit in the very violence it condemned (De Gruchy 1997, 22). Thus, the *Kairos Document* concluded, the state and church had betrayed the citizens of South Africa (1986, 22–23). The grounds of collective action, not to mention the possibility of its justification, had been subverted by a "theological tyranny."

To the state's heresy and the "cheap grace" of reconciliation, the *Kairos Document* juxtaposed a prophetic theology. Placed in the context of human suffering and oppression, the theologians argued that the potential for liberation appeared as the (hermeneutic) interpretation of prophetic narratives revealed the basis for redemptive action. In short, prophetic theology was a "doing theology" that eschewed political neutrality and endeavored to eliminate "structural injustice" (1986, 17–18; Borer 1998, 102). Essential to this work was the *act* of naming.

The evil forces we speak of in baptism must be named. We know what these evil forces are in South Africa today. The unity and sharing we profess in our communion services or Masses must be named. It is the solidarity of the people inviting all to join in our struggle for God's peace in South Africa. The repentance we preach must be named. It is repentance for our share of the guilt for the suffering and oppression in our country. (1986, 29)

Turning between God, state, and civil society, the threefold movement of this passage deserves close scrutiny. What is the power of the name? The power of naming?

First, the name recovers the potential to make history from within the experience of violence. Evil is known. Masked by the state, it has not been fully spoken. The content of speech, an infusion of experience into knowledge, naming manifests this evil. In the name, the presence of evil is rendered present. This appearance constitutes a situation, a time of choice. While opportune, this time is and is not extra-ordinary. As baptism re-collects or remembers sin at the very point when God's grace "gives humanity time," the situation is a time within time (Migliore 1991, 218). The naming of evil brings a history to presence in the name of a future. In this time for the making of time, the past is the potential for the future. Perhaps both prophetic and messianic, the name thus figures a time of transition, a turning between past evil and the promise of God's word.[10] Here, recalling Walter Benjamin's important work on language, the name stands in relation to the divine word, its connection to knowledge given standing by the creating/creative word of God (1996, 69). As an outpouring (*kenosis*) of divine love, this *Logos* is a potential for action.[11] In the assumption of history, the naming of evil as evil against God, the potential for history-making appears as that name that embodies and moves between past experience and present faith.

The naming of violence and oppression *figures* a temporal referent for choice. In its second line of argument, the *Kairos Document* held that this potential could be rendered actual as the name performed a re-presentation of experience. As named, the "solidarity of the people" facilitates the "struggle for God's peace." More directly, naming funds the formation of individual and collective identity. The "experience of suffering" exposes how and why oppression is a shared condition (1986, 18). Individual histories reveal common ground and crystallize purpose. At first, this collective action is confrontational. The promise of peace requires struggle against a state that has supplanted God's word with the instrumental violence of human law. Severed from its relational character, concerned more with subjection than the cultivation of shared (interdependent) subjectivity, the state is illegitimate. Thus, solidarity is possible only outside and against law.[12] As an expression of collective meaning and purposes, the name invokes a space for unity and opposition to injustice.

Against apartheid, the name invents and sustains a common and oppositional identity. The risk of this stance is that it replicates the *form* of the injustice to which it is opposed. Identities of opposition may harbor the will to violence. In the third movement of the *Kairos Document*'s position, this identitarian dilemma is turned to a practice of identification. While identity sustains collective struggle against oppression, the *Kairos Document* holds that this oppression is partly self-created. Across society, the theologians saw widespread support for either a theo-political regime that equated its own power with a divine capacity for creation or a form of religious resistance that traded reconciliation for political action. Both commitments justified confession. An act of contrition that concedes the fallibility of human principle and renders self-certainty contingent on God's grace, confession serves several ends. It challenges the "absolute and universal" principles that legitimized apartheid (1986, 22). Equally, it places the work of liberation under the banner of faith. Left without the unquestioned concepts that endow human law with its violent form, the same concepts that appropriate the divine Word and undermine humanity's relationship with God, the vulnerability induced by confession infuses the struggle against oppression with an *attitude* of forgiveness (34).

The logic of this claim is subtle. Naming performs a critique of both state and church theology. It establishes a common basis for struggle, showing that state institutions and religious communities have failed those whom they claimed to serve. This betrayal of faith was evidence that the private domain of authentic experience was less than a pure and liberating reserve. If so, the development of human identity—self-certainty— becomes the need for identification; as humans relate to God, they must relate to each other. In secular terms, the risks of identitarian violence are resolved only as concrete opposition to apartheid is infused with an *attitude* of sacrifice. Anathema to liberalism, this attitude does not fate self-denigration. Instead, it marks an *ethos* of oppositional argumentation, ɛ commitment to the idea that social justice is a relational good that canno be imposed but must be built through interactions in which violence anɩ animosity may be all that oppressed and oppressor have in common. Iᵣ these terms, forgiveness does not fiat over opposition as much as it use opposition—as a shared condition—to prompt dialogue. Not found iɩ mainstream theology, far from a "third way" mediation that "cover₅ over" oppression in the name of stability (1986, 29), the *Kairos Docu-*

ment held that "true" reconciliation is the struggle for "truth, repentance, justice, and love" from *within* "conflict, disunity and dissension" (11).

The name turns between moments of opposition and unity. In the *Kairos Document*, this movement was both performed and advocated. The text named a situation of injustice, enacted critique, and linked its oppositional stance to the need for collective political change. Moreover, the document called on citizens to undertake this same work. It was, according to Charles Villa-Vicencio, a theologian who helped draft the text and who was later appointed to head the TRC's Research Department, "a revolutionary document without violence." What's more, he notes, the *Kairos Document* was partly addressed to the "edges of civil society," the spaces of creativity that flourished in the midst of oppression and violence.[13] Thus, against the state and dissatisfied with how the religious organs of civil society had defined the role of reconciliation in the struggle against apartheid, the *Kairos Document* enacted an opposition within an opposition. It attempted to undermine the state's legitimacy while challenging citizens and civic organizations to remake the form of their resistance. With this argumentation, the *Kairos Document* makes the situation it names. It opens a moment in which speech-action must both invent the grounds of identity and secure the basis for identification. Against violence and quietude, a public interpretation of reconciliation names this potential, the potential to overcome apartheid by converting the force of its oppression to the power of representation. In this turn, the arguments presented in the *Kairos Document* resemble the (verb/al) action of counterpublicity. Set in the between of human relations, the faith of invention names the work of politics.

CODA

Closure ought not mean synthesis. In this essay, my aim has been to work between counterpublic theory and a rhetorical investigation of counterpublicity. In this (excluded) middle, I have sought to consider the *problem* of how (subaltern) counterpublics speak. Concerned that the naming of counterpublics invokes an idealism that supplants the contingency of public speech-action with an orientation that fixes the expression of "marginal" identity, the essay has endeavored to show why counterpublic theory might benefit from a rhetorical turn. Between its general and local commitments, and caught between a concern for the form of public deliberation and the mystery of how it begins, critique faces a double problem of representation. It must detail how groups define situations of violence and use the representation of experience to enact opposition that challenges the form and content of collective interest in the name of political representation. Thus, as the public is and is not, my suggestion has been that counterpublic speech-action may appear as a varied set of rhetorical practices. Rhetorically, a counterpublic is both less and more than public. It is less because it is outside the public, separated by and opposed to the exclusivity of its discourse. It follows from the public, a derivative. But, simultaneously, this spatial and temporal distance is a relation, a promise that can be both oppositional and forgiving. With an impulse to counter the public without forsaking its name, a counterpublic is more public than public. It harbors the founding promise that the public could not keep, a beginning that bears the dream of that very thing to which it reacts.

In the middle of counter/public life, there appears the potential for relation. In South Africa, the *Kairos Document* was one voice among many in the opposition that brought the end of apartheid. It sat between the state and civil society, addressing and challenging both. In this middle, we find the development of a situation in which individuals appealed to reconciliation as a way to move between moments of oppositional identity formation and collective identification. In retrospect, it is difficult not to wonder if this rhetorical logic can be brought to other local and international conflicts (du Toit 1999, 51). Developed in a time of democratization, counterpublic theory feeds this interest, provoking us to ask after its contribution to a global culture of human rights and democratic politics. At both the particular and general level, the question is premature. The rhetorical performance of counterpublicity sheds light on how citizens and groups employ communication to create, challenge, and redefine their personal and civic relationships. Inside and outside the commons, it appears in myriad tropologies that turn our individual and collective commitments inside out. We should pursue this variety, examining the occasions of its appearance, how it enacts the (re)constitution of public life, and the ways in which it alters the practice of democratic representation. In this way, we might better grasp that the potential for unity, a philosophical-poetic seed of globalism, may appear only as it remains energized by the expression of difference. Between public and counterpublic, linking what is opposed and opposing what is linked, the work of counterpublicity begins in the faith that we can reconcile opposition and consensus without inaugurating a mediation in which one of these goods is subsumed into the other.

NOTES

    The author acknowledges the MacArthur Foundation and the Social Science Research Council for their generous support of this research.

1. The choice to bracket "subaltern" simply indicates that counter-public theory is not always addressed to the subaltern per se.

2. In this essay, I am primarily concerned with the problem of how counterpublics use opposition to generate the grounds of agreement with their dominant counterparts. As Asen and Brouwer note in their introduction to this volume, this focus accounts for only one mode of counterpublic communication. In other work (2000), I have plotted how this dimension of counterpublic theory is tied to the struggle for recognition delineated by both Honneth (1997) and Fraser (1995).

3. One doubts that Fraser's call to disseminate discourse means only flying (e-mailing) over the town square (cyber-community), dropping leaflets (data packets) that may or not be picked up (opened) and read (decoded). While such action might raise *awareness* of an issue, it would not necessarily yield any sort of interaction between a counterpublic and its public "audience." As well, such an "informational" aspiration does little to explain why Fraser makes the strong claim that counterpublics are a kind of public. On my reading, Fraser's claim about the publicist orientation of counterpublics implies a desire to reach a base level of understanding, a sort of "weak consensus" in which participants grasp what is being discussed even as they may disagree about what it means, for instance, if there is really a "problem." On a somewhat related track, this view is supported by Fraser's admittedly puzzling appeal to discourse, the process of communicative interaction that Habermas characterizes as an attempt to create the *basis* for consensus through debate over the "validity conditions" of competing proposals. Consistent with my position here, I have argued elsewhere that this procedure can deter inquiry into the generative functions of opposition and conflict (1993).

4. See Spivak (1988, 274). David Lloyd has worked out this idea in his brief discussion of the "subalternity effect" (1996, 263). One might also compare Judith Butler's discussion of a constitutive exclusion for reasons why an ideal attribution of counterpublicity may dampen political participation (1993, 189–190). Bernstein (1996) also has an excellent discussion of this issue.

5. For discussions of tropology see Butler (1997), White (1978), and Ricoeur (1996).

6. Due to space limitations, I can only sketch how this agenda might be pursued along three heuristic lines of inquiry. First, it seems important to identify the kinds of situations in which counterpublics appear. The occasion of counterpublicity is a perceptual-historical exigence that motivates announcements about the deficiency of public discourse, the need for individuals to identify as members of a counterpublic, and the need for oppositional action. These signs may appear as counterpublic theory begins

with the study of rhetorical history (Zarefsky 1998; Doxtader 2001).
Second, the situations of counterpublicity mark opportunities to investigate
the ways in which counterpublics invent oppositional arguments, how
these modes of contestation challenge dominant visions of the common
good, and whether such claims seed collective interaction and agreement.
This is local work. The communicative movements that enact counterpublicity appear in rhetorical arguments that address a variety of audiences.
The force of these arguments, the ability to advocate, be heard, and affect
change, may be a function of how counterpublics define and justify particular agendas. Named interests may be justified by values that are drawn
from the public itself, or counterpublicity may gather its power by claiming
that the public has betrayed its own word or history. As moments when
taken-for-granted norms of deliberation are seen to betray *both* their supporters and their critics, such "oppositions in common" may contain a
potential or motive for dialogue (Havel 1990; Bernstein 1996). Third, a
critical analysis of counterpublicity entails inquiry into the problem of
whether strategies of contestation enhance the quality of democratic deliberation. One measure of this potential is the complex notion of representation. Discussed at length by Spivak (1988), representation refers both to
the ability of individuals to re-present their experiences and interests and to
the activity in which the needs of a constituency are "served" by a desig-
nated authority. Interdependent, these senses of representation can serve as
a benchmark for evaluating the relative success of counterpublicity. More
precisely, as Hannah Pitkin has noted, the possibility of representation rests
on the ability of political systems (actually existing democracies?) to cultivate the potential for argumentation: "Representing seems to consist in
promoting the interests of the represented, in a context where the latter is
conceived as capable of action and judgment, but in such a way that he
does not object to what is done in his name. What the representative does
must be in his principal's interest but the way he does it must be responsive
to the principal's wishes. He need not actually and literally act in response
to the principal's wishes, but the principal's wishes must be potentially
there and potentially relevant. Responsiveness seems to have a kind of negative criterion: conflict must be possible and yet nevertheless not occur"
(1972, 155). In these terms, counterpublicity is an argumentative challenge
to the delegation and practice of institutional-public authority *and* an
attempt to preserve the potential for argumentation about how a society
constitutes norms of political power. Consistent with Arendt's understanding of speech and action, counterpublicity is important precisely because it
introduces a sense of contingency into taken-for-granted standards of consent and participation. Opposition is productive to the degree that its risk
constitutes a motive and means of collective engagement.

7. While there are some who underscore that the concept of "civil society" contains a colonial legacy and has limited applicability in African politics (Simone 1995), there are many others who argue that the term does represent accurately the nature of South African politics (Friedman and Reitzes 1996; Friedman 1991). Here, however, there is substantial debate over how to define its precise nature. See Friedman (1995), Drah (1995), and Naidoo (1995) for three reviews of this debate.

8. There is a very interesting debate over how to define the nature and operation of reconciliation. Elsewhere, I have overviewed this controversy (2001). For other treatments see the respective works of Schreiter (1992), Shriver (1995), and Taylor (1960).

9. Desmond Tutu made very specific claims as to why reconciliation was an effective means of resisting apartheid. According to Michael Battle, one of the Archbishop's former students, Tutu's theology is a mixture of Anglican doctrine and mediation theology. Unique to Africa, the latter rests on a principle of *Ubuntu*. The plural form of *Bantu*, ubuntu connotes both "humanity" and a "similar linguistic bond between African speakers" (Battle 1997, 39). Evident in Tutu's activist preaching, *ubuntu* theology holds that individuals are human only insofar as they establish relations with and concede their dependence on others. As a "self-sufficient human is subhuman," Tutu's defense of reconciliation rests on a complex critique of identity. Bound by a "delicate network of interdependence," individuals have a coherent identity only as they are able to identify with others. Difference is the substance of shared meaning.

10. I am grateful to Giorgio Agamben for his insights on these matters, especially his provocative reflections into the temporal movements of New Testament discourse.

11. This line of argument is a basic element of Tutu's *ubuntu* theology (Battle 1997, 74).

12. The argument is thus very similar to the one presented by the young Hegel.

13. Generously, Professor Villa-Vicencio offered these reflections during a 1999 interview in Cape Town.

REFERENCES

Adorno, Theodor. 1973. *Negative dialectics*. Translated by E. B. Ashton. New York: Continuum.

African National Congress. 1955. *Freedom charter*. http://www.anc.org. za/ancdocs/history.charter/html (26 June 1999).

——. 1985. National Executive Committee. "The future is in our grasp." Lusaka, SA: African National Congress.

Arendt, Hannah. 1958. *The human condition.* Chicago: University of Chicago Press.

——. 1965. *On revolution.* New York: Viking Press.

Aristotle. 1958. *The politics.* Translated by Ernest Barker. Cambridge: Cambridge University Press.

Asmal, Kader. 1997. *Reconciliation through truth.* Cape Town: David Philip Publishing.

Balcomb, Anthony. 1993. *Third way theology: Reconciliation, revolution, and reform in the South African Church during the 1980's.* Pietermaritzburg, SA: Cluster Publications.

Battle, Michael. 1997. *Reconciliation: The Ubuntu theology of Desmond Tutu.* Cleveland: Pilgrim Press.

Benhabib, Seyla. 1986. *Critique, norm and utopia: A study of the foundations of critical theory.* New York: Columbia University Press.

Benjamin, Walter. 1996. Critique of violence. In *Walter Benjamin: Selected writings, volume 1, 1913–1926,* edited by Michael Bullock. Cambridge, MA: Harvard University Press.

Bernstein, J. M. 1996. Confession and forgiveness: Hegel's poetics of action. In *Beyond representation: Philosophy and poetic imagination,* edited by Richard Eldridge. Cambridge: Cambridge University Press.

Beyerhaus, Peter. 1987. *The Kairos Document: Challenge or danger to the church?* Cape Town: Gospel Defence League.

Bohman, James. 1996. *Public deliberation: Pluralism, complexity and democracy.* Cambridge: Massachusetts Institute of Technology Press.

Borer, Tristan. 1998. *Challenging the state: Churches as political actors in South Africa, 1980–1994.* Notre Dame, IN: Notre Dame University Press.

Burke, Kenneth. 1969. *Rhetoric of motives.* Berkeley: University of California Press.

Butler, Judith. 1993. *Bodies that matter: On the discursive limits of 'sex.'* New York: Routledge.

——. 1997. *The psychic life of power: Theories in subjection.* Stanford, CA: Stanford University Press.

De Gruchy, John. 1997. The dialectic of reconciliation: Biblical perspectives on forgiveness and grace. In *The reconciliation of peoples: Challenge to the churches,* edited by Gregory Baum and Harold Wells. Maryknoll, NY: Orbis Books.

De Klerk, Willem. 1994. The process of political negotiation: 1990–1993. In *Birth of a constitution,* edited by Bertus De Villiers. Kenwyn, SA: Juta.

De Villiers, Bertus, ed. 1994. *Birth of a constitution*. Kenwyn, SA: Juta.

Derrida, Jacques. 1998. Faith and knowledge: The two sources of 'religion' at the limits of reason alone. In *Religion*, edited by Jacques Derrida and Gianni Vattimo. Stanford, CA: Stanford University Press.

Doxtader, Erik. 1993. The entwinement of argument and rhetoric: A dialectical reading of Habermas' theory of communicative action. *Argumentation and Advocacy* 28:51–63.

———. 2000. Characters in the middle of public life: Consensus, dissent, and ethos. *Philosophy & Rhetoric* 33:336–369.

———. 2001. Making rhetorical history in a time of transition: The rhetorical occasion, constitution, and representation of South African reconciliation. *Rhetoric & Public Affairs* 4:223–260.

Drah, Kofi. 1995. Lessons and comparisons from elsewhere in Africa. In *Civil society after apartheid: Proceedings of a conference convened by the Centre for Policy Studies on the role and status of civil society in post-apartheid South Africa*, edited by Richard Humphries. Doornfontein, SA: Centre for Policy Studies.

du Toit, Fanie. 1999. Seeking to establish democratic values in South Africa: Can truth help us? *Journal of Theology for Southern Africa* 103:49–63.

Fraser, Nancy. 1985. What's critical about critical theory: The case of Habermas and gender. *New German Critique* 35:97–132.

———. 1992. Rethinking the public sphere: A contribution to the critique of actually existing democracy. In *Habermas and the public sphere*, edited by Craig Calhoun. Cambridge, MA: Massachusetts Institute of Technology Press.

———. 1995. From redistribution to recognition: Dilemmas of justice in a post-socialist age. *New Left Review* 21:68–93.

Friedman, Steven. 1991. An unlikely utopia: State and civil society in South Africa. *Politikon* 19:5–19.

———. 1995. Introductory perspectives. In *Civil society after apartheid: Proceedings of a conference convened by the Centre for Policy Studies on the role and status of civil society in post-apartheid South Africa*, edited by Richard Humphries. Doornfontein, SA: Centre for Policy Studies.

Friedman, Steven, and Maxine Reitzes. 1996. Democratization or bureaucratisation? Civil society, the public sphere, and the state in post-apartheid South Africa. *Transformations* 29:55–73.

Gastrow, Peter. 1995. *Bargaining for peace: South Africa and the national peace accord*. Washington, DC: U.S. Institute of Peace Press.

Goodnight, G. Thomas. 1991. Controversy. In *Arguments in controversy: Proceedings of the seventh SCA/AFA conference on argumentation*, edited by Donald W. Parson. Annandale, VA: Speech Communication Association.

Habermas, Jürgen. 1971. *Knowledge and human interests*. Translated by Jeremy Shapiro. Boston: Beacon Press.

———. 1987. *The theory of communicative action, lifeworld and system: A critique of functionalist reason*, vol. 2. Translated by Thomas McCarthy. Boston: Beacon Press.

———. 1989. *The structural transformation of the public sphere: An inquiry into a category of bourgeois society*. Translated by Thomas Burger and Frederick Lawrence. Cambridge: Massachusetts Institute of Technology Press.

Hart, Lynda. 1998. *Between the body and the flesh: Performing sadomasochism*. New York: Columbia University Press.

Havel, Vaclav. 1990. The power of the powerless. In *Without force or lies: Voices from the revolution of Central Europe in 1989–1990*, edited by P. Wilson. San Francisco: Mercury House.

Hegel, Friedrich. 1961. The spirit of Christianity and its fate. In *On Christianity: Early theological writings*. Translated by T. Knox. New York: Harper.

Honneth, Axel. 1997. *The struggle for recognition: The moral grammar of social conflicts*. Translated by Joel Anderson. Cambridge: Massachusetts Institute of Technology Press.

Jay, Martin. 1993. Experience without a subject: Walter Benjamin and the novel. *New Formations* 20:145–155.

Johns, Sheridan, ed. 1991. *Mandela, Tambo and the African National Congress: The struggle against apartheid 1948–1990, a documentary survey*. Oxford: Oxford University Press.

Kairos Theologians. 1986. *The Kairos Document: Challenge to the church*, 2d ed. Grand Rapids, MI: Eerdmans.

Kant, Immanuel. 1983. What is enlightenment? In *Perpetual peace and other essays on politics, history and morals*. Translated by T. Humphrey. Indianapolis: Hackett Publishing.

Kinghorn, Johann. 1997. Modernization and apartheid: The Afrikaner churches. In *Christianity in South Africa: A political, social and cultural history*, edited by Richard Elphick and Thomas Davenport. Berkeley: University of California Press.

Klaaren, Eugene. 1997. Creation and apartheid: South African theology since 1948. In *Christianity in South Africa: A political, social and cultural history*, edited by Richard Elphick and Thomas Davenport. Berkeley: University of California Press.

Kotze, Hermien. 1998. Civil society: Setting the record straight. In *Creating action space: The challenge of poverty and democracy in South*

Africa, edited by Conrad Barberton. Cape Town: Institute for a Democratic South Africa.

Krog, Antjie. 1998. *Country of my skull: Guilt, sorrow and the limits of forgiveness in the new South Africa*. New York: Random House.

Lloyd, David. 1996. Discussion outside history: Irish new histories and the 'subalternity effect.' In *Subaltern studies: Writings on South Asian history and society*, edited by Shahid Amin and Dipesh Chakrabarty. Dehli: Oxford University Press.

Lotter, Hennie P. P. 1991. Some Christian perceptions of social justice in a transforming South Africa. *Politikon* 19:45–65.

Mansbridge, Jane. 1996. Using power/fighting power: The polity. In *Democracy and difference: Contesting the boundaries of the political*, edited by Seyla Benhabib. Princeton, NJ: Princeton University Press.

Marais, Hein. 1998. *South Africa: Limits to change—the political economy of transition*. London: Zed Books.

McCarthy, Thomas. 1994. Legitimacy and diversity: Dialectical reflections on analytical distinctions. *Protosoziologie* 6:199–228.

McKeon, Richard. 1990. *Freedom and history and other essays: An introduction to the thought of Richard McKeon*. Edited by Zahava McKeon. Chicago: University of Chicago Press.

Migliore, Daniel. 1991. *Faith seeking understanding: An introduction to Christian theology*. Grand Rapids, MI: Eerdmans.

Naidoo, Jayendra. 1995. How much of civil society could be included in a corporatist-type agreement or structure? In *Civil society after apartheid: Proceedings of a conference convened by the Centre for Policy Studies on the role and status of civil society in post-apartheid South Africa*, edited by Richard Humphries. Doornfontein, SA: Centre for Policy Studies.

Pitkin, Hannah F. 1972. *The concept of representation*. Berkeley: University of California Press.

Reitzes, Maxine. 1995. How should civil society formations relate to structures of representative government? In *Civil society after apartheid: Proceedings of a conference convened by the Centre for Policy Studies on the role and status of civil society in post-apartheid South Africa*, edited by Richard Humphries. Doornfontein, SA: Centre for Policy Studies.

Ricoeur. Paul. 1996. Between rhetoric and poetic. In *Essays on Aristotle's Rhetoric*, edited by Amelie Rorty. Berkeley: University of California Press.

Rose, Gillian. 1996. *Mourning becomes the law: Philosophy and representation*. Cambridge: Cambridge University Press.

Rubenstein, Sue. 1995. What role exists for civil society formations in the development process? In *Civil society after apartheid: Proceedings of a conference convened by the Centre for Policy Studies on the role and status of civil society in post-apartheid South Africa*, edited by Richard Humphries. Doornfontein, SA: Centre for Policy Studies.

Schreiter, Robert. 1992. *Reconciliation: Ministry and mission in a changing social order*. Maryknoll, MD: Orbis Books.

Shriver, Donald. 1995. *An ethic for enemies: Forgiveness in politics*. Oxford: Oxford University Press.

Simone, Abdou. 1995. Revisiting South African conceptions of civil society. In *Civil society after apartheid: Proceedings of a conference convened by the Centre for Policy Studies on the role and status of civil society in post-apartheid South Africa*, edited by Richard Humphries. Doornfontein, SA: Centre for Policy Studies.

Sparks, Allister. 1996. *Tomorrow is another country: The inside story of South Africa's road to change*. Chicago: University of Chicago Press.

Spivak, Gayatri Chakravorty. 1988. Can the subaltern speak? In *Marxism and the interpretation of culture*, edited by Cary Nelson and Lawrence Grossberg. Urbana: University of Illinois Press.

Taylor, Charles. 1995. *Philosophical arguments*. Cambridge, MA: Harvard University Press.

Taylor, Vincent. 1960. *Forgiveness and reconciliation: A study in New Testament theology*. London: MacMillan.

Thompson, Leonard. 1995. *A history of South Africa*, rev. ed. New Haven, CT: Yale University Press.

van Tonder, Joh. 1996. The salient feature of the interim constitution. In *South Africa: Designing new political institutions*, edited by Murray Faure and Jan-Erik Lane. London: Sage.

Waldmeir, Patti. 1997. *Anatomy of a miracle: The end of apartheid and the birth of the new South Africa*. New York: W.W. Norton.

Walshe, Peter. 1997. Christianity and the anti-apartheid struggle: The prophetic voice within divided churches. In *Christianity in South Africa: A political, social and cultural history*, edited by Richard Elphick and Thomas Davenport. Berkeley: University of California Press.

White, Hayden. 1978. *Tropics of discourse: Essays in cultural criticism*. Baltimore: Johns Hopkins University Press.

———. 1992. Writing in a middle voice. *Stanford Literature Review* 9:179–187.

Young, Iris Marion. 1987. Impartiality and the public sphere. In *Feminism as critique*, edited by Seyla Benhabib. Minneapolis: University of Minnesota Press.

————. 1997. Asymmetrical reciprocity: On moral respect, wonder and enlarged thought. *Constellations* 3:340–363.

Zarefsky, David. 1998. Four senses of rhetorical history. In *Doing rhetorical history: Concepts and cases*, edited by Kathleen Turner. Tuscaloosa: University of Alabama Press.

3 ACT-ing UP in Congressional Hearings

DANIEL C. BROUWER

On 10 March 1987, playwright and AIDS activist Larry Kramer presented a fiery speech in New York City criticizing not only the city
and federal governments' inexcusably poor responses to the AIDS epidemic but also the queer community's own play-by-the-rules approach to
the epidemic. Building on the awakened anger of his audience, Kramer
challenged them: "Do we want to start a new organization devoted solely
to political action?" (quoted in Crimp and Rolston 1990, 27). An overwhelming number of people responded affirmatively, and on 12 March
1987, the first chapter of the AIDS Coalition to Unleash Power (ACT UP)
was formed in New York City.[1] Only twelve days later, ACT UP members
staged their first demonstration on Wall Street, protesting what they perceived as an overly cozy relationship between the federal Food and Drug
Administration (FDA) and the pharmaceutical company, Burroughs Wellcome, maker of azidothymidine (AZT).[2] An effigy was burned, traffic was
snarled, and arrests were made. More important, ACT UP gained national
attention through coverage of the demonstration, and the FDA soon after
changed its policy in question.

A sudden emergence as a potentially volatile force with which to
reckon and a growing presence in the national mediascape characterize
the first several years of ACT UP's existence. That first Wall Street demonstration set the tone: ACT UP came to be known as an activist group that
employed disruptive, unruly, and often highly performative modes of
protest in public spaces. Establishing a precedent later followed by such
queer activist groups as Queer Nation and Lesbian Avengers, ACT UP
often invaded seemingly apolitical or restricted sites (Gamson 1989, 86).[3]
In fact, to the casual observer, these kinds of public demonstrations—

heckling the president, disrupting a service at St. Patrick's Cathedral in New York City, interrupting trading at the New York Stock Exchange— have come to stand in for all of the group's political activity. But this casual observation is reductive, for ACT UP is remarkable for its employ- ment of a wide variety of sites for its activist energies. While much schol- arly and popular attention has been granted to the group's unruly public performances, in this essay I cast my gaze away from these more familiar public demonstrations and instead examine members' less-well-known participation in the state-sponsored forum of U.S. congressional hearings. While ACT UP participation in congressional hearings is infrequent and spans a period of only two and a half years, scholarly examination of these hearings provides an opportunity to examine counterpublic and state interactions under conditions regulated by, and thus ostensibly favor- able to, the state; in such a forum, what can and what do these activists make of their participation?

A mutual unease between ACT UP members and federal officials charges the hearings: on the one hand, ACT UP fears for co-optation by virtue of merely appearing in the forum; on the other hand, the threat of a disruptive violation of the discursive norms of the hearings might rightly set the representatives on edge. I argue that textual evidence from witnesses' testimony shows that ACT UP members hold a profoundly ambivalent view about their participation. There is a cautious recognition among ACT UP members of the potential benefits of "oscillation" between such distinct sites as the group's relatively enclaved organiza- tional, committee, and affinity group meetings, public demonstrations "in the streets," and state-sponsored congressional hearings. But there also exists a strong current of frustration with the highly choreographed nature of the hearings, as well as a concern that participation in the hear- ings is inevitably an exercise in co-optation. In addition, I argue that ACT UP members' participation instigates a critical publicity and pro- vides a mechanism by which members gain access to stronger publics; in this way, what might be gained in the near future becomes more impor- tant than the results of the immediate discursive exchange between repre- sentatives and activists.

By way of building support for these arguments, I first briefly note practices of counterpublicity by ACT UP. Second, I provide a brief history of the interactions between ACT UP and institutions and representatives of the federal government, which leads to a narrowing of my focus on the congressional hearing as a particular site of discursive activity. Locating the hearings within the theoretical rubric of public sphere studies, I argue that the hearings constitute a "weak" public nested within the strong pro- cedural public of Congress. Having established this foundation, in the fourth section I amplify key themes of the testimony by ACT UP members. Finally, I note the ways in which textual evidence from the hearings and extratextual evidence about the organization help us to understand reasons for members' participation in this forum.

ACT UP AND COUNTERPUBLICITY

Initiated by Rita Felski (1989) and catalyzed into theoretical currency by Nancy Fraser (1992), the category of the "counterpublic" illuminates the workings of marginal peoples. Felski defines a counterpublic as an "oppositional discursive space" (1989, 155) and counterpublic spheres as "critical oppositional forces within the society of late capitalism" (166). For Felski, a counterpublic sphere is "counter" because it is *partial*—partial because it consciously and unapologetically concerns itself with the emancipation of particular identities/groups rather than orienting itself to the goal of universal human emancipation endemic to some liberal political theory (167). Yet a counterpublic sphere is "public" because it directs its discourse outward into society. Fraser's explanation of the dual character of subaltern counterpublics—as "spaces of withdrawal and regroupment" on the one hand, and as "bases and training grounds for agitational activities directed toward wider publics" (124) on the other hand—emphasizes the publicist orientation of the counterpublic. Amplifying the dangers of overemphasis on withdrawal and regroupment, Jane Mansbridge (1996) joins Felski and Fraser in positing an imperative that links counterpublics to other public arenas. "For participation to help people understand their interests better," Mansbridge argues, people may find it necessary "to oscillate between protected enclaves . . . and more hostile but also broader surroundings in which they can test those ideas against the reigning reality" (57).

Oscillation guarantees neither short-range nor long-range victories for activists, but without it counterpublics forego the possibilities of their critical and expansive work. In the case of ACT UP, I argue that members' oscillations between spheres and fora revitalize public discourse.[4] In the "bases and training grounds" (Fraser 1992, 124) of organizational meetings, committee meetings, caucus meetings, and affinity group meetings, members choose enemies, suggest alliances, propose direct actions, debate means and ends, praise and condemn each other, articulate visions of justice, and engage in a multitude of other activities that foster the creation and refinement of oppositional discourses that are counter to dominant and mainstream discourses about AIDS. Activists employ those oppositional discourses during their appearances in the wider publics of talk shows, community meetings, medical symposia, and "the streets."

Reference to specific acts of *counterpublicity* (see Doxtader elsewhere in this volume) by ACT UP members verifies their success not only in expanding discursive space but also in gaining material victories. As an activist group committed to direct action, the group's appearances in wider publics often take the form of public demonstrations: targets of the group's ire are legion and include local, state, and federal governments; private industry; and religious figures and institutions. Demonstrations at the New York Stock Exchange in 1987, 1988, and 1989 dramatized the culpability of the nation's private sector in the AIDS crisis. Just weeks after the 1987 demonstration (the organization's first), the Food and Drug Administration announced that it would speed up the approval process for anti-HIV drugs. Similarly, one result of the 1989 Wall Street demonstration (involving activist invasion and interruption of the floor of the New York Stock Exchange) was Burroughs Wellcome's subsequent decision to reduce the price of AZT by 20 percent. A 10 December 1989 protest against the incursions of New York City's John Cardinal O'Connor into the city's political arena involved a massive demonstration outside St. Patrick's Cathedral as well as a disruption of the Mass services inside the Cathedral. While most accounts portrayed the actions as anti-Catholic and disrespectful of the freedom of religious worship, in the view of many ACT UP activists the actions signaled their willingness to use whatever means necessary, excepting physical violence, to achieve their goals and served notice to future targets. More recently, in the spring and summer of 1999, activists pestered Vice-President and presidential candidate Albert Gore along his campaign trail, disrupting his speeches and accusing him of malignant neglect in his seeming unwillingness to encourage pharmaceutical companies to release anti-HIV drugs at affordable rates to African countries. Under pressure from activists and political leaders here and abroad, the Clinton administration chose Al Gore to deliver the first ever health-focused address before the United Nations Security Council on 10 January 2000. Such acts of counterpublicity demonstrate how ACT UP members' oscillation toward wider publics expands discursive space and wins material gains.

ACT UP's participation in congressional hearings is another example of the group's oscillation between spheres of human activity. In the next two sections, I provide a very brief description of ACT UP's activities on a federal level and then locate the forum of the congressional hearing within the rubric of public sphere theory.

ACT UP AND THE STATE

While federal officials and institutions were early and frequent targets of the group's anger, the group made efforts to intertwine itself with federal officials and federal institutions through deliberation and negotiation. Archival records (ACT UP/New York Records, box 29) indicate that during the 11 January 1987 ACT UP general meeting, House Representative Theodore Weiss (D, NY) spoke to the membership and fielded questions. Further evidence of the group's willingness to work earnestly with Congress appears in a 1990 document by the Congressional Action Working Group in which the Group announces its purpose "to work with Congress in formulating a Congressional Agenda for action to end the AIDS crisis" (n.p.). And a flier in the fall of 1992 announces the revitalization of a congressional working group "to create specific legislative proposals, and use direct action to force Congress to implement them" (n.p.).

In addition to these efforts at earnest collaboration, ACT UP activists also mounted lively demonstrations staged at federal institutions such as the White House and at venues where federal officials like then–President Ronald Reagan and then–Food and Drug Administration chief Frank Young appeared.[5] One of the most pivotal events to accelerate the entrée of ACT UP into fora at the federal level was the 11 October 1988 demonstration at the Food and Drug Administration (FDA) headquarters in Rockville, Maryland. Organized by a national coalition of AIDS activist groups, the protest drew nearly one thousand demonstrators in an effort to "seize control of the FDA." Two key factors contributed greatly to the unarguable success of the demonstration: first, ACT UP members had reached a compelling level of competency with regard to medical knowledge and research protocol as a result of their rigorous autodidacticism; second, the demonstration was meticulously plotted and campaigned, a process that included the development of a press kit distributed to the media and to the FDA (Crimp and Rolston 1990, 76). While technically the demonstrators did not infiltrate and seize control of the FDA, they did interrupt the business of the day, managed to place graphics and banners on the entrance to the building, and staged numerous activist performances before a large media contingent. Shortly after the demonstration, the FDA met activist demands by making significant changes to its AIDS drug research and distribution policies. Over the next year, ACT UP members benefited from a marked increase in federal officials' and pharmaceutical company representatives' willingness to listen to them and to invite them to participate in discussions about research.

Crimp and Rolston (1990) proclaim the FDA demonstration to be "unquestionably the most significant demonstration of the AIDS activist movement's first two years" (76), in large part because it propelled activists into more fora, including congressional hearings, at the federal level. Indeed, the first ACT UP–affiliated activist testified at a congressional hearing just six months after the demonstration. Like Crimp and

Rolston, I argue that well-timed and well-plotted demonstrations serve a critical function: although as discursive phenomena they are profoundly antideliberative, ironically the demonstrations help activists gain access to previously restricted fora, such as hearings.[6]

SITUATING CONGRESSIONAL HEARINGS AS PUBLICS

Recent work by Jürgen Habermas, particularly his discourse theory of democracy elaborated in *Between Facts and Norms* (1996), provides a way of recognizing the United States Congress as a state-sponsored procedural public. Habermas joins Fraser (1992) in recognizing the multivariate interwranglings of state and civic bodies in parliamentary and representative democratic governments.[7] His discourse theory distinguishes between constitutionally guaranteed, decision-oriented *procedural* publics that serve as "contexts of justification" (307) and as safety mechanisms for social cohesion, and informal, opinion-forming *general* publics that serve as "contexts of discovery" (307). Especially during House and Senate floor debate, the function of Congress as a procedural public becomes clear. Thus, similar to Fraser's description of sovereign parliaments as "a public sphere *within* the state" (134), we can describe the floors of Congress as a public nested within the state.

The various House and Senate committees and subcommittees play extraordinary roles in the functioning of the federal government. Indeed, Woodrow Wilson's famous utterance in 1895 that "Congress in its committee rooms is Congress at work" (1925, 79) holds true today. Joseph Bessette (1994), writing about the quality and character of deliberative democracy in the history of the United States, claims that "by design it is in committees and subcommittees that the most detailed and extensive policy deliberation occurs within Congress" (156). Essential to the ability of committees to craft public policy are hearings. Hearings conducted by various House and Senate committees function as "contexts of discovery" in which citizens, experts, academics, and elected representatives (not mutually exclusive identities) participate in discursive wrangling designed to elicit information and arguments, to publicize issues, and to mobilize support for specific policies. And while Bessette concedes that hearings sometimes serve nondeliberative functions such as enhancing a representative's public profile or embarrassing the presidential administration, still he argues that they are "eminently suited for investigating the merits of pending proposals" (156).

Witnesses at congressional hearings provide arguments, statistics, personal narratives, and other data that not only aid committee members in formulating and revising the language of their bills but also provide members with rhetorical resources during their discursive performances on the floors.[8] In this way, "hearings serve the rhetorical function of invention for committee members" (Rives 1967). In addition, hearings participate in a critical publicity. Habermas's (1996) insistence that legislative branches of constitutional governments keep "institutionalized opinion- and will-formation open to the informal circulation of general political communication" (183) betrays his hope that a critical publicity can emerge from publics. In congressional hearings, critical publicity operates on three levels. On one level, during the immediate, face-to-face interactions between witnesses and state representatives, witnesses can "publicize" their "criticism" of the state. On another level, as noted above, the likelihood exists that representatives will transport and translate portions of witness testimony to the House or Senate floor. On a third level, because of the presence of media representatives, witnesses are almost guaranteed that their testimony will be disseminated to wider, mediated audiences.[9] As I argue later, ACT UP members exploit these levels of critical publicity to help them advance their critique of the state.

Despite these possibilities to inflect significantly the nation's discourse about public policy, obstacles exist for witnesses who serve as activists for social change. A significant impediment to deliberation in the hearings is the fact that state representatives determine and enforce norms of discourse. In the forum of the congressional hearing, status inequities between state officials and civilian and professional witnesses mean that state officials dictate the format of the hearings, the content of the hearings, and to some extent the modes of expression (Davis 1981). Witnesses do not have the power to dictate the overarching course of the hearing, to challenge the rules or norms of the setting, to engage in (excessively) nonnormative modes of expression without the threat of expulsion, or to engage in extended cross-examination with other witnesses or with representatives.[10] (The architecture of hearing rooms, where seating for members of Congress is elevated, conveys this inequity.) Another obstacle is the fact that hearings function as a "weak" public, an arena whose discursive activities are oriented to opinion-formation, in contrast to "strong" publics wherein both opinion-formation and decision-making activities occur (Fraser 1992, 134). As such, activist witnesses do not directly participate, through voting, in the final determination of policy proposals.

In summary, hearings constitute a "weak" public—preparatory and interstitial, occurring after an agenda has been set but before decision making has begun—nested within the strong, procedural public of Congress. With these understandings of the nature of the forum—its possibilities and limitations—I now turn my attention to elaboration of the qualities of testimony among the ACT UP activists.

IN THEIR OWN WORDS: TESTIMONY OF ACT UP
MEMBERS IN CONGRESSIONAL HEARINGS

ACT UP members are not the first individuals affected by AIDS to offer testimony at congressional hearings. The precedent of having people with AIDS testify before Congress was established in August 1983, when such individuals participated in hearings held to evaluate the "Federal Government's Response to AIDS." In 1985, another round of hearings to evaluate the federal government's response to AIDS was held, and this round included testimony from people with AIDS as well as advocates from AIDS-related organizations (not mutually exclusive categories). In short, a precedent had been set for having people with AIDS (PWAs) and AIDS activists offer testimony four years before the formation of ACT UP and five years before members of the group began testifying before Congress.

A review of Congressional Information Service (CIS) indexes from 1987 through 2000 indicates that during the nearly fifteen years of ACT UP's existence, five individuals explicitly affiliated with ACT UP have testified. The first to testify, Iris L. Long, PhD, the founder of ACT UP/NY's Treatment and Data Committee, did so on 28 April 1988, on the issues of development, testing, and availability of therapeutic drugs for AIDS. Two other witnesses, Martin Delaney and Jim Eigo, testified on behalf of ACT UP at the 20 July 1989 hearing, on the issue of parallel-track research designs for clinical drug development. On 21 March 1990, Jim Davis from ACT UP/NY testified on the housing needs of people with AIDS. Later that year, Tony Davis, a member of ACT UP/NY's Treatment and Data Committee, testified before a House subcommittee convened to discuss drug availability and research for opportunistic infections.[11]

ACT UP members' testimony is notably different from the testimony of the PWAs who had testified before them, especially with regard to topic and style of address. This is so, I argue, for three distinct reasons: first, ACT UP members and PWAs are specifically requested by congressional representatives to speak about different aspects of AIDS; second, ACT UP members and PWAs often view their political relationship with the federal government from different perspectives; and third, none of the ACT UP members identifies as seropositive or AIDS-diagnosed. While most ACT UP–ers express some sense of frustration or anger with the federal government, most do so in restrained and reasonable tones. Except for one person, these witnesses express their dissent and agitation respectfully. All adhere to a loose five- to seven-minute time frame for their opening statements and answer questions earnestly, and all but one avoid interruptions or diversions in the course of the deliberations. Finally, all ACT UP witnesses avoid the more unruly types of behavior typical at their demonstrations—shouting slogans, shouting others down, chaining oneself to heavy, immovable objects—and thus avoid being ejected from the hearings.

ACT UP members' remarks that most illuminate counterpublic participation in this state-sponsored forum coalesce around five distinct themes: expertise, dialogue, surveillance, access to strong publics, and use of multiple fora. The struggles and successes of AIDS activists to enter the privileged realm of medical expertise are well-documented, and in ACT UP testimony we find assertive confirmations of the expertise of people with AIDS and AIDS activists.[12] Iris Long, for example, calls for the government to submit its protocols for placebo-based studies to "a panel of expert AIDS patient advocates" (House 1988, 194) and notes that the Reagan-appointed Presidential Commission on HIV had included among its recommendations an ACT UP–authored proposal for an electronic registry of all clinical drug trials in the New York City area (195). Nearly two years later, in what must have registered as a fit of humorous presumption to the representatives present, Jim Davis kindly offers the services of ACT UP expertise: "The People with AIDS Housing Committee of ACT UP New York is available to consult with any Member of Congress on this or any future legislation regarding housing for people living with AIDS" (House 1990a, 76). Related to the theme of expertise is the theme of dialogue; Long's model of dialogue in which activists set agendas, present them to the public and to government officials, and debate as rough equals with officials (House 1988, 193) begins to resemble Habermas's (1996) account of the long road from "general publics" to procedural publics (314).

The theme of surveillance arises as ACT UP members reverse the putative spying relations between counterpublics and states. In the hearings, both Jim Eigo and Long announce to federal officials and wider audiences (via media publicity about the hearings) that it is the federal government that is under surveillance by ACT UP. "ACT UP was the first organization to monitor the status of the AIDS treatment program of NIAID [National Institute of Allergic and Infectious Diseases]" (House 1988, 193), Long notes. The irony of her assertion is that it is typically government (federal, state, or local) that monitors people with AIDS both epidemiologically and politically. Indeed, in addition to the ostensibly benign data gathering of the Centers for Disease Control and Prevention, Federal Bureau of Investigations officers (as well as local police officers) have been known to infiltrate chapter meetings (Bull 1991; Osborne 1993). Aware that it is being watched, the group watches back. Iterating the group's commitment to future publication of federal misdirection or inaction, Long's reversal of the direction of scrutiny posits ACT UP as a savvy watchdog.

The fourth theme of access to strong publics asserts the significance of oscillation to the group. On 20 July 1989, testimony by Martin Delaney on behalf of Project Inform and ACT UP/San Francisco is most notable for its explicit commentary on the difference between "weak" and "strong" publics and its criticism of the government for excluding PWAs and AIDS activists from stronger, decision-making publics or bodies. Delaney holds out hope for productive dialogue by noting a "good spirit of collaboration currently between activists and regulators" (House 1989, 27) despite previous vilification and frustration. Still, Delaney laments that few inroads have been made in gaining PWAs and AIDS activists greater access to opinion-forming *and* decision-making bodies. Straining at the boundaries of his earlier acknowledgment of "a spirit of collaboration," Delaney concludes his testimony with a demand and a threat:

> We feel it's time for the voice of patients to be given first authority here. We've waited for 8 years, patients have cooperated, and we're increasingly dissatisfied with the results. Fortunately, this frustration comes at a time when there do appear to be signs of real progress on the horizon, but so far, it's only rhetoric, not the results, and we believe it's Congress' duty to regularly check in and put some accountability into the system. If we fail to do that, I think you're going to see the greatest explosion of community unrest here since the Vietnam War. (30)

Bracketing the unfortunate characterization of rhetoric as mere words divorced from the realm of action, we find in Delaney's unveiled threat a significant shift in strategy. A frustration derived in part from continued exclusions from strong publics shall, if left unaddressed, foment radical activity in multiple general publics.

This threat and a similar assertion by Tony Davis in 1990 serve to alert federal officials that AIDS activists will not be mollified by occasional participation in congressional hearings; rather, they will, to turn to the fifth theme, continue to employ multiple arenas for the accomplishment of their agendas. Speaking at hearings to discuss drug availability and research for opportunistic infections on 1 August 1990, Davis gives equal emphasis to ACT UP's participation both within the politically sanctioned forum of the hearing and outside of that political avenue via demonstrations and protests. Toward the beginning of his testimony, Davis reviews the past two years of the Treatment and Data Committee's activities.

We have met with researchers, clinicians, and pharmaceutical companies. We have lobbied and demonstrated against the lack of interest in treatments for opportunistic infections. In the last 6 months, AIDS activists from across the nation have mounted demonstrations at the Centers for Disease Control in Atlanta and the National Institutes of Health in Bethesda. (House 1990b, 26)

In this review, Davis clarifies the broad range of communicative avenues and communicative styles of which ACT UP is capable and in which it is willing to engage. Not so subtly, Davis warns that even when they finally gain entry to the fora to which they have demanded access, activists will neither evacuate previously employed fora nor inhabit the new fora as polite guests. ACT UP's refusal to allow Secretary of Health and Human Services Louis Sullivan to present the closing address at the Sixth International AIDS Conference in San Francisco in July of 1990 verifies these points.[13]

In their testimony, ACT UP members address an immediate audience comprised of other witnesses and federal officials; to the federal officials present, they direct accusations and warn of continued scrutiny and dissent in general publics. However, they exploit the principle of publicity that inheres in the forum in order to gain wider audiences for their denunciations of federal inaction and injustice. Furthermore, they explicitly thematize and critique the conditions and limitations of the very forum in which they have agreed to participate.

Of equal significance to the particular ways in which they use the forum is the basic fact *that* they use forum. An alternative, politically viable response to an invitation to appear at the hearings would be refusal: to refuse an invitation would dramatize one's profound lack of faith in the forum. Instead, activists not only accept but also seek out invitations to hearings. At this juncture, I explore in more detail the political stakes involved in participation in the hearings by way of arriving at a more thorough and nuanced account of their presence.

THE PROMISES AND PITFALLS OF PARTICIPATION

As I noted earlier, ACT UP is remarkable in its successful endeavor to seek out and use a vast array of arenas and fora. Some of those fora, like congressional hearings, are extant sluices and canals of the political system; as such, they are imagined in a radical political worldview as "inside." Deemed the radical wing of the AIDS social movement since its formation in 1987, ACT UP has garnered, not surprisingly, both praise and condemnation from other AIDS activists for their pointed, disruptive, performative public demonstrations and for their occasional refusal to work through the standard, liberal channels for amelioration. But it should be noted that early in its history, largely as a result of its persistence, the group gained entry to fora from which it had previously been excluded.

A tension between working inside the system and outside of the system has concerned the group since its earliest days (Cohen 1997, 98; Golden 1992).[14] Handelman (1990) writes about this tension as it has been manifested in ACT UP meetings: "Frequently, the meetings wallow in virulent disagreement over side issues. Is ACT UP co-opted by being granted a seat on a government panel?" (85). More specifically, Handelman quotes ACT UP member Jim Eigo in direct reference to the tension between radical and liberal tactics:

> He [Eigo] disagrees with those who would rather ACT UP remain a radical street organization and never have any members on government panels. "You're only co-opted if you're forced to mute your criticisms," he says. "I just see it as direct action of a different sort." (89)

Eigo's own participation in 20 July 1989 House subcommittee hearings shows him refusing to mute his criticism: in addition to his warning about surveillance and critical publicity, he more than any of the other ACT UP witnesses amplifies moral and ethical criticism of federal practices. Emphasizing the urgency of getting drugs to those whose health is precarious, Eigo asserts that "people whose only alternative is death or deterioration cannot ethically be asked to wait for bureaucratic niceties" (House 1989, 39) required in placebo studies. And against those physicians who complain about the daunting task of conducting efficient research on a parallel-track model, Eigo argues that their opposition to a "humanitarian plan to ease my community's suffering, saying it might prevent them from doing a job they've been unable to do thus far, is a measure of the distance they stand from my community" (41). Eigo's critics within the group might discern in his position a political naïveté, a brazen faith in the power of individuals to resist deep structures of power and discipline. To these critics, the well-being of the group depends critically on maintaining its staunch outsider status. Indeed, as chapters in numerous cities have disbanded and as the media presence of the group has diminished from the mid-1990s on, many (including Larry Kramer) argue that rapid and excessive moves to insider politics have enervated the group (Farber 1995).[15]

Besides the political threat of co-optation through participation in a state-sponsored forum, AIDS activists risk the emotional threat of disidentification. In addressing a body that does not necessarily respect you and in abiding by that body's norms of discourse, the sacrifices can be great. Cindy Patton (1997) notes these sacrifices when she writes about the oscillation of queer activists: "Sometimes we must make sense to government agents, but we shouldn't confuse this reeling moment of apparently transparent communication with a true recognition of queer presence by forces who generally oppose us" (209).[16] Although Patton writes more broadly of queer activism, her warning against a facile assumption that invitation or permission to address the state is an authentic acknowledgment of respect holds for radical AIDS activists, many of whom are queer.

Despite these stakes and activists' keen awareness of them, ACT UP members' participation in congressional hearings over a two-and-a-half-year period can be explained in large part by the multiple benefits accrued and potentially accruable to the group through oscillation. In my reading, there are several possible benefits of oscillation, each of which is borne out of the testimony discussed in the previous section. First, participation in the hearings gains the group wide, national publicity, thus enhancing the group's credibility to elected officials and to the nation at large. Indeed, the fact that the immediate audience is not necessarily the most significant audience to activists who testify is an important rhetorical feature of the encounter. Elected representatives and invited witnesses alike frequently indicate that they are speaking past or beyond those who are immediately present and are addressing instead a wider, mediated audience. When news of activists' participation in the hearings reaches members of this mediated audience, the activists' discourse is legitimated by virtue of being invited by the state.

Similarly, the hearings provide yet another forum for recognition and repetition of the group's messages in local, regional, or national media. However, as I mentioned earlier, the group neither ceases its participation in other fora nor sacrifices its prerogative to be dissatisfied. Although group members do not "act up" (in the colloquial sense) at the hearings, Martin Delaney and Tony Davis exploit their presence at the hearings to express their displeasure with the nature of the hearing as a forum and to broadcast threats and warnings about future activist interventions.

Another significant reason for ACT UP's oscillation is the fact that implementation of the group's recommendations, particularly their calls for new protocols for drug trials, is dependent on federal resources, notably federal money. Until—that is, *unless*—activists, researchers, and health care providers can gain enough funds through private sources, dependence on the state will remain inextricable. Tony Davis admits as much in his testimony when he says "although we AIDS activists have been and will continue to be critics of NIAID [National Institute of Allergy and Infectious Diseases], we do recognize the fact that Congress must provide the funding to enable NIAID to keep pace with research opportunities" (House 1990b, 27). Furthermore, activists recognize that through appeals to the state they can put more pressure on private industry, particularly pharmaceutical companies. Profoundly skeptical of pharmaceutical companies' concern for anything other than profits, ACT UP members frequently demonstrated against the companies in order to compel them to reduce drug prices and to commence a more vigorous research regimen, but they also called on the state to regulate the profit-driven industry. As Eric Sawyer succinctly noted at a 1993 demonstration: "The [pharmaceutical] industry can't regulate itself. The federal government is going to have to step in" (quoted in Sanchez and Wheeler 1993, A1). In order to have their demands met, AIDS activists cannot afford to repudiate the state as an interlocutor, nor can PWAs stop being clients of a welfare state simply because that is what they prefer. Not surprisingly, inextricable dependence on the state foments a profound ambivalence among PWAs and activists. Lauren Berlant (1997) explains:

> Disidentification with U.S. nationality is not, at this moment, even a theoretical option for queer citizens: as long as PWAs (People with AIDS) require state support, as long as the official nation invests its identity in the pseudoright to police nonnormative sexual representations and sexual practices, the lesbian, gay, feminist, and queer communities in the United States do not have the privilege to disregard national identity. We are compelled, then, to read America's lips. (150)

And when marginal individuals like PWAs and AIDS activists do address the nation in a state-sponsored forum such as hearings, Berlant discerns "acts of strange intimacy between subaltern peoples and those who have benefited by their subordination" (222–223).

Finally, oscillation benefits ACT UP because it enables the group to push for access to strong publics. As Cohen (1997) argues, "activist pressure in the form of demonstrations made opportunities to sit down with policy makers more available, and activists took eager advantage of them" (98).[17] During (but especially after) the two-year period of ACT UP testimony, various agencies of the federal health complex invited members of ACT UP and other activist organizations to participate as observers or as voting members of treatment and prevention committees. Of particular significance was the decision by National Institutes of Health (NIH) leaders to permit full activist participation in AIDS Clinical Trial Groups (ACTGs). This decision, made in early 1991 just a few months after the last ACT UP member testified at a hearing, was particularly bold, for it recognized PWAs and activists as possessors of a kind of medical expertise. Furthermore, it provided PWAs with the opportunity to discuss the viability of treatment options before release and to question researchers and direct the course of discussion. Most important, the decision extended equal voting power to PWAs and activists (d'Adesky 1991, 158). In short, the ACTGs were the first federal, "strong" procedural public to which activists gained access—access that participation in the "weak" procedural publics of congressional hearings facilitated.

CONCLUSION

On 1 October 1991, at the U.S. Capitol, members of ACT UP demonstrated both outside and inside of the building. As 300 protesters stood on the Capitol steps shouting and chanting in a legal demonstration sanctioned by an official permit, one demonstrator inside the building interrupted the flow of Senate floor debate by shouting from the public gallery (Associated Press 1991).[18] The events of this day synecdochically represent the long-term political strategy of many members of ACT UP: this strategy seeks to work inside and outside of extant channels of political activity simultaneously. I have argued that as a group ACT UP holds a profoundly ambivalent attitude toward the congressional hearing forum. Although ACT UP members participate in this forum at the state's invitation, they remain skeptical of the efficacy of both the forum *in toto* and their own participation in the forum. However, these activists use the forum of the hearings to strive to gain greater access to "stronger" procedural publics where they can be involved in decision-making as well as opinion-forming endeavors. Furthermore, because the very nature of the forum guarantees dispersal of ACT UP discourses to wider audiences, and because the discourses that members produce, however strident, still bear the mark of state tolerance, the benefits of oscillation are too compelling for activists to ignore.

The case of ACT UP participation in congressional hearings informs and revises studies in the public sphere in at least two ways. First, it demonstrates that when counterpublics stand in an antagonistic relationship with a state, activists' alliances with a few politically sympathetic elected officials can set in motion an impressive penetration of the state. At the federal level, Theodore Weiss of New York and Henry Waxman of California have proven to be these sympaticos, convening hearings in the early 1980s the main purpose of which was to give expression to the federal government's poor response to AIDS. Before the formation of ACT UP in 1987, these and other members of Congress invited people with AIDS and AIDS activists to testify and to scrutinize and critique the federal government. At hearings chaired by these representatives, oppositional discourse was neither squelched nor contained, for the chairmen pursued lines of questioning with the witnesses, and the presence of media representatives guaranteed wider publicity. When ACT UP formed, activists in the organization were able to exploit extant, amicable relations with state representatives in order to gain their access to hearings. Second, we find that counterpublic agents can be as strategic as states in the employment or exploitation of specific fora. Whereas states have often been accused of extending fora to dissidents and marginals for the purpose of strategic dilution of political opposition, the testimony of ACT UP members in congressional hearings betrays a calculating orientation. I do not mean to say that activists sought to deceive elected officials. Rather, the strategic orientation inheres in the exploitation of their participation as a tool for further penetration of the state. As strategic acts, ACT UP members' appearances before the state are far from mythic notions of the citizen's trip to Washington, DC. In an important sense, hearing testimony functions as a ritual of citizenship. But the relationship that activists presume with their government is a far cry from grateful supplication. As autodidactic medical experts and as accomplished veterans of civil disobedience, ACT UP activists approach the state as critics and reformers.

NOTES

Portions of this essay were presented at the 1996 Speech Communication Association national convention in San Diego, CA, the 1998 National Communication Association convention in New York, NY, and colloquia at Northwestern University. The author wishes to thank David S. Birdsell, Robert Asen, and Jean Goodwin for their helpful comments; and John Milton Hendricks and the staffs at Northwestern University's Government Publications and Maps Department and the New York Public Library Manuscripts and Archives Division for their gracious assistance.

1. Kramer is often incorrectly named the sole founder of ACT UP/New York. While his 10 March speech was an extraordinary catalyst for the formation of the group, and while his was an especially vibrant voice in the group for almost two years, Kramer should be recognized as

one of several cofounders of the group. Other cofounders include Maxine Wolfe, Bradley Ball, Eric Sawyer, and Michelangelo Signorile. Members chose the name of the group at the 19 March 1987 meeting.

2. AZT, also known as azidothymidine or zidovudine, was the first anti-HIV drug released by the federal Food and Drug Administration. The drug was originally developed in 1964 as a possible cancer treatment, was shelved when proven ineffective, and was retested in the mid-1980s as a possible anti-HIV treatment. Burroughs Wellcome obtained the patent and marketed the drug as Retrovir.

3. These tactics are hardly new to oppositional politics; indeed, ACT UP members, some of whom participated in social movements in the 1960s and 1970s, owe a great debt to the spirit and the practices of earlier politics. ACT UP was the first organization to mobilize these tactics in the fight against AIDS.

4. Valeria Fabj and Matthew Sobnosky argue that ACT-UP's dismantling of technical, public, and private sphere boundaries serves to rejuvenate the public sphere. Against Jürgen Habermas, who interprets the inclusion of private interests into the public sphere as detrimental and damaging to the public sphere (Habermas 1989, 132, 198), Fabj and Sobnosky (1995) interpret ACT UP's "translat[ion of] private concerns of people with AIDS into public issues" (172) as an enhancement to the development of AIDS public health policies and the practice of medical AIDS research. Following Fabj and Sobnosky, I have argued that through oscillation activists succeeded in both challenging and expanding notions of "expertise," in democratizing health care formulation and provision, and in reconfiguring boundaries between private, public, and technical spheres (Brouwer 2000).

5. Accounting for the quantity and quality of all ACT UP activities oriented toward the nation and the federal government is far beyond the scope and means of this study. However, brief mention of a few salient activities is warranted. A protest at the U.S. Capitol building in September 1990 resulted in the disruption of federal proceedings. In that protest, ACT UP members disrupted a Senate Judiciary Committee hearing on the nomination of Judge David Souter for the Supreme Court; protestors' shouts denounced the harm to women that Souter's anti-abortion views would occasion (Souter Day 1 1990). Thousands of demonstrators at the April 1993 March on Washington for Lesbian and Gay Rights linked arms and encircled the Capitol to dramatize a demand for more spending on AIDS research; one organizer of the demonstration asked demonstrators to stand with their backs facing the Capitol in a symbolic reversal of congressional betrayal against people with AIDS (Sanchez and Miller 1993, A1). More recent instances of ACT UP "presence" in or around

Congress include ACT UP/New York's Eric Sawyer criticizing the low level of U.S. funding for global AIDS at a state department briefing on World AIDS Day, 1 December 1997, and the pronouncement of a brief eulogy for Steve Michael, founder of ACT UP/Washington [D.C.], by Eleanor Norton Holmes on 3 June 1998.

6. Here, I am corroborated by ACT UP member Mark Smith (quoted in Weinraub 1991, E1) and scholar Peter Cohen (1997, 98, 100–101). However, contrary views—that unruly civil disobedience forestalls, if not corrodes, possibilities for discussion and debate between ACT UP members and officials and researchers—are more numerous. For popular accounts of this argument, see Cotton (1990); Leo (1990, 1992); and Labash (1996). The threat of such an unrecoverable loss of an audience as the aftermath of disruption was made manifest in 1990 when, during the closing address of the Sixth Annual International AIDS Conference, ACT UP protesters prevented Secretary of Human Health and Services Louis Sullivan from speaking by shouting him down; later that day, Sullivan announced, "I will not in any way work with those individuals" (quoted in Zonana 1990, A3).

7. Habermas's early configuration of the relationship between the state, civil society, and the private sphere called for a strict, normative demarcation of those entities. Criticism of this demarcation has been ample. Fraser (1992), for example, points to the existence of parliamentary forms of government and their unsettling of strict demarcations between state and civil society as evidence of the inadequacy of that model. To a significant degree, Habermas has revised his theories in recognition of such criticism (see, e.g., Habermas 1996).

8. A brief description of the procurement and management of witnesses is warranted: Both majority and minority party committee members invite witnesses to testify. Interested parties who have not been invited to testify may request the opportunity. When the testimony of a particular witness is deemed crucial but that witness rejects an invitation to testify, committees are accorded the power to compel the witness to testify through a subpoena. Witnesses are required to submit in advance a written copy of their testimony, and both the written and spoken testimony appear in published transcripts of committee hearings (Goehlert and Martin 1989, 15).

9. Miller (1978) and Keefer (1993) express skepticism about the critical role of publicity generated by congressional hearings. Miller notes that committees sometimes establish hostile relations with media representatives (658). Meanwhile, Keefer argues that media's efforts to generate participation actually hinder citizen participation in public policy processes (421). Despite this skepticism, I strive to show through textual

and extratextual data that ACT UP witnesses successfully exploit the possibilities for critical publicity at the hearings.

10. A pointed critique of these rules of discourse comes from Martin Delaney, founder of Project Inform in San Francisco, during 20 July 1989 hearings on revising federal research practices: "I came here today with great frustration because, as I say, we have been through so many other commissions, Congress people and meetings over the last few years, that we feel after awhile our words are going on deaf ears here. On many occasions when we get through this process, no matter what we say, Dr. Fauci and Dr. Young come up after us and have the last word and there's never an opportunity to cross examine them from our point of view" (House 167).

11. No ACT UP–affiliated witnesses are listed in the CIS Index after 1990. All four of the hearings at which ACT UP members appear were convened by House committees: Government Operations; Banking, Finance, and Urban Affairs; and Energy and Commerce.

12. Some of the most important work on AIDS and expertise is by Patton (1990), Treichler (1991), and Epstein (1995, 1996). For studies that foreground the communicative dimensions of AIDS expertise, see Brashers and Jackson (1991) and Fabj and Sobnosky (1995).

13. In 1988, at the Fourth International AIDS Conference in Montréal, ACT UP famously stormed the main stage of the conference, demanding, among other things, a greater role in planning and administrating the conference. The next year and ever since, ACT UP members have played key roles in the conferences. The apparent irony that emerges in a comparison of the 1988 and 1990 conferences derives from juxtaposing the group's demand for gaining access and being allowed to participate with their disruption of a public address and their refusal to allow Louis Sullivan to participate.

14. Research through the ACT UP/NY archives at the New York Public Library corroborates this claim. A review of minutes of the meetings from March 1987 through December 1994 indicates that frequent debates, some of them virulent, occur between members over the ideological purity and efficacy of insider versus outsider politics. Minutes of the meetings do not, however, indicate debate over participation in congressional hearings. For example, in May of 1988, minutes of the meeting indicate that "Iris Long reported about a Congressional hearing where she and others testified," but there is no indication of discussion or debate. Of course, this could be attributed to the weariness or inattention of the note-taker.

15. To members of ACT UP/Paris during a speech in 1995, ACT UP/New York cofounder Larry Kramer advocated the following: "If you

have a choice of being on the inside or being on the outside, stay on the outside. . . . You must be very careful not to become researchers who take the place of researchers, or doctors who take the place of doctors. Remain activists" (quoted in Tinmouth 1995/1996, 52).

16. The term *queer* is not unproblematic. Throughout this essay, I have been using the term broadly to refer to theories and practices that are critical of and resistant to the normative, in a way similar to Michael Warner's description of queer as "an aggressive impulse of generalization . . . [that] rejects a minoritizing logic of toleration or simple political interest-representation in favor of a more thorough resistance to regimes of the normal" (1993, xxvi). In this sense, *queer* refers neither exclusively nor inherently to same-sex erotics and sexuality.

17. Provocatively, Cohen (1997) describes ACT UP street activism as "bourgeois militancy" (105), and he links male ACT UP activists' eagerness to work on the inside to class style and class privilege.

18. For accounts of this demonstration, see Associated Press (1991), Wilgoren (1991), and Foerstel (1991).

REFERENCES

ACT UP/New York Records. Manuscripts and Archives Division. New York Public Library.

Associated Press. 1991. AIDS protesters arrested at Capitol, 1 October. http://web.lexis-nexis.com (10 December 1998).

Berlant, Lauren. 1997. *The queen of America goes to Washington City: Essays on sex and citizenship.* Durham, NC: Duke University Press.

Bessette, Joseph M. 1994. *The mild voice of reason: Deliberative democracy and American national government.* Chicago: University of Chicago Press.

Brashers, Dale, and Sally Jackson. 1991. "Politically-savvy sick people": Public penetration of the technical sphere. In *Argument in controversy: Proceedings of the seventh SCA/AFA conference on argumentation,* edited by Donn Parson. Annandale, VA: Speech Communication Association.

Brouwer, Daniel C. 2000. Representations of gay men with HIV/AIDS across scenes of social controversy: A contribution to studies in the public sphere. Ph.D. diss., Northwestern University.

Bull, Chris. 1991. Spy allegations pit Pennsylvania police against activists. *Advocate,* 26 February, 22.

Cohen, Peter. 1997. 'All they needed': AIDS, consumption, and the politics of class. *Journal of the History of Sexuality* 8:86–115.

Cotton, Paul. 1990. Scientifically astute activists seek common ground with clinicians on testing new AIDS drugs. *Journal of the American Medical Association* 264:666–669.

Crimp, Douglas, and Adam Rolston. 1990. *AIDS demographics*. Seattle, WA: Bay Press.

d'Adesky, Anne-Christine. 1991. Empowerment or co-optation? AIDS activists. *Nation*, 11 February, 252:158.

Davis, Kristine M. 1981. A description and analysis of the legislative committee hearing. *Western Journal of Speech Communication* 45:88–106.

Epstein, Steven. 1995. The construction of lay expertise: AIDS activism and the forging of credibility in the reform of clinical trials. *Science, Technology, & Human Values* 20:408–437.

———. 1996. *Impure science: AIDS, activism, and the politics of knowledge*. Berkeley: University of California Press.

Fabj, Valeria, and Matthew J. Sobnosky. 1995. AIDS activism and the rejuvenation of the public sphere. *Argumentation and Advocacy* 31:163–184.

Felski, Rita. 1989. *Beyond feminist aesthetics: Feminist literature and social change*. Cambridge, MA: Harvard University Press.

Foerstel, Karen. 1991. Hill AIDS protest brings 74 arrests and a foul smell. *Roll Call*, 3 October.

Fraser, Nancy. 1992. Rethinking the public sphere: A contribution to the critique of actually existing democracy. In *Habermas and the public sphere*, edited by Craig Calhoun. Cambridge: Massachusetts Institute of Technology Press.

Gamson, Joshua. 1989. Silence, death, and the invisible enemy: AIDS activism and social movement 'newness.' *Social Problems* 36:351–367.

Goehlert, Robert U., and Fenton S. Martin. 1989. The legislative process and how to trace it. In *Congress and law-making: Researching the legislative process*, 2d ed. Santa Barbara, CA: ABC-CLIO.

Golden, Mark. 1992. ACT UP redux. *QW*, 11 October, 22–25.

Habermas, Jürgen. 1989. *The structural transformation of the public sphere: An inquiry into a category of bourgeois society*. Translated by Thomas Burger and Frederick Lawrence. Cambridge: Massachusetts Institute of Technology Press.

———. 1996. *Between facts and norms: Contributions to a discourse theory of law and democracy*. Translated by William Rehg. Cambridge: Massachusetts Institute of Technology Press.

Handelman, David. 1990. ACT UP in anger. *Rolling Stone*, 8 March, 80–82, 85–86, 89–90, 116–117.

Keefer, Joseph D. 1993. The news media's failure to facilitate citizen participation in the Congressional policymaking process. *Journalism Quarterly* 70:412–424.

Labash, Matt. 1996. ACT-UP vs. PETA: Clash of the titans. *Weekly Standard*, 8–15 July, 28.

Leo, John. 1990. When activism becomes gangsterism. *U.S. News & World Report*, 5 February, 18.

——. 1992. The politics of intimidation. *U.S. News & World Report*, 6 April, 24.

Mansbridge, Jane. 1996. Using power/fighting power. In *Democracy and difference: Contesting the boundaries of the political*, edited by Seyla Benhabib. Princeton, NJ: Princeton University Press.

Miller, Susan H. 1978. Congressional committee hearings and the media: Rules of the game. *Journalism Quarterly* 55:657–663.

Osborne, Duncan. 1993. ACT UP and the FBI. *Advocate*, 29 June, 60–61.

Patton, Cindy. 1990. *Inventing AIDS*. New York: Routledge.

——. 1997. *Fatal advice*. Durham, NC: Duke University Press.

Rives, Stanley G. 1967. Congressional hearings: A modern adaptation of dialectic. *Journal of the American Forensic Association* 4:41–46.

Sanchez, Rene, and Bill Miller. 1993. Gay activists carry protests to Capitol and White House; demonstrations focus on AIDS, rights for lesbians. *Washington Post*, 25 April, A1.

Sanchez, Rene, and Linda Wheeler. 1993. On the march, in joy and pain; gay activists begin gathering amid celebrations and protests. *Washington Post*, 24 April, A1.

Souter day 1: 'Silent on abortion,' backs privacy rights. 1990. *Abortion Report*, 14 September.

Tinmouth, David. 1995/1996. POZ honors. *POZ*, December/January, 45–53.

Treichler, Paula. 1991. How to have theory in an epidemic: The evolution of AIDS treatment activism. In *Technoculture*, edited by Constance Penley and Andrew Ross. Minneapolis: University of Minnesota Press.

U.S. House. 1988. Subcommittee on Human Resources and Intergovernmental Relations of the Committee on Government Operations. *Therapeutic drugs for AIDS: Development, testing, and availability*. 100th Cong., 2d sess. 28 and 29 April.

——. 1989. Subcommittee on Health and the Environment of the Committee on Energy and Commerce. *AIDS issues (Part 2)*. 101st Cong., 1st sess. 20 July and 18 September.

——. 1990a. Subcommittee on Housing and Community Development of the Committee on Banking, Finance and Urban Affairs. *Housing needs of persons with Acquired Immune Deficiency Syndrome (AIDS)*. 101st Cong., 2d sess. 21 March.

————. 1990b. Subcommittee on Human Resources and Intergovernmental Relations of the Committee on Government Operations. *Drugs for opportunistic infections in persons with HIV disease*. 101st Cong., 2d sess. 1 August.

Warner, Michael. 1993. Introduction. In *Fear of a queer planet: Queer politics and social theory*, edited by Michael Warner. Minneapolis: University of Minnesota Press.

Weinraub, Judith. 1991. AIDS activists' routes of pain; from all walks of life, marching on a disease. *Washington Post*, 1 October, E1.

Wilgoren, Debbi. 1991. 74 AIDS activists arrested in Capitol protests. *Washington Post*, 2 October, A24.

Wilson, Woodrow. 1925. *Congressional government*. Boston, MA: Houghton Mifflin.

Zonona, Victor F. 1990. Did AIDS protest go too far? Conference: ACT UP draws fire and praise after activists shouted down a cabinet official in San Francisco. *Los Angeles Times*, 2 July, A3.

4 The Black Press and the State

Attracting Unwanted (?) Attention

CATHERINE SQUIRES

INTRODUCTION

Much of public sphere theory is interested in the moments when the public develops its opinions and then moves to present them to the state. Theorists have also asked whether marginalized publics have "safe spaces" to engage in deliberation or enjoy material resources and legal protections to safely and effectively transmit opinions to the state and wider publics (Dawson 1995; Felski 1989; Fraser 1992; Young 1990). However, the histories of marginalized publics also instruct us that it is often the state that moves to the public. For example, Dawson (1995) explains how various agencies of the United States government bombarded Black Power-oriented institutions of the Black public sphere with a variety of oppressive strategies, including heavy surveillance, infiltration, and physical violence. These state-sponsored strikes are not unique to the 1960s and 1970s but are only one example of the state's willingness to interfere directly with the mechanisms of a marginal public sphere. The Black populace has long been subject to state interference and oppression. From the slave codes to the intransigence of Southern governors, from COINTELPRO to the battles over fair housing and affirmative action, Black publics have lived with the reality of the state's ability to intrude on and affect Black life—for ill and for good. This chapter focuses on one particular form of movement, or oscillation, of the state to the Black public sphere: government attempts to censor and intimidate the Black press from 1917–1945. Through these oscillations, the state threatened to curtail the fast-growing power of the mass-distributed urban Black newspapers, attempting to stifle or eliminate this new voice of dissent and positive racial identity.

As I have argued elsewhere (Squires 1999), publics formed by marginalized peoples take on particular genres of discourse and action depending on culture, relations with the dominant public and the state, and socioeconomic forces: enclaved, oscillating, counterpublic, and parallel.[1] I contend that from the years 1917 to 1945, the Black public sphere mainly exhibited the characteristics of the oscillating genre, where members of a marginalized public systematically project their previously enclaved ideas toward the state and wider publics. In this period, Black newspapers and new civil rights organizations vigorously exercised their right to speak against racism and racist policies to both Black and white audiences aided by newly successful mass-printed, Black-owned newspapers. The bold rhetoric from these Black public sphere institutions drew the attention of the state. This resulted in oscillations of various state apparatuses to the publicity organs of the Black public sphere. Three issues in particular drew local and national oscillations of the state: mass migration of Blacks from the South; alleged communist and antiwar sympathies during World War I; and protests against discrimination in the New Deal, armed forces, and war industries during World War II. However, rather than creating egalitarian opportunities for whites in power and Blacks to discuss race relations, much of these movements were encroachments on the Black public sphere that reinforced the oppressive nature of government's role in Black life and sought further restriction of Black voices. These controversies provide us with stark examples of the state's impact on the institutions of marginal public spheres and their everyday activities.

THE RISING BLACK PUBLIC:
MIGRATION AND EMPOWERMENT IN URBAN ARENAS

Pushed by racism and economic concerns and pulled by promises of a better life, Blacks left the rural South in droves for the cities of the North and the growing urban areas of the South. In cities such as Chicago, Memphis, New Orleans, Detroit, New York, and Baltimore, African Americans created large enclaves. Bronzeville and Harlem, East Baltimore and other urban "black belts" became cultural and political centers for the New Negro era. The great migrations of Blacks from rural to urban areas put Blacks in a stronger position to consolidate identity and circulate ideas and opinions in a wider arc than in the nineteenth century. Congregated in cities, Blacks had more numerical power, and those with access to the vote had newfound voting power. New political organizations such as the NAACP and Black unions emerged and grew. Greater editorial and financial control over communication industries created new opportunities to express dissent and project a militant oppositional discourse into wider publics. These enclaves, enjoying more economic and civic freedoms, were stronger, more diverse, and afforded Blacks a solid platform from which to launch more frequent and bolder oscillations into the white public arena.

Thus, not only were segregated enclaves of the Black public strengthened and diversified, but a national Black public and identity could emerge, linked by the new communication and social institutions founded in the early part of the century. This could only occur in an environment where public assembly, speech, and consolidation of various resources did not inspire intense white reprisal. A national Black public did not arise immediately after slavery; instead, the brief period of Reconstruction was transformed into a reign of terror in the South and reversal of the few civil rights provisions enacted after the Civil War. Although Black newspapers emerged in this period, many did not survive the fall of Reconstruction, and others were forced to mute their protests for fear of violence. All in all, the Black public still acted more like an enclaved public for the remainder of the nineteenth century, expressing its oppositional consciousness mainly in safe spaces and rarely supporting open confrontations with the white public. It was not until the Great Black Migration to the cities and Ida B. Wells's antilynching crusade that the Black public began to take the shape of an oscillating public, one that would no longer settle for the public scripts of the white majority in public confrontations outside Black enclaves.[2] This new Black public created out of its own traditions of struggle a new sense of publicity, purpose, and organization. Between 1905 and 1915, the Black press and its sister forms of mass communication became solid institutions that were able to impact a wider range and larger number of Black folks than ever imagined in the previous century. In addition, Black literacy rates soared in the early years of the twentieth century, providing a larger audience for the new papers. These developments coincided with and accelerated the development of independent Black political organizations and thought in Black enclaves, providing the foundation from which to launch challenges at the white public sphere and its government agencies and officials. The first such challenge examined here is the encouragement of Blacks to leave the South, a message that was countered by Southern white governments and newspapers.

THE PRESS AS RACE ADVOCATE AND GRAPEVINE: BRINGING BLACKS NORTH

In the press of America, all that the Negro gets is headlines for his faults, 'BIG BURLY BLACK BRUTE DOES THIS AND

HUGE BLACK NEGRO FIEND DOES THAT.' This is the advertisement and the only sort of introduction that the Negro daily gets to white masses. . . . The Negro's real heart and virtue rarely ever is exposed to America. We have a right to proper representation before the bar of public opinion, but we have not had it.[3]

Blacks gained better representation at that bar with the emergence of a national Black press. After the death of Booker T. Washington, the Black press supported a wider range of attitudes and political programs. Unlike Washington, who urged Blacks to "cast down their bucket" in the South, the new urban newspapers advocated northern migration. Prior to and during the First World War, the growing northern Black press created campaigns and worked with northern labor agents to bring Black southerners to cities. Papers such as the Chicago *Defender* created pro-North propaganda that emphasized the better wages and racial climate of the North, and continued to rail against lynch law and the rule of Jim Crow to convince sharecroppers and others to migrate. In addition, the papers criticized segregation in the Armed Forces, and some suggested draft resistance. Printing articles about the greater freedoms of the North and selling advertising space to labor agents, papers depicted a developing Black urban culture that appealed to many Blacks. Even some southern Black weeklies, still relatively muzzled by threats of white violence, mildly encouraged the drive North, as did the *Southern Indicator* in this statement from 1919:

> We are told, and we read it for ourselves, too, that the North is still inviting our people to come up and fill the vacancies made by the foreigners daily. And of course the invitation will be accepted more readily the more the law is laid aside. . . . Our good white friends of the South had better awake and demand a stop, else the North will grow in prosperity upon the wickedness . . . of the South. (quoted in Kerlin 1920, 12)

Between 1915 and 1920 alone, over one-half million Blacks left the South. This mass exodus left whites flabbergasted and without their expected pool of cheap labor. The bold public statements of the Black press were read North and South by thousands of Blacks—and many suspicious whites. This unprecedented level of oscillation of "New Negro" militant ideology into the white public sphere in turn sparked a set of oscillations from the state. Rather than engage with Blacks in dialogue to solve the problems of lynchings, unfair sharecropping contracts, and poll taxes, the governments of many states and the southern press attacked Black newspapers and those who read and distributed them.

Southern politicians and newspapers railed against the "militant" content of the northern papers and accused them of slandering the South and tricking Blacks into moving North. In 1920 an attempt was made by Southern Congressmen to pass a law prohibiting the use of the U.S. mail to any "Negro publication" that was deemed to advocate "racial violence" (Vincent 1973, 34). This law, if it had been successful, would have ended all mailings of Black publications if defining what content "advocated racial violence" was left to Southerners. Although the laws were not passed, the South found other ways to intimidate Blacks from moving North. The Chicago *Whip*, in its 21 August 1919 issue, reported the beating and arrest of a northern labor agent in the South for trying to get workers to move north, and also noted that Louisiana passed a law preventing labor agents from doing business in the state. Additionally, the Southern press created a counterpropaganda campaign. As the *Kansas City Sun* reported:

> The Press despatches [*sic*] this week say that the Southern Newspaper Publishers' Association would spend a hundred thousand dollars this year advertising the South. 'Tisn't necessary, brother, your rough necks and lynchers have advertised the South so thoroughly that there isn't any danger or possibility of any immigration setting in toward that benighted section of our fair land. (quoted in Kerlin, 139)

Some states sent their own labor agents North and paid Blacks there to tell stories of freezing temperatures and joblessness. The findings of these "Colored commissions" were publicized through the Associated Press (AP). Not that these portrayals of hardship weren't partly true, as Blacks did suffer hiring prejudices in the North, but the Black papers ridiculed the AP's exaggerated portrayal of northern cities as too much for southern Blacks to handle. The following excerpt comes from an article that was reprinted widely:

> The commissions have an entirely different way of viewing the state of affairs here [in the South] from the way Negroes on the ground here view it. I have interviewed Negro laborers, Negro mechanics, Negro porters . . . [names many other professions], and I have been unable to discover one who would agree that he finds conditions better now than they were a year ago.[4]

Furthermore, the new Black journalism was committed to smashing Southern stereotypes of passive, happy Southern Negroes. In reaction to an article by the *Weslyan*, a white religious publication claiming that good ol' Mammy didn't want to go North, the Black-owned New Orleans *Southwestern Christian Advocate* wrote the following:

> The *Weslyan* is dead right when it says that the 'Black Mammy' would not give a penny for more rights than she has had. . . . All that we can say is that that is the attitude of the 'Black Mammy' as far as outside appearances are concerned. There were those of this class who were absolutely satisfied with their subordinate relations but when they get out from under the roofs of their master their attitude is entirely different. The 'Black Mammy' is going and we bid her an affectionate good-bye and a long farewell. (quoted in Kerlin, 30)

The *Washington Bee* attacked Republican Blacks who let their votes be bought for a pittance, declaring that "it is the young colored Americans who are defending the rights and the liberties of their people, and the old school [Black] politician is the dangerous element in society."

Unlike the Black papers of the nineteenth century, which emphasized the American in the label "Colored American," the new papers trumpeted the notion of a separate Black identity and culture that its readers subscribed to heartily. The majority of the new Black papers self-identified as "militant" in their approach to racial discrimination. This militancy was not limited to males. Black women, both in male-owned periodicals and Black women's magazines, wrote of Ebony queens and the need to protect Black women from white rapists and to debunk the myth that lynching was done in reaction to Black rapists' attacks on white women. Ida B. Wells stated the problem succinctly:

> The Lynching record for a quarter of a century merits the thoughtful study of the American people. It presents three salient facts:
> First: Lynching is a color-line murder
> Second: Crimes against women is the excuse, not the cause
> Third: It is a national crime and requires a national remedy.[5]

Wells's campaign against lynching and its related racial and sexual myths continued despite the destruction of her paper, *Free Speech*, by a white mob, and her writings and speeches inspired thousands and jump-started the NAACP's antilynching campaign. She embodied the spirit of the new

Black woman, public and proud, who was the partner to the "race man" whose image eclipsed hers in the dominant public sphere in the coming years of expanding Black political action. Although these women's contributions were often overlooked, male-edited and -written press accounts of white excuses of lynching reflected the analyses of Ida B. Wells, Anna Julia Cooper, and other early Black feminists. A 1919 article in the *Cleveland Gazette* reported the following on race riots and lynching in Omaha:

> A U.S. Senator 'justified' the Omaha tragedy. He 'justified' it as a 'means of protecting white women.' We venture the assertion that ninety-five percent of the outrages reported in Omaha were committed, if at all, by white men. Besides, readers of the press see daily occurrences of white men outraging even thirteen-year old white and black girls. Southern Senators should shut their mouths and cover their own nakedness in this matter. (quoted in Kerlin, 137)

In addition to these antilynching "radicals," nationalists were also able to thrive in the Black public sphere. Marcus Garvey's brand of nationalism was widely distributed through his organization's paper, the *Negro World*, which enjoyed high circulation rates (Moses 1996; Vincent 1973; Wintz 1996). John Albert Williams, founder of the Omaha *Monitor*, regularly published a section titled "General Race News," showcasing race heroes and promoting racial pride (Paz 1996, 223). The *Monitor* was also a strong supporter of Garvey's Universal Negro Improvement Association (UNIA), and published articles and columns regarding African history penned by UNIA members and *Negro World* reporters. Other papers printed leftist columns: the Omaha *Guide* subscribed to the Communist-operated Crusader News Service and the socialist- and anarchist-staffed Federated Press. In the 1930s, the *Guide* also threw its support behind the League of Struggle for Negro Rights, a Communist-supported group (Paz 1996, 224). So not only were the larger papers in the biggest cities providing a range of "radical" opinions, but regional papers contained a mix of political thought. And the reach of these thoughts was substantial.

INCREASED CIRCULATION, INCREASED ATTENTION

In the introduction to his 1920 survey of the Black press, Robert Kerlin wrote the following:

> The Negro seems to have newly discovered his fourth estate, to have realized the extraordinary power of his press. . . . Into

> every town and village of the land, and into many a log cabin
> in the mountains, come the colored papers, from all parts of
> the country, and these papers are read, and passed from hand
> to hand, and re-read until they are worn out. (1968, ix)

Indeed, the reach of the Black press contributed to a growing "imagined community" (Anderson 1991) of Blacks who shared a set of news texts. By 1920, both the Pittsburgh *Courier* and the Chicago *Defender* posted paid circulations in excess of 200,000. By 1944, the combined circulation of the *Defender*, the *Courier*, the Norfolk *Journal & Guide*, Harlem's *Amsterdam News*, and the *Afro-American* was 740,282, and combined circulation of all Black weeklies was around two million. However, "unlike the daily paper that is discarded at the end of each day, the Black weeklies tended to be held longer and passed around more," and so these figures only reflect the holders of subscriptions, not the actual readers who eventually read or had the paper read to them (Finkle 1975, 52). Scholars such as Lawrence Hogan (1984) and Lee Finkle (1975) suggest multiplying official circulation numbers by three or four—and in the case of the *Defender*, five—to get a better estimate of how many Blacks got the information in these papers. So between 1920 and 1940, we can estimate that around five million Blacks were getting information from the Black weeklies either through their own subscription or by sharing with others. Considering that the Black population numbered 10.4 million to 12.8 million during this period, this estimate would mean nearly half of Black citizens were exposed to the content of the new Black press.

Northern papers did not only sell in their own cities but in the South as well. An estimated two-thirds of the copies of the *Defender* were sent out of the city to be sold in other regions (Hogan 1984, 23). While southern Blacks with subscriptions to northern papers were often persecuted, there were other ways of slipping in news from outside. Relatives and other visitors from the North transported articles, both in print and in memory, passing along tales of better economic opportunities, famous Black entertainers, and voting victories like the election of Oscar DePriest as the first Black alderman, and later congressman, in Chicago. A modern and ingenious version of the Black grapevine was facilitated by the wider range of jobs open to Blacks in the North: Black train porters were employed as subscription agents and distributors of papers like the Chicago *Defender*.

In addition to having railroad workers and travelers distributing the paper, entertainers and speakers on tour collected news, solicited subscriptions, and picked up copies of smaller local papers to bring back to the Chicago *Defender*'s offices to be reworked and published in its pages.

Walker (1996) describes the *Defender*'s content as the result of "a collective effort" between the "professional" newsmakers in the *Defender*'s offices and the traveling "news gatherers" (24). These cooperative processes were augmented by the nationwide network of local journalists and columnists working for the Associated Negro Press (ANP), founded in 1919 by Charles Burnett. The following are among the well-known "stringers" for the ANP: William Pickens, NAACP Field Secretary; poet Langston Hughes; and Jessie Fauset, author of *The Chinaberry Tree* (Hogan 1984, 143–147). In the first half of the century, Black reporters were still not given press passes or even allowed into the press gallery in the Congress, so ANP reporters relied on other methods. Correspondent Alvin White often got Black office workers and messengers to open files and memos they were delivering to congressional offices. Some Black federal employees, such as Numa Adams, wrote for ANP as well (Hogan 1984, 91). Blacks used these grapevine-like methods to skirt segregation in the Capitol and to provide reliable information for readers.

The widespread involvement of people of so many different ideological and professional backgrounds enhanced the sense of a national Black public, which was truly community-based as so many folks from different walks of life contributed to the creation and success of Black papers. The papers' demands for racial justice were welcomed by Blacks who were tired of accommodation and white hypocrisies. Even though the southern Black papers were not able to write as militantly for fear of violence, the radical messages of race pride from the North seeped into southern Black minds. This was very key to the further development of the Black public sphere, for the wide range of the news media affected the scope of the Black public's imagination North and South; Black people nationwide read similar news of Black accomplishment, outrage, and creativity.[6] Southern Blacks, mired in Jim Crow, could imagine allies in the North working in new organizations like the NAACP, and Blacks voting without literacy tests or fear of lynching in Chicago and New York; and they could experience pride in seeing alternative images to the racist projections of whites.

In her ethnographic studies during the 1930s, sociologist Hortense Powdermaker "detected more aggressive attitudes emerging among [southern] Blacks" especially in the younger generation (Powdermaker 1968, 328). She described this generation as more literate and exposed to Black papers as well as radio and film. Through this media exposure and education, she concluded, they were more likely to believe that they were equal to whites. Furthermore, while they continued to enact the "public transcript" of subservience expected by whites, they were quick to explain this behavior as necessary performance, not as a true reflection of their identity. "The Negroes always have the laugh on the whites," said one interviewee, "because the whites are always being deceived but never know it" (330). Resentment of white paternalism and violence prevailed over acceptance in the "hidden transcript" of Black life.[7] Thus, the Black press facilitated the growth of the internal aspects of the public sphere through its production and transmittal of alternative Black identities and fostering the imaginations and discussions of Blacks across the nation. But these new alternatives and their related politics were not well-received in other arenas, particularly the agencies of the state and other white public institutions.

WORLD WAR I: FEAR OF BLACK COMMUNISM AND DISSENT

The "radical" Black press was gaining the attention of the federal government. As the New Negro press attacked racist federal government policies, the federal government became concerned that such editorial content would hamper war strategy and international affairs during both World Wars. In addition, northern and national white-owned papers, not just southern ones, increased their scrutiny of Negro periodicals dramatically during the war years. While this heightened surveillance was intended to be punitive by the initiators, it provided an avenue for oscillation of Black ideas into the white public sphere.

During both world wars, the Black press devoted many pages to the exploits of Black GIs and wrote scathing editorials on the hypocrisy of Blacks fighting for democracy abroad when Jim Crow laws still reigned at home. During the First World War, some papers even applauded draft resisters for not fighting for a government that allowed lynching (Vincent 1973, 35). At the federal level, the Executive Branch and the Army worried about Black opinion adversely affecting the war effort. Fearing disruption, the federal government began to survey the output of the Black press. President Wilson held a conference with the editors and owners of the major Black papers to plead for their "cooperation." This cooperative effort, however, was a one-sided affair with the burden laid at the feet of the owners' editors: the heads of the Black newspapers were told to end their attacks on segregation in the Armed Forces. This oscillation toward the Black press, which at first looked like a true attempt at dialogue, was accompanied by coercive actions that spoke louder than Wilson's words. Black papers were banned from several army bases in both wars for periods of time. The FBI and Postmaster General were used to halt the spread of what some politicians considered sedition and treason. Accusing them of treason and communist sympathies, the government took away the second class mailing privileges from periodicals like the *Richmond Planet* and the *Messenger* (Vincent 1973, 36). In the process of espousing socialism as the best strategy for Blacks, the young editors of the *Messenger*, A. Phillip Randolph and Chandler Owen, were arrested for their socialist writings and had their postal privileges rescinded. Interestingly, the judge let them off, having decided that Negroes were not capable of the sophisticated socialist reasoning found in the propaganda that Owen and Randolph were (correctly) accused of authoring and distributing.

Washburn's (1986) study of recently released federal documents reveals how a consistent pattern of surveillance and intimidation of the Black press was practiced by the FBI from 1918 through the civil rights movement. During the First World War, such interference and threats did not affect the content of most Black papers, especially the powerhouses of the North. Indeed, the charges of communism were refuted with wit, as here in the *Courier*:

> Until recently no one would have thought of calling Negroes Bolshevists, and yet the Negro is no different now from what he has been with respect to his duty toward his government. He has always been a loyal citizen, and he is none the less loyal now. . . . We never heard of a Negro Bolshevist as long as the Negro remained quiet. . . . But when the Negro went to France and there laid down his life along with all other Americans . . . [w]hen the Negro returned home and observed the attitude of the American white man toward him, when he observed the unhampered program of the lynchers . . . [h]e at once began to fight back. He decided that Liberty is Liberty wherever found. Then went up the cry from all over the country: The Negro is joining the Bolshevists. (quoted in Kerlin 1920, 150–151)

Despite pressure from the president and the FBI, most large papers did not change their editorial style. DuBois, under pressure from the NAACP Board and the government, adopted a temporary "close-ranks" editorial policy during the war that was heavily criticized by papers like the *Defender*, *Amsterdam News*, and the *Messenger*. However, when Black regiments were created, most papers supported the soldiers and sent correspondents to cover their battles in Europe and Africa. Still criticizing the racism within the Army, the Black press and the Black public gave servicemen a hero's welcome, staging parades and reporting on their valor and patriotism.

During and after the war, many white publications criticized the Black press for heightening racial tensions between Black soldiers and whites. Similar to their responses to charges of Bolshevism, the Black papers answered these attacks with their own version of the racial violence that escalated after the war. Known as "Red Summer," the season after the war was stained by the blood of race riots often started by whites determined to keep recently returned Black GI's "in their place." The *Denver Star* railed against the white press's complicity with the white mobs:

> "U.S. Troops Ordered to Shoot Negroes," "Negro Rapes White Woman," "Negroes Plan to Kill Whites in South." . . . All these glaring headlines were made to discredit the Negro in the Community in which he lives. . . . It has a tendency to heat our enemies and cool our friends and the Negro in all parts of the United States pays dearly, even for the slightest racial misunderstanding. The Negro must keep his ear close to the ground. (quoted in Kerlin, 7)

Reframing the skewed vision of race riots in the white press, the Black papers between the wars continued to advocate self-determination, self-defense, and protest. The *Journal and Guide* reported Blacks fighting off lynch mobs in Washington not as aggression but as self-defense motivated by white refusals to act civil.

> White enthusiasm in the lawless slaughter began to freeze as soon as the blacks began to shoot and cut to kill. . . . The outcome of the rioting at Washington, and at Longview, Texas, is that the black masses driven to desperation by white mobs have reached the conclusion that the only way left to them is to meet the white mob lawlessness with black mob lawlessness. (quoted in Kerlin, 18)

The racial violence of the Red Summer convinced many Blacks that war service was no guarantee of civil rights, and activist strategies were preferred. The press remained in favor of boycotts, strikes, and other demonstrations, culminating in their support for Randolph's 1942 March on Washington Movement (MOWM) and the "Double V" editorial strategy.

WORLD WAR II: RENEWED FEAR OF BLACK PROTEST

Randolph's MOWM was the first glimpse of a possible national Black movement, and it woke up the Roosevelt administration. Like other Blacks, Randolph was frustrated with the racism in the New Deal agencies, particularly with the lack of racial equity in hiring by government agencies for the defense buildup. After the NAACP's "National Defense Day," a day of protest meetings in twenty-three states (and a departure from its usual legalistic methods), failed to get the notice of the government, Randolph began his call for a massive march on Washington, DC. Garfinkel describes the MOWM as

> a radical departure from what had previously characterized even more militant Negro protest activities. The scope of such an undertaking is one of important difference. To be successful, a vast amount of organizational work would be required on a grass-roots level. . . . Also, people who were ordinarily apathetic and apolitical would have to be simultaneously stimulated. (1959, 41)

That "stimulation" came from the Black press. Garfinkel found that "overwhelmingly, the sentiment of these newspapers favored the March. . . . During the last months before the March deadline the MOW was easily the major news item in the entire Negro press" (55). By May of 1941, the *Defender* was reporting the organization of a branch of the MOWM that "met with enthusiastic response" from Black Chicagoans. Other papers also reported packed meetings, but an official count was never done of prospective marchers. However, with all of the hype of the march in the Black press, it must have seemed to outsiders that there would be hundreds of thousands of Blacks on the capitol in July 1941. Even major organizations such as the National Council of Negro Women, Alpha Kappa Alpha sorority, and the Negro Elks planned to hold their meetings in Washington so that their members could attend the March.

Through the publicity of the threat of an amazing gathering of disgruntled Negroes, Randolph, his organizers, and the Black press forced the federal government to address Black workers' needs. On 18 June, President Franklin Delano Roosevelt personally conferred with the leaders and strongly urged them to cancel the March. Their condition was an executive order to desegregate the war industries. They finally achieved that goal, without marching, when FDR signed Executive Order 8802, which created the Fair Employment Practice Committee (FEPC) to curtail discrimination in the defense industries, on 25 June 1941.[8] This victory secured Randolph's place as an important figure in Black political life. More important, the March also highlighted the powers of one of the most important new institutions of the time: the Black press. The popularity and assumed influence of the Black newspapers prompted further government oscillations. As with earlier interactions, these movements were made for surveillance and censorship, not dialogue.

By the beginning of the Second World War, whites' heightened awareness of the Black press and related organizations, combined with the economic opportunities of the war economy, changed the interaction between the white public sphere and the Black public's institutions. The government was increasingly aware of and concerned with the expanding volume and visibility of the New Negro. As during the First World War, the government feared that a discontented Black public would breed troubles for the war effort. Certainly memories of the treatment received by Black GIs returning from World War I had not dissipated in the Black community by 1941. After Pearl Harbor, many Blacks were extremely skeptical that their involvement in the war effort would result in anything different than another series of race riots and Jim Crow in the military. The Office of War Information (OWI) conducted a survey in early 1942 to assess the level of Black support for the war and found it was low.

> This study concluded that "resentment at Negro discrimination is fairly widespread throughout the Negro population." When those who were interviewed were asked if they were better off before the war, more responded that they were either the same or worse off than they had been. The answer to the question, "Would you be better off if America or the Axis won the war?" was especially revealing. Most believed that they would be treated either the same or better under Japanese rule [but worse under the Germans]. . . . [O]nly 11 percent responded in the affirmative when asked if conditions would improve for blacks if the United States won the war. (Finkle 1975, 102–103)

Official summaries of the survey downplayed the level of Black resentment, describing the Black population as having "less enthusiasm" for the war than whites.[9] These reports of low morale and the Black press's policy of criticizing Jim Crowism in the New Deal, the armed forces, and the war industries convinced the white press and government that Blacks had to be won over—or silenced.

In a time when Hitler's propaganda machine was seen as central to the rise of the Third Reich, the Office of War Information and the FBI were particularly sensitive to issues of press activism and rhetoric. President Roosevelt himself contacted the editors of the five largest Black papers and asked them to tone down their criticism for the sake of the war effort. Both criticism and cooperation emerged between the Black and white public as the country geared up for the Second World War. Black editors were invited to speak with government officials, but then their papers were charged with taking advantage of the crisis to pursue their racial aims. Others accused them of trying to incite a race war with their insistent demands for equality. The Black press responded to these criticisms with editorial statements such as the following from the *Journal and Guide:*

> We are no bolder now in our demands . . . than we were prior to the first world war, and during the two decades which elapsed between 1918 and 1939. . . . We are on the spot. Our people cry out in anguish: This is no time to stick to a middle of the road policy; help us get some of the blessings of Democracy here at home first before you jump on the free [*sic*] the other peoples' bandwagon. (quoted in Finkle, 64)

Despite these protestations, the government continued its investigations of and pressure on the press. Meetings were set and letters were exchanged between sympathetic members of the administration to warn editors that the Post Office was targeting Black publications (Washburn 1986, 66–97). Certain issues of the *Courier* were declared "unmailable" in 1942, and the *New Negro World* was almost suppressed for sedition after an investigation held up its mailing pending a decision from the Justice Department. Luckily, Attorney General Francis Biddle was adamant about First Amendment rights and curtailed as much of the censorship activities launched at the Black press as he could. Military Intelligence also saw the Black press as a "major factor of Negro unrest," and the War Department created a committee to decide how to deal with Black reporters' and papers' presence in the camps (150). Although none of the major papers was suppressed entirely, many were heavily censored before reaching GI hands. There was constant contact between Black aides in the War Department and the editors concerning possible censorship, artificial shortages of newsprint, and pending investigations of content.

The amount and intensity of federal attention made some editors nervous, and they constantly reinforced their position of loyalty to the war effort—although they could not claim the same level of loyalty for the Black populace. The editors portrayed themselves and Black leaders as preventing violent outbreaks in the Black masses, not fomenting them. Writing in May of 1942, Pittsburgh *Courier* columnist George Schuyler explained that "Negro leaders and editors caution their people to use organized protest and . . . the courts," and warned "who will do this if these spokesmen are squelched?" (Finkle 1975, 67). These spokesmen were taking heat on two sides: the government, who wanted full compliance with the war effort, and their readers, who expected the press to continue to report on racial injustices and advocate for change. William Hastie, racial adviser to the secretary of war, called a conference of Black leaders, which included many newspaper editors, on 10 January 1942. When he polled them on the question of whether Blacks supported the war fully, thirty-six said Blacks were not behind the war, five said they were, and fifteen abstained—later these silent fifteen were said to claim they believed Blacks did not support the war effort (107).

The Black masses were much more militant than the leaders assembled by Hastie; as a result, the editors were unwilling to merely "close ranks" and put aside racial issues. Many of the editors saw the government's need for Black support as an opportunity to make political gains and were tentatively supportive of the New Deal and the war. Thus, they concocted a strategy to gain favor both with their readers and the government. The stance taken by the majority of remaining papers was to present a united front with the war effort while simultaneously promoting racial equality, albeit in a less radical way. Quickly the press realized that the Allies' anti-Nazi rhetoric could be used to critique America's racism. But unlike in 1918 when Du Bois's "close ranks" editorial was widely disparaged, the majority of the press in the 1940s followed a route of cooperation. The "Double V" strategy, which stood for victory abroad against Nazi tyranny and victory at home against white racism, was coined by James G. Thompson on 31 January 1942, when he wrote the following words in a letter to the *Courier*:

> Let Colored Americans adopt the Double VV for a double victory. The first V for our enemies from without, the second V for victory over our enemies from within. . . . This should not and would not lessen our efforts to bring this conflict [from without] to a successful conclusion. (quoted in Washburn 1986, 55)

The next *Courier* edition displayed a large "Double V" on the front page, and the campaign was on. Even though they pledged to fight both fronts equally, the Double V was a hard sell to the Black public, not to mention the white public sphere and the federal government.

In addition to contending with government censors, Black editors had to work hard to get the Black public to overcome their critical memories of past Black war service being rewarded with more racism and violence. Journalists tried to convince Blacks that things would be the same or worse if the Axis powers (who also practiced racist doctrine) won, so both victories had to be won to ensure that Black freedom struggles would be fruitful and continue. Editor Charlotta Bass of the California *Eagle* was initially skeptical that the Double V would work. She feared that the VV strategy would put too much emphasis on the war and not enough on discrimination (Bass 1960). While she eventually threw her support behind the Double V, other Blacks were suspicious, and it took much time, effort, and many column inches to win over Black readers. To get their support, Black journalists had to consistently lobby the war industries and the armed forces to rid themselves of Jim Crow.

> The wartime position of the Black press was determined by the belief among Black editors and leaders that Blacks would have to serve as equals in the armed forces in order to gain eventual equality, and by the militancy of its readers. The Black press would continue to protest, and the Black population had to support the war effort and participate equally in combat action against the foreign enemy. These aims were not mutually exclusive; in fact they complemented each other. A double victory—one at home and one abroad—was the answer. (Finkle 1975, 110)

Despite the creation of the Double V, the government's pressure on the Black press continued. A series of meetings in the first half of 1943 between the editors of the largest Black publications and Vice-President Henry Wallace, Biddle, and officials from the OWI, the Navy, and other war departments cleared up some of the conflicts. But Black editors still had to contend with threats, warnings, and suppressions of particular mailings. The Office of Censorship did not end mandatory inspections of Black publications until 1944. Additionally, J. Edgar Hoover launched his own investigation and attack on the Black press in September of 1943, producing a 714–page report and asking Attorney General Biddle to prosecute the Black press for sedition. Biddle refused to do Hoover's work, but the FBI Director continued to seek indictments well into 1945 (Washburn 1986, 166–202).

But the papers did not back down from their criticism of the racism that continued to surface in New Deal and war programs. After the Detroit Race Riot of 20–21 June 1943, the editor of the Michigan *Chronicle* "believed that the riot created a 'more nationalistic and more chauvinistic and anti-white' mood among Blacks than ever before. Even those of us who were half liberal and were willing to believe in the possibilities of improving race relations have begun to have doubts—and worse, they have given up hope" (Thompson 1996, 145). While endorsing him in

1936, immediately after the election the *Afro-American* challenged Roosevelt to deliver on promises that he made during the campaign, forcefully reminding him that Black voters had contributed to his reelection and were owed more equity in the New Deal (Farrar 1998, 74). But Roosevelt failed to live up to their expectations, and the paper endorsed Wendell Willkie in 1940 and further lambasted FDR for tolerating racism in New Deal agencies.[10] And despite the continued concern by the OWI and War Department over Black newspapers, these agencies also saw mass media as an opportunity to gain Black war support.

SOLICITING BLACK SUPPORT: BLACK-ORIENTED RADIO PROGRAMMING DURING WARTIME

Since the 1930s, Ambrose Caliver, a Black employee in the Office of Education, had tried to convince radio networks to broadcast "educational programming" he devised about Blacks, but many were scared of low ratings and southern affiliate backlash. When the Army and War Department began looking for ways to increase Black war morale, Caliver was ready with proposals for radio programming targeted at Black audiences—and the education of whites. NBC had already broadcast "America's Negro Soldier" on 12 August 1941, for the Army, and the broadcast was a success (Meckliffe and Murray 1998). Government support for Negro programming along with the prospect of having popular Black musicians perform led NBC to agree to carry Caliver's first show, the Negro segment of "Americans All," a program dedicated to demonstrating the contributions and equality of America's ethnic groups. Contingent on the success of the segment, NBC agreed to broadcast more on Black history and culture (Savage 1995, 161).

Caliver stacked the deck in his favor. He solicited the free involvement of Cab Calloway, Count Basie, and other performers for the cultural segment. He also got higher-ups in the Office of Education to ask the Roosevelts to preview the broadcast. Eleanor Roosevelt gave the show a positive review in her national column, "My Day," a week before the scheduled broadcast. Her endorsement plus the involvement of popular jazz musicians and actors such as Paul Robeson drew automatic attention from the Black and white press (161). The show was a hit: the Office of Education and NBC were deluged for requests for the educational materials made for the show, and *Variety* and *Time* magazine both gave it rave reviews. Caliver's next program, "Freedom's People," garnered similar acclaim, even though the program ended with a close-to-defiant speech from labor organizer A. Philip Randolph.

Yes, the Negro people, loyal and patriotic citizens of America, stand ready, with brain and brawn, *when the barriers of race discrimination are broken down, opening up more opportunities*, to give without stint or limit of their sweat, toil, tears, treasure and blood to enable our country . . . to avenge the treachery of Japan and destroy the menace of Hitler and preserve democracy and liberty *for all Americans without regard to race, creed, color, or national origin.* (emphasis added, quoted in Savage 1995, 185)[11]

That such a "radical" was given federally sponsored, national airtime was the direct result of Caliver's positioning and desire to use that position to uplift the race. That the series did so well commercially and critically was also a boon, Savage argues, as it inspired a new generation of talk programming targeting "the race problem."[12] Caliver's programs and their inheritors created a new venue for Black oscillation and racial discussions in the media institutions of the white public sphere, providing more opportunities for Black voices to be heard by and converse with whites. But radio was not the only conduit for oscillation into media controlled by whites. The white press was increasingly aware and concerned with the increasing volume and visibility of wartime Negro protests, especially those reported in the popular Black press.

THE WHITE PRESS (RE-)EVALUATES THE BLACK PRESS

Predating Gunnar Myrdal's (1944) declaration of the Negro press's importance, northern white journalists finally paid attention as the South had been doing since the beginnings of the migration. The *Atlantic Monthly*, *Saturday Review of Literature*, and the *New York World Telegram* devoted space to critiquing their Black counterparts. However, through this barrage of editorials and counter-editorials, some white journalists and editors changed their negative stance towards Black papers. Westbrook Pegler of the *New York World Telegram*, after lambasting the Black weeklies in a series of 1942 columns, conceded the following by July of that year: "If I were a Negro, I would live in constant fury. . . . I would not be a sub-American, a sub-human being, and in docile patience forever yield my rightful aspiration to be a man" (quoted in Finkle 1975, 67). The *New Republic* ran a series of six articles on the Negro press in 1943, asserting that the publications were raising the war morale of Blacks. Editor Thomas Sancton admitted "when a white man first reads a Negro newspaper, it is like getting a bucket of cold water in the face," but he

acknowledged the importance of getting that wake-up call to Black sentiments (Finkle 1975, 78). Due to this increased publicity in the white press,
either for good or ill, most of the white public knew of the Double V campaign by the end of 1943, the largest "hearing" of Black opinion since the
antilynching crusade. And despite the continued criticism from many
whites, Blacks were unwilling to back off of the home front component of
the V: in a 1943 readers poll, *Negro Digest* reported that the majority of
those polled favored a continuance of their militant stance (Lee 1943, 31).

The surveillance and study of the Black press created more oscillation of ideas between the Black and white public, exposing more white
Americans to Black thought. While this engagement did not originally
arise out of a desire to facilitate egalitarian, interracial discussions, it did
spark debates and thinking that would not have occurred if Blacks had
backed down from their position. The sympathetic words of certain white
editors and writers identified new allies and signaled a greater willingness
of whites to consider questions of Black equality.

CONCLUSION

These oscillations between the Black press and the state remind us that we
must look not just to how marginalized publics address the state and
dominant public, but also to the reaction those oscillations bring. As
Dawson (1995) has shown in his work on the "decline" of the Black
public sphere in the 1970s and 1980s, institutions that serve members of
public spheres can be targeted by the state just as easily as individuals, and
assaults on these institutions can have dire consequences for the collective.
Despite the myth of the free press and an egalitarian public sphere free of
state intervention, the quality of the government oscillations encountered
by the Black press threatened to hinder the ability of the Black public to
gather and transmit information through the press. While government
oscillations meant that white officials were evaluating indigenous expressions of Black public opinion, the great majority of those opinions were
defined as dangerous and fit for suppression, not discussion. Furthermore,
the white press made similar conclusions about the Double V, although
these were discussed and challenged over the duration of the war.

One major aim of any marginalized public sphere is to be able to
project its ideas and interests into the larger public to affect changes in
dominant opinion and policy. The Great Black Migration of the early
twentieth century ushered in a new era of consolidation and oscillation
for the Black public. New forms of transportation, labor, and media distribution brought the North and South Black populations together in

larger combinations, creating economies of scale to support various organizational endeavors. These developments made it possible for Blacks to strengthen their institutions and to begin larger and lengthy discussions concerning their identity and place in America. The increased sense of independence that arose out of these conditions boosted the Black press's confidence to speak truth to power, directly engaging whites in debate in the vocabularies of the New Negro, not the public transcripts scripted by whites.

While the fact that oscillations occurred more frequently was heartening, we must still judge their quality, acceptance, and their successes. When the government and the white press chose to oscillate and react to the critique of the Black press, it was usually an attempt to repress, not discuss, Black opinions and political demands. Furthermore the exchanges occurred between Black press elites, government officials, and white press elites. This was not large-scale, democratic discourse between the masses. Rather, the oscillations of the era covered here are examples of *integrative marginalization* (Cohen 1999), whereby elites of the marginal public are allowed some access to power, but the majority of the marginalized group is left out of discourse and decision-making processes. Hence, the discursive opportunities of Black newspaper owners, editors, and writers changed, but many Blacks, especially those in the South, were not in a position to confront the white public and the state.

On a more positive note, Blacks, with the awesome resources of publicity and organization newly at their disposal, were able to experiment with many more forms of counterdiscourse and action. Negotiations with the state and debates with the white press allowed further circulation of Black thought and highlighted new tools: the threat of Black organized protest and an enhanced sense of racial identity and solidarity. In these oscillations between the state and Black public sphere, we see the limits of these tactics as well as parts of the process of building an oppositional consciousness and group identity. Taylor and Whittier (1992) reveal that group identity and consciousness are better conceptualized as negotiations occurring both within marginal groups and in relations with outsiders. The New Negro consciousness and related critiques of the state and dominant public were shaped both by the actions of the press and the desires of its readers and the reactions of the state. Threats of censorship and violence narrowed the scope of printed Black dissent, thereby slowing the development of some forms of critique and protest. Despite these roadblocks, the Black public's desire for increased rights and the willingness to vocalize those desires grew, both in and out of the state's view.

The interactions between the Black press and the state during the world wars provide us with an example of the growth of the Black public and its increasingly public displays of dissatisfaction with the racial status quo. New urban-based institutions such as the press and civil rights organizations were able to solidify their positions and provide outlets for the Black public's ideas, frustrations, and plans. Those newspapers demanding equal rights were subjected to repressive state tactics, but most were never completely silenced due to the government's fear of mass Black uprisings damaging the war effort. The restricted yet continually critical voices of the Black press, along with ethnographic and poll data, indicate that there was much more dissent brewing in the local enclaves of the Black public than was seen by outsiders. In safer spaces, Blacks continued to hone their options and make plans even though the leaders of the major national groups and the press were not always willing to publicize plans for mass protests. The works of Aldon Morris (1981, 1984) and Charles Payne (1995) reveal how crucial behind-the-scenes activities were to the next phase of the civil rights struggle. Most of these activities remained within safe enclaves in the years leading up to the modern civil rights movement. This is precisely why the local mass actions in the South in the 1950s took most of white America by surprise—because their surveillance had missed the level of resentment of white supremacy and willingness to confront it head-on.

NOTES

1. So we can speak of a public *enclaving* itself, hiding its antiestablishment ideas and strategies in order to avoid sanctions, but internally producing lively debate and planning; we can also imagine a public *oscillating* to engage in debate with outsiders and to test ideas. A public that engages in mass actions to assert its needs would be a *counterpublic*, utilizing disruptive social movement tactics to make demands on the state. Finally, we can envision a public working in conjunction with others on equal footing enjoying a *parallel* status. Utilizing these four labels, I hope to offer scholars a more flexible and descriptive vocabulary to employ when analyzing the various actions of a particular public or group of publics.

2. I take the term *public script* from the work of James Scott (1990) who describes the public transcript as that which is approved by the dominant public. "Hidden transcripts" are created by subordinate publics in safe spaces to express discontent with the status quo.

3. This extended quote comes from the 10 October 1919, edition of Oklahoma City's *The Black Dispatch* (Kerlin 1920, 3).

4. This article was printed widely, notes Kerlin (1920, 134). This particular reprint was taken from the Baltimore *Afro-American*, 29 August 1919.

5. Wells's passage here comes from "Lynching, Our National Crime," a speech given to the NAACP's founding conference in 1909 and reprinted in Walker (1992), *The Rhetoric of Struggle: Public Address by African American Women*.

6. This argument follows Benedict Anderson's (1991) argument in *Imagined Communities*. Anderson describes the importance of the press to creating a sense of nation and belonging among geographically dispersed peoples who share a language. Arjun Appadurai (1993) also comments on the importance of the imaginary to the public sphere in his discussion of globalization and public spheres.

7. Other studies of Black sharecroppers reflect this sentiment, also finding that Blacks preferred to eliminate as much contact with whites as possible to avoid having to play expected public roles of subordination. See, for example, Payne (1995), who summarizes many studies of southern Blacks that found a major shift in attitudes during the 1930s and 1940s.

8. Other branches of the MOWM did march in the coming years, however, as the Executive Order was not being enforced readily. In Chicago and St. Louis, MOWM Committees marched on the Merchandise Mart and a defense plant, respectively (Garfinkel 1959, 98).

9. These summaries neglected to report the anger contained in responses such as this one from a student: "I have no interest in the kind of war they are fighting; I'd like to wage a little war on some of these white people here."

10. Even before these events, the Baltimore *Afro-American* was particularly tenacious in its criticism of FDR. In 1933, the newspaper harshly criticized the National Recovery Administration for replacing Black workers with whites, and declared that Black workers have "every right to look upon the Blue Eagle as a vulture feasting on the pungent bones of racial hatred" (Farrar 1998, 73).

11. The emphasized phrases indicate that Randolph was treading the line. As Savage (1995) notes, "it was a challenge for Randolph to stay within the political borders of a federal broadcast considering his own criticisms of President Roosevelt" (185).

12. Among those analyzed in Savage's dissertation are ABC's "Town Meeting on the Air" and the University of Chicago's "Round Table," both of which devoted multiple sessions to race relations and Black guests. In addition, independent stations also took the initiative to create race-based programming, such as New York's WMCA series "New World A' Coming." The show was the brainchild of Black author Roi Ottley;

WMCA's liberal white owners, Nathan and Helen Straus; and the City-Wide Citizens Committee on Harlem, "an interracial civic and political group which co-sponsored the series" (Savage 1995, 417). The series was modeled after Ottley's book of the same name and covered culture, politics, and history, as well as current events.

REFERENCES

Anderson, Benedict. 1991. *Imagined communities: Reflections on the origin and spread of nationalism*, rev. ed. London: Verso.

Appadurai, Arjun. 1993. Disjuncture and difference in the global cultural economy. In *The phantom public sphere*, edited by Bruce Robbins. Minneapolis: University of Minnesota Press.

Bass, Charlotta. 1960. *Forty years: Memoirs from the pages of a newspaper*. Los Angeles: Charlotta Bass.

Cohen, Cathy. 1999. *The boundaries of blackness: AIDS and the breakdown of black politics*. Chicago: University of Chicago Press.

Dawson, Michael C. 1995. A black counterpublic?: Economic earthquakes, racial agenda(s), and black politics. In *The black public sphere*, edited by the Black Public Sphere Collective. Chicago: University of Chicago Press.

Farrar, Hayward. 1998. *The Baltimore Afro-American, 1892–1950*. Westport, CT: Greenwood Press.

Felski, Rita. 1989. *Beyond feminist aesthetics: Feminist literature and social change*. Cambridge, MA: Harvard University Press.

Finkle, Lee. 1975. *Forum for protest: The black press during World War II*. London: Associated University Presses.

Fraser, Nancy. 1992. Rethinking the public sphere: A contribution to the critique of actually existing democracy. In *Habermas and the public sphere*, edited by Craig Calhoun. Cambridge, MA: Massachusetts Institute of Technology Press.

Garfinkel, Herbert. 1959. *When Negroes march: The March on Washington Movement in the organizational politics for FEPC*. Glencoe, IL: Free Press.

Hogan, Lawrence D. 1984. *A black national news service: The Associated Negro Press and Claude Barnett, 1919–1945*. London: Associated University Presses.

Kerlin, Robert Thomas. 1920. *The voice of the Negro, 1919*. New York: E. P. Dutton.

Lee, Wallace. 1943. Negro Digest Poll: Will Negro achievement curb race discrimination? *Negro Digest* 17:31–32.

Meckliffe, Donald, and Matthew Murray. 1998. Radio and the black soldier during World War II. *Critical Studies in Mass Communication* 15:337–356.

Morris, Aldon D. 1981. Black southern sit-in movement: An analysis of internal organization. *American Sociological Review* 46:744–767.

———. 1984. *The origins of the Civil Rights Movement: Black Communities organizing for change*. New York: Free Press.

Moses, Wilson Jeremiah, ed. 1996. *Classical Black Nationalism: From the American Revolution to Marcus Garvey*. New York: New York University Press.

Myrdal, Gunnar. 1944. *An American dilemma: The Negro problem and modern democracy*. New York: Harper.

Payne, Charles. 1995. *I've got the light of freedom: The organizing tradition and the Mississippi Freedom Struggle*. Berkeley: University of California Press.

Paz, D. G. 1996. The black press and the issues of race, politics and culture on the Great Plains of Nebraska, 1865–1985. In *The Black Press in the Middle West, 1865–1985*, edited by Henry Lewis Suggs. Westport, CT: Greenwood Press.

Powdermaker, Hortense. 1968. *After freedom: A cultural study in the Deep South*, 2d ed. New York: Russell & Russell.

Savage, Barbara Dianne. 1995. Broadcasting freedom: Radio, war, and the roots of civil rights liberalism, 1938–1948. PhD diss., Yale University.

Scott, James C. 1990. *Domination and the arts of resistance: Hidden transcripts*. New Haven, CT: Yale University Press.

Squires, Catherine. 1999. Searching black voices in the black public sphere: An alternative approach to the analysis of public spheres. PhD diss., Northwestern University.

Taylor, Verta, and Nancy E. Whittier. 1992. Collective identity in social movement communities: Lesbian feminist mobilization. In *Frontiers in social movement theory*, edited by Aldon Morris and Carol McClurg Mueller. New Haven, CT: Yale University Press.

Thompson, Julius Eric. 1996. An urban voice of the people: The black press in Michigan, 1865–1985. In *The Black Press in the Middle West, 1865–1985*, edited by Henry Lewis Suggs. Westport, CT: Greenwood Press.

Vincent, Theo. 1973. *Voices of a black nation: Political journalism in the Harlem Renaissance*. Trenton, NJ: Africa World Press.

Walker, Juliet E. K. 1996. The promised land: The *Chicago Defender* and the black press in Illinois, 1862–1970. In *The Black Press in the Middle West, 1865–1985*, edited by Henry Lewis Suggs. Westport, CT: Greenwood Press.

Walker, Robbie Jean, ed. 1992. *The rhetoric of struggle: Public address by African American women*. New York: Garland.

Washburn, Patrick Scott. 1986. *A question of sedition: The federal government's investigation of the black press during World War II*. New York: Oxford University Press.

Wintz, Cary B., ed. 1996. *African American political thought, 1890–1930: Washington, Du Bois, Garvey and Randolph*. London: M. E. Sharpe.

Young, Iris Marion. 1990. *Justice and the politics of difference*. Princeton, NJ: Princeton University Press.

5 Representing the State in South Central Los Angeles

ROBERT ASEN

In fall 1996, a political controversy erupted over allegations first reported in the *San Jose Mercury News* that during the 1980s a CIA-backed drug ring introduced crack cocaine into Los Angeles to finance the Contra war against the communist government of Nicaragua. The allegations appeared in a three-part investigative series titled "Dark Alliance" by *Mercury News* reporter Gary Webb which, as the series' subtitle suggested, purported to tell "the story behind the crack explosion." In dramatic fashion, Webb (1996a) charged in the series' first installment that this "dark alliance" produced disastrous consequences for African-American communities. This alliance "opened the first pipeline between Colombia's cocaine cartels and the black neighborhoods of Los Angeles, a city now known as the 'crack' capital of the world. The cocaine that flooded in helped spark a crack explosion in urban America and provided the cash and connections needed for LA's gangs to buy automatic weapons."[1]

Despite the grave nature of these allegations, mainstream media initially ignored the "Dark Alliance" series. Its charges circulated instead through the Internet and talk radio. African-American community leaders expressed outrage as they learned of the allegations. As public awareness grew, government officials and agencies called for investigations. House and Senate committees announced hearings. The Justice Department and the Central Intelligence Agency launched separate investigations. At the same time, major news organizations exhibited skepticism in their coverage of the allegations. Newspapers such as the *New York Times* and the *Washington Post* reported a disposition among African Americans to believe such charges. These newspapers and others investigated the *Mercury News*' reporting and found evidence lacking.

At the height of the controversy, Juanita Millender-McDonald, a representative for portions of South Central Los Angeles as a member of the California congressional delegation, invited CIA Director John Deutch to speak to community members to address their questions and concerns (CIA chief 1996). This chapter examines their encounter, which took place on 15 November 1996, in the Locke High School gymnasium in the Watts section of South Central Los Angeles. Tension and contention permeated an encounter shaped by a palpable sense of momentousness. Participants advanced assertions of anger and mistrust amid expressions of pain and calls for understanding. Their encounter materialized a scandalous confluence of forces: a secretive and sometimes suspect agency, a beleaguered community, and a destructive drug associated in the public imagination with deviant low-income urban residents.

This encounter is important for several reasons, not the least of which is that the allegations, if true, were damning—the allegations suggested a fundamental delusion among those responsible for national policy priorities. Beyond this, the encounter has theoretical significance for studies in the public sphere. First, the controversy that sparked this encounter supports a conception of the public sphere as consisting of counterpublic spheres and larger public spheres. The differing responses of skepticism by mainstream media and anger in segments of the African-American community reveal that the public sphere is not a singular, stable entity but a dispersed, ephemeral phenomenon that produces public opinions that are complex, textured, and often competing.

Second, this encounter discloses the inadequacy of current theories of the public sphere to account for the manifold, overlapping relations between the public sphere and the state. This literature has focused on the question of whether and to what extent lines between the public sphere and the state are permeable. On the one hand, theorists like Jürgen Habermas insist on a strict separation between the public sphere and the state. In his model of deliberative democracy, Habermas distinguishes contexts of justification from contexts of discovery. He locates contexts of justification in legislative bodies, where deliberations have "less to do with becoming sensitive to new ways of looking at problems than with justifying the selection of a problem and the choice among competing proposals for solving it" (1996, 307). The dispersed, relatively autonomous communicative flows of the public sphere constitute a context of discovery. On the other hand, theorists like Michael Schudson view the public sphere as consisting of a "set of activities that constitute a democratic society's self-reflection and self-governance" (1994, 530). Schudson subsumes the deliberative fora of the state under the public sphere and regards legislatures as privileged public spheres operating within a state. The encounter between Deutch and South Central community members presents a case addressed by neither position. Deutch represented the state in his appearance at the Locke High School gymnasium. His representation demonstrates that the state itself may participate in public or counterpublic spheres as a deliberative agent.

State participation is complicated, however, by a fundamental tension in representation between absence and presence, between standing for something and embodying that something. The representative is and is not the person, object, or idea represented (Williams 1983; see also Derrida 1982). At Locke High School, Deutch stood in for the state and yet his physical presence embodied the state. Standing in for the state, Deutch stood in for larger forces—the federal government most directly, but also other social and political institutions that audience members perceived as acting against their interests. His embodiment of the state offered a focal point for audience anger, frustration, and suspicion. Yet his representation of state authority, as an important source of social legitimation, created opportunities for moments of recognition. As community members appealed for recognition as capable, integral agents, they anticipated successful negotiation of the potentially competing claims of a politics concerned with group identity and a politics oriented toward socioeconomic transformation.

In focusing on the absence and presence of representation, this chapter pursues a dimension of what has been referred to more broadly as the "politics of representation" (see, e.g., Hinz 1998; Stimpson 1988). To assert that representation enacts a politics is to assert that all representing is interested, tendentious. As Linda Hutcheon explains, "there is no value-neutral, much less value-free, place from which to represent" (1989, 41). Representations grant social values and, in turn, communicate and perpetuate social values. If representing does not present a person, object, or idea as it is, then representing consists of contest and struggle as advocates advance potentially conflicting representations in the multiple and overlapping arenas of the public sphere.[2] This process of public dialogue has important implications as representations circulate in social and political debates and link up with various policy initiatives. Along these lines, Richard Dyer holds that the treatment of social groups by larger societies may be based on representations and that "representations delimit and enable what people can be in any given society" (1993, 3). In the Locke High School gymnasium, representing implicated South Central Los Angeles residents in matters of national security and the U.S. war on drugs.

In what follows, I first reconstruct the context of the town hall meeting by describing the "Dark Alliance" series and recounting various reactions to its allegations. I then examine the town hall meeting by attending to the participation of Millender-McDonald, Deutch, and community members. Ambiguity and tension characterized the contributions of all. Millender-McDonald served dual roles as a representative of the state and a member of the community. Deutch represented the state as both a concerned and capable participant and a defensive, distant, and controlling power. And community members exhibited skepticism about and hope for positive recognition from Deutch and those he represented.

* * *

The controversy prompting Deutch's appearance in South Central foretold a turbulent encounter. The "Dark Alliance" series implicated the Central Intelligence Agency directly and indirectly in a host of illegal and grossly improper activities: the CIA likely knew that persons affiliated with the agency engaged in drug dealing; the CIA compromised local police department investigations and arrests of suspected drug dealers associated with the agency; the CIA obstructed persons seeking to uncover links between the agency and drugs; and the CIA permitted shipments of drugs to enter the United States. Three disreputable figures played crucial roles in the *Mercury News* account. Ricky Donnell Ross, "Freeway Rick," whom the series described as "a dope dealer of mythic proportions in the LA drug world" (Webb 1996a), sold vast amounts of crack cocaine to Los Angeles street gangs. His supplier was Oscar Danilo Blandon Reyes, a Nicaraguan expatriate who, after settling in Los Angeles, decided to raise money for the Contra war effort by dealing cocaine. Blandon's key contact was Juan Norwin Meneses Cantarero, a major international drug dealer who introduced Blandon to drug trafficking and whom the series identified as a director of "intelligence and security" in California for the largest Contra group, the Fuerza Democratica Nicaraguense [Nicaraguan Democratic Force].

The series highlighted the disproportionate suffering experienced in African-American communities as a result of the crack epidemic. Webb (1996a) observed that although the Contra war had long since passed, African Americans still grappled with its "poisonous side effects." Homeless crack addicts populated some urban communities in large numbers, and thousands of young black men convicted on drug charges sat in prison cells. These and other ills were wrought by the widespread distribution of a drug that "was virtually unobtainable in black neighborhoods before members of the CIA's army started bringing it into South Central in the 1980s at bargain-basement prices" (Webb 1996a). The series detailed how Blandon developed a successful marketing strategy that targeted poor urban communities as "vast, untapped markets" (1996b). The emergence of crack cocaine transformed the drug from an indulgence of rich celebrities and business executives to an affordable, highly addictive drug for the urban poor. The series also illustrated the comparatively high price paid by African Americans in the war on drugs. Focusing on an issue that "outrages many in the African-American community" (Kornbluh 1997, 35), the third installment addressed sentencing disparities between blacks and whites for cocaine trafficking by recounting the different fates of Ross and Blandon after their business relationship ended (Webb 1996c). Charged in a 1994 Drug Enforcement Agency sting carried out in large measure with the participation of Blandon, Ross was convicted and faced a possible sentence of life imprisonment without parole. In contrast, Blandon served twenty-eight months in prison after he was convicted in a separate case. Blandon then became a highly paid government informant, receiving more than $166,000 from federal agencies in the eighteen months leading up to the *Mercury News* investigation. From targeting to sentencing, the series demonstrated that African Americans were the clear victims of a "dark alliance."

Major news media ignored the "Dark Alliance" series at first. Awareness of the series and its allegations spread through the Internet and black radio. Indeed, the "Dark Alliance" series presented a number of journalistic innovations. The on-line version permitted readers to link to many of the documents and materials cited in the story—photographs of the key players, congressional transcripts, Federal Bureau of Investigation reports, a federal arrest warrant, and audio-recordings of court testimony. The web site also included an on-line forum that permitted readers to respond to and raise questions about the allegations. As awareness of the story spread, "hits" to the on-line Mercury Center increased by 15 percent (Kornbluh 1997). Both regular readers of the *Mercury News* and those following the special series posted links to the web site on hundreds of Internet news groups. Black radio bolstered this heightened reception as talk show hosts gave out the web site address and read excerpts from the series. Radio talk shows themselves became forums for discussion as hosts used their programs to discuss the allegations with listeners and black elected officials appeared on these shows to lend credence to the charges. The importance of black radio may be illustrated in the response to Representative Maxine Waters's mid-September announcement to a Washington, DC, radio audience that the Congressional Black Caucus planned to address the matter at an upcoming open meeting. Two-thousand people instead of the expected 200 attended (McCoy 2001). These responses evidence that the allegations contained in the "Dark Alliance" series struck a chord for many African-American readers. The allegations confirmed the suspicions of some that the desperate plights of poor black communities could not have arisen through isolated incidents alone; the series provided explanations, however disturbing, for the troubling developments witnessed and experienced by some members of African-American communities.

While reactions in African-American communities demonstrated the strong resonance of the allegations with the experiences of many community members, reactions in the mainstream press suggested a starkly different outlook. Major newspapers eventually responded to the *Mercury News* allegations in October. Coverage in these newspapers exhibited a pronounced skepticism. Articles ascribed to African Americans a disposition to believe such charges without any corroborating evidence. The *Washington Post* published two front page articles refuting the "Dark Alliance" series titled "The CIA and Crack: Evidence of an Alleged Plot Is Lacking" and "Conspiracy Theories Can Often Ring True." The first article reported that a *Washington Post* investigation found no conclusive evidence that CIA-backed Contras or Nicaraguans in general played key roles in the emergence of crack as a widely used narcotic across the U.S. Instead, the investigation attributed the rise of crack to a broad-based phenomenon driven in numerous locations by persons of different nationality, race, and ethnicity (Suro and Pincus 1996). The second article observed that "in the African American community the allegations have hit a nerve, highlighting an inclination, born of bitter history and captured in the polls, to accept as fact unsubstantiated reports or rumors about conspiracies targeting blacks" (Fletcher 1996, A1). The article enumerated several such rumors, including ones that purportedly had led some African Americans to boycott certain soft drink and fast food products in the belief that these products contained secret ingredients designed to sterilize black men. The article surmised that "often, the history of victimization of black people allows myth—and, at times, outright paranoia—to flourish" (Fletcher 1996, A18). Similarly, the *Los Angeles Times* refuted the allegations published in the *Mercury News*. The newspaper relayed the findings of its own investigation that viewed the crack epidemic as a dispersed, multiform phenomenon rather than a government-sanctioned plot. Yet it conceded that "for many African Americans, such a scenario is within the realm of belief, even if the details might be inaccurate or unverified" (Katz 1996, A1). In an article titled "Though Evidence Is Thin, Tale of CIA and Drugs Has a Life of Its Own," the *New York Times* reiterated these themes as it added a focus on the role of the Internet in the controversy. The newspaper rejected the charges of the *Mercury News* sharply, noting that "there is scant proof to support the paper's contention that Nicaraguan officials linked to the CIA played a central role in spreading crack through Los Angeles and other cities" (Golden 1996, A14). The *Times* characterized the controversy as a "jolt enhanced by the Internet."

Different reactions to the series displayed contrasting perceptions of government and media credibility and culpability.[3] Even as it refuted the allegations, the *New York Times* observed that "by its disparate impact, the story has underscored both the profound mistrust of government that history has engendered among many blacks and the difficulty that many whites have in understanding their views" (Golden 1996, A14). The negative media response to the allegations may have suggested to some readers if not a widening conspiracy than a perfunctory interest in an issue of deep concern to many African-American communities. Indeed, as newspapers regularly reported an African-American proclivity to believe unsubstantiated rumors, they displayed a patronizing attitude toward persons in whom reporters discerned suspicious attitudes—in effect legitimating suspicion as they sought to dispel it. These varied community and media reactions to the "Dark Alliance" series prefigured the diverse and often competing attitudes, beliefs, and perceptions that circulated through the Locke High School gymnasium as John Deutch met South Central community members.

* * *

As participants settled into their places in the crowded gymnasium, Juanita Millender-McDonald called the town meeting to order. An aura of state authority permeated the proceedings from the outset. Deutch and members of Congress sat at a head table located on a stage at the front of the room. Placards placed on the table stated their names and titles. They spoke to community members from a podium bearing the Official Seal of a Member of Congress. Behind the head table and scattered throughout the room sat and stood congressional staffers and a conspicuous security detail. Deutch and members of Congress reproduced protocols of state discourse in their interactions. They addressed each other in their official and institutional positions and acknowledged each other's stature and areas of expertise. For example, Millender-McDonald introduced Julian Dixon, a congressman in attendance, as the senior member on the Permanent Select Committee on Intelligence. Such performances of state authority were not entirely unwelcome, however, for they presented to community members opportunities for recognition.

These opportunities were not presented without qualification. Deutch traveled to Locke High School to articulate the CIA's position and to answer community members' questions. But Deutch and other representatives assumed a measured stance. State participation appeared to proceed only through certain modes of engagement. Gestures of openness and secrecy implied that state participation might be withdrawn if its authority came under too great a perceived threat. Openness was invoked in the statements of members of Congress, who repeatedly referred to the meeting as "unprecedented" and "extraordinary." For example, in her opening remarks, Millender-McDonald described the encounter as a "town hall meeting unlike ever held before, for this town hall meeting allows the South Central community to interact solely with the Director of Central Intelligence—an unprecedented moment in time."[4] News accounts presented similar analyses. The *Los Angeles Times* referred to the encounter as a "dramatic break with tradition for America's most secretive government agency" (Mitchell and Zamichow 1996, A1). Some participants discerned openness not only in the meeting, but in Deutch himself. Jane Harman, another member of the California congressional delegation in attendance, characterized Deutch as a person who had demonstrated a record of concern for the inner city. She asserted: "I doubt that any of John Deutch's predecessors would have come to such a meeting, but I'm not at all surprised that he is here."

Representatives retreated from these claims of openness during confrontational moments, intimating a return to the tradition of secrecy noted by the *Times*. As Deutch approached the speaking podium, several audience members booed loudly. Millender-McDonald returned to the podium to quiet the audience. One young woman persisted, shaking her head "no" as Millender-McDonald asked her to stop shouting. To the woman and others, Millender-McDonald exhorted that "you must realize that we did not have to do this. . . . Wait a minute, wait a minute. We did not have to do this. We could have continued to allow you to not see the face of the person who is going to launch this investigation, not know what he is going to do, how he is going to do it. But I saw the need for him to come so that you could raise those questions."

Millender-McDonald's role in the meeting manifested difficulties in encounters between counterpublics and the state. She occupied an intersectional position. In Washington, she represented community entry into the formal and informal flows of state discourse. Enacting tensions of representation, she both stood for the community and manifested the community to state actors. During the town meeting at Locke High School, Millender-McDonald represented the state as a member of the South Central community set apart from the community by her association with state authority. Her efforts to regain calm so that Deutch could speak evidenced this multidirectional process. Millender-McDonald explained that often she had heard speakers whom she did not like but nevertheless listened to respectfully. Setting herself as an exemplar of the community, she asked the audience to do the same: "I have asked you to please give the respect of this congresswoman." The respect of "this congresswoman" was important for the well-being of the South Central community. As her stature rose or fell in the eyes of state representatives, so, too, did the community's stature. Disruptions persisted, and Millender-McDonald explained that the town meeting did not have to happen, as I noted above. She continued in this manner to distinguish herself from the community, explaining that "I have to take a red-eye out tonight to Washington to start your work." Appealing for quiet one final time before relinquishing the podium, Millender-McDonald attempted to reconnect with the audience. A shift in pronouns from "your" to "our" signaled a shift in standing as she repositioned herself as a community member. She exhorted: "So please, for the sake of our community, if you don't want to give the respect, then you might want to exit at this time."

Millender-McDonald struggled as she sought to negotiate her potentially conflicting identities. As a member of the community, she shared the audience's shock and disgust on learning of the allegations: "The mere idea that our government could have in any way been involved in the distribution of this horrendous drug throughout our community is repulsive." At the same time, she acknowledged her distinct role in resolving this controversy. She recognized that "we need to uncover the truth behind these reports if the federal government and those of us who are representatives are to continue to hold the trust of the people." In conducting the town hall meeting, Millender-McDonald assumed the role of state representative as she sought to maintain order by monitoring turn-taking among questioners, admonishing participants who uttered offensive language, and seeking calm at various moments so that participants could be heard by others.

Deutch spoke after Millender-McDonald's intervention, but his speech admits no easy judgments. Deutch represented the state variously. His speech highlighted four main points: he shared the audience's concern regarding the drug epidemic; he relayed CIA actions to combat drug lords; he explained the nature of the CIA's investigation into the charges; and he asserted that no available evidence substantiated the charges, though the investigation would continue to pursue all possible leads. From one perspective, Deutch represented the state as a concerned and capable agent determined to uncover the truth regarding potential agency wrongdoing. He sought common ground with community members in his first main point. He insisted that "the people of the Central Intelligence Agency and I understand the tremendous harm that drugs do to America, that drugs do to families and to communities and the ways that drugs kill babies. We understand how ravaging drugs are to this country. The CIA employees and I share your anger at the injustice that drug victims encounter." Here and elsewhere, Deutch spoke indignantly about the ills suffered by community members. He displayed passion and resolve to halt the flow of drugs into the country. He appeared at times deeply disturbed by the allegations. Referring to the drug dealing charge, he asserted: "It is an appalling charge. It is an appalling charge that goes to the heart of this country. It is a charge that cannot go unanswered. It says that the CIA— an agency of the United States government founded to protect Americans—helped introduce drugs and poison into our children and helped kill their future." Deutch understood the significance of the allegations. He knew that his credibility and the credibility of his agency were at stake.

Deutch offered the audience examples of successful agency actions against drug lords to demonstrate the capabilities and intentions of the CIA. He recounted that the agency had captured all of the drug lords in the Cali cocaine cartel and had seriously disrupted the flow of materials necessary for cocaine production among the countries of South America. Also, Deutch presented details lending credibility to the CIA's investigation. He announced that the investigation would be conducted by the CIA Inspector General, and he explained that the Inspector General possessed the legal authority to access all records and documents of all classification levels and to interview all persons deemed relevant to the investigation. Moreover, Deutch's well-organized presentation suggested an overall measure of competence.

Yet Deutch also represented the state as a defensive, distant, and controlling power. His tone was at times strident. He pointed his finger at the audience and pounded the podium with his fist. He shouted throughout much of the speech. His attitude was at times patronizing. At one point in the speech, Deutch pointed to a lack of public understanding of the covert activities of the CIA. He conceded that public suspicion was not unreasonable, but his explanation implied that CIA operations were too intricate to be understood by the general public. He disclosed that "in the course of recruiting agents to penetrate drug cartels to break up those groups that bring drugs to the United States, our case officers, our men and women, deal with bad people, very bad people." The nature of the drug trade required the agency to work with these "very bad people," but these joint efforts often produced misinformation as a consequence. The CIA's contacts "frequently lie about their relationships with us for their own purposes. So it is hard for the members of the public to know what's true and what is not true." At other points in the speech, Deutch waited out audience outbursts like a disappointed parent. Further, in illustrating the "proven track record" of the Inspector General in prosecuting fraud in the agency, Deutch cited a case ill-proportioned to allegations of drug dealing. He reported that just recently the Inspector General discovered CIA employees misusing credit cards and sent those employees to jail. The example drew laughter from some audience members. Moreover, though Deutch sought common ground with community members in his first point, his expressions of concern exhibited a detachment from the audience. He dissociated "the employees of the CIA and I" from "your anger." He did not connect the drug epidemic to his own life experiences. He did not, for instance, share a story of a family member, colleague, associate, old friend, or acquaintance who had battled drug addiction and the pain this person had suffered as a result.

These varying representations signaled differences in how the state could have been perceived. Portions of Deutch's speech represented the state as an interested participant engaged in a dialogue oriented toward mutual understanding and action. Other portions represented state entry in this counterpublic sphere as an attempt to deflect community members' concerns or manipulatively suggest that these concerns already had been addressed or that they were unfounded. Neither representation dispensed with the other. Both circulated in the town hall meeting at Locke High School. The very ambiguity of state representation invoked particular contexts of memory and experience to establish audience interpretations. For some observers, Deutch may have been seen as a reasonable representative addressing an unreasonable audience. A news article reporting the encounter in the *Los Angeles Times* the next morning suggested this viewpoint. The article recounted that "the gathering of 800 at Locke High School quickly deteriorated into a shouting match" (Mitchell and Zamichow 1996, A1). An accompanying picture of Deutch pointing toward the audience included the caption "Deutch . . . stresses a point in Watts speech." Yet many persons in attendance at Locke High School may have seen Deutch as simply another in a long line of well-dressed state representatives who made promises to South Central and similar communities only to break these promises subsequently. This sort of response engages a "critical memory" of state intervention in African-American communities, a "critical memory [that] judges severely, censures righteously, renders hard ethical evaluations of the past that it never defines as well-passed" (Baker 1995, 7). Such hard ethical evaluations informed the responses of many in the Locke High School gymnasium.

In a one-hour question-and-answer session that followed the speech, many community members exhibited mistrust and suspicion. Their questions focused mostly on these doubts. Some wondered how the CIA could be trusted to investigate itself. They contended that the agency would attempt to protect itself from public censure if it discovered that the allegations were true. Others pointed to the historical misdeeds of the federal government as well as the Central Intelligence Agency as evidence that neither could be trusted to examine the charges honestly. The first questioner eloquently addressed the issue of mistrust as she reminded Deutch of the historical betrayals of African Americans by government agencies. She invoked the notorious Tuskegee experiment, where doctors working under the auspices of government agencies at Tuskegee University permitted syphilis in African-American males to go untreated to study the long-term effects of the disease. She asked: "Sir, I'd like to know how this incident differs from my school, what happened at my school at Tuskegee University where for twenty years the government denied inflicting syphilis among African-American men until they died. And then they agreed that yes they had something to do with it. . . . So I want to know from you how what you're saying now differs when the government said that for twenty years until the men were dead, because we're alive now." Deutch's response did not acknowledge the depth of injury and mistrust manifested in this woman's question. Indeed, she refused to state her name for fear of being subjected to an IRS audit. Deutch asserted that he hated "as much as you hate" past actions at Tuskegee. But he seemed satisfied to contrast the Tuskegee incident with the present controversy by noting that no one stepped forward twenty years ago to launch an investigation. Moreover, the question itself suggested that as audience members invoked particular contexts of memory even the most impressive speech could not escape the mistrust produced through a history of betrayal.

Insinuations of conspiracy pervaded the meeting. These insinuations took two forms: "malicious intent" and "benign neglect." In her study of rumor in African-American culture, Patricia Turner (1993) notes that "malicious intent" conspiracies portray the government as channeling drugs into African-American communities in an active attempt to destroy these communities.[5] "Benign neglect" conspiracies view the government as doing little if anything to prevent the flow of drugs into African-American communities because African-American well-being is a low national priority. Benign neglect conspiracies emerged in questions like the one asked by a woman who wondered how a nation that defeated Russia in the Cold War could not defeat third-world nations in the war on drugs. Ascription of malicious intent covered a wide range of topics. One audience member asked Deutch if Walter Pincus, a *Washington Post* reporter who co-authored one of the newspaper's investigations of the "Dark Alliance" series, conspired with the CIA as a paid asset. Another charged that President Reagan wished to break up the air traffic controllers' union in the early-1980s to ease the flow of cocaine into this country. Another accused major U.S. oil companies of supplying drug dealers with chemicals needed to produce crack cocaine. And still another insisted that the Reagan administration set up a parallel government in 1988 to privatize U.S. intelligence operations.

The charge that produced the greatest audience outcry came from a white man who identified himself as Mike Ruppert, a former Los Angeles Police Department (LAPD) narcotics detective. He maintained unequivocally that the CIA had been dealing drugs for a number of years: "I will tell you, Director Deutch, as a former Los Angeles police narcotics detective that the agency has dealt drugs throughout this country for a long time." His revelation drew hoots, hollers, and whistles. A few audience members chanted, "Whoomp! There it is!" Ruppert explained that as a detective assigned to South Central Los Angeles, he was approached regularly by CIA personnel seeking to recruit police officers for agency drug operations. Asserting his views, Ruppert assumed the persona of an insider disclosing classified information. He named specific operations (Amadeus, Pegasus, and Watchtower), referred to the CIA Inspector General by name, and employed police jargon. Ruppert stated that his own life had been placed in jeopardy when he made his allegations public. He recounted that "I did bring this information out eighteen years ago, and I got shot at and forced out of the LAPD because of it." Audience reaction to Ruppert's claims did not, of course, signify gladness that the CIA may have been implicated in drug dealing. Rather, many in the audience viewed his remarks as confirmation from an apparent insider in an important public forum. His statement belied establishment dismissals and attributions of irrationality in community members.

Though Deutch's embodiment of the state presented a focal point for audience mistrust and suspicion, his standing in for larger forces created an opportunity for recognition. The aura of state authority permeating the proceedings functioned crucially in this regard. As a powerful institution, the state confers legitimacy on groups and their members through recognition (as an important complement to its policy programs and other initiatives). Even though South Central community members believed that the state and the forces it represented had betrayed them, they wished to be affirmed as participants in a larger society. Some community members beseeched Deutch and assembled news media to see South Central residents not through the distorted lens of disparaging media stereotypes but as integral, capable agents dedicated to the well-being of their community. One young man, noting the television cameras broadcasting the town meeting, called for a different kind of nationally televised program: "We need a camera right in the heart of South Central." He exhorted media representatives to return with their cameras even after the controversy had subsided to see South Central residents as they are. "We have a lot of talent here," he proclaimed, "We have a lot of hard working people in this community who have worked with these kids on drugs that you guys never talk to. It's time for you to bring your cameras back to our community and let everybody in the other parts of the world know that we are not all on drugs, we are not all gangbangers, we are not all murderers."

Seeing community members as they are also meant seeing the harms inflicted on them by the forces Deutch represented. One older woman wept as she described the condition of her neighborhood and its children: "In Baldwin Village where I live, there are no jobs for the children. And our kids are commodities. They're being cycled through the prisons. They come back to the street and they're marked and scarred for the rest of their life." Illustrating these points, she described the struggles of one of her sons. He served the nation in the Navy aboard a nuclear submarine. When he returned home, he could not secure employment because of racial discrimination. The woman sought Deutch's assistance in alleviating the ills that plagued the South Central community. She implored: "I hope that you'll help put an end to it because we're tired, and we're hurt, and we're angry." The woman's comments implied that community members were neither cynical in their mistrust nor naive in their suspicions. Yet she "hoped" that Deutch's visit could contribute to a positive transformation of their community. The woman suggested that grounds existed for societal recognition of the harms suffered by the community as well as recognition of the abilities of its members. Moreover, calls to see community members as capable and willing agents asserted a link between recognition and action. Demanding jobs for their children, community members understood that socioeconomic amelioration required the larger society to see the needs, interests, and capacities of South Central as community members saw them.

Others doubted that Deutch and those he represented could see South Central community members except through the lens of negative stereotypes circulating in mass media channels and political institutions. In the view of some audience members, outside observers' attachment to negative images arose in the absence of shared experiences. Outsiders did not know of or did not understand the experiences of South Central residents. At various points in the meeting, audience members shouted questions intimating this ignorance, such as "Have you ever seen a crack baby?" Audience members contrasted the privileged backgrounds of Deutch and his constituents—their access to superior education, well-paying jobs, safe neighborhoods—to the historical subjugation and everyday struggles of African Americans. One angry man, who identified himself as Matthew Dylan, rebuked Millender-McDonald for bringing Deutch to the community in the first place. He characterized the town meeting as an empty gesture designed to quell community outrage. He insinuated that Deutch had no intention of discovering the truth behind the allegations. Dylan denounced Deutch's visit: "This man coming into this community at this time, as far as we are concerned most of us in this audience, is a mandate to close this investigation and prepare us for him to say six months down the line that the CIA didn't do anything." Irate, Dylan wondered with whom Millender-McDonald had consulted before extending an invitation to Deutch. He queried incredulously, "How in, my God, who did you in your constituency, Juanita, did you consult with to bring this man into this community at this time?" The use of pronouns in his statement—"this man coming into this community at this time"—was revealing. His repetition of the word "this" to introduce elements in the series particularized each and implied an impossible synthesis of the three. At the very least, the exigencies of the situation undermined discourse oriented toward mutual understanding. But Dylan's statement also advanced a stronger claim: that an insuperable gap in understanding existed between Deutch and the community. Dylan suggested that Millender-McDonald betrayed the South Central community when she invited Deutch to speak to them. He described himself as a solid supporter of Millender-McDonald—until the meeting: "Anything that happens next is terribly anti-climatic and you know it." In response, Millender-McDonald, supported by audience applause, held that "there are some constituents here who appreciate this director coming to this community."

The implication that the town hall meeting was only perfunctory in nature offended audience members. They desired recognition from Deutch and the forces he represented, but they sought genuine recognition entailing respect, not insincere recognition displaying dismissal. The demands articulated by long-suppressed groups for recognition from social orders has been described by Charles Taylor as a "politics of recognition." He holds that its practitioners make crucial distinctions between judgments of worth rendered on demand and judgments offered after earnest engagement with the perspective of another. He characterizes judgment on demand as "an act of breathtaking condescension. No one can really mean it as a genuine act of respect. It is more in the nature of a pretend act of respect given on the insistence of the supposed beneficiary" (1995, 70). Rather than appreciating and elevating others, judgments cursorily made deprecate and demean others. Audience members discerned this quality in the hearings. One man charged that Deutch did not intend to engage the community seriously, but that his actual interests lay elsewhere. "You see," he observed, "you coming in this community today in this way is nothing more than a public relations move for the white people of this country because you know as well as everyone else that the CIA has been dealing drugs throughout the world and bringing drugs into this country since the Vietnam War." Far from addressing audience concerns, Deutch's effort to maintain his agency's innocence and his promise to conduct an independent internal investigation insulted audience members and denied them recognition as capable, integral agents seeking to repair their community. The man repudiated assurances offered by Deutch: "So you're going to come in this community and insult us, and tell us that you're going to investigate yourselves. You've got to be crazy." The respect entailed in genuine recognition intimates a sustained engagement of the parties involved. Michael Walzer holds that the respect that emerges in recognition cannot be willed. Rather, "in any substantive sense, it is a function of membership" (1983, 278). Discerning a perfunctory quality to the town meeting, some community members doubted that Deutch would sustain any commitments made during the meeting.

As audience members debated Deutch's capacity to recognize them as they wished to be seen, Deutch failed to recognize his own role as state representative. He did not see himself as standing in for larger forces. Focusing on his physical body and the specific charges against his agency, Deutch asserted what he could not attain—an unmediated presence that could resolve the tensions of representation. At one point during the town hall meeting, a young man who identified himself as a documentary filmmaker described interviews he conducted with former CIA agents in which they recounted a host of illegal agency activities ranging from attempted assassinations and government overthrows to spying on U.S. college campuses. His frustration apparent, Deutch acknowledged the strongly held skepticism of the audience yet reasserted his purpose in attending the town hall meeting. He disclosed that "I did not come here thinking that everybody here was going to believe me. I came here for a much simpler task. I came here to stand up on my legs and tell you what I was doing to investigate horrible allegations." Deutch represented himself as presenting himself to his audience. He emphasized the significance of his actual participation: "I want you to know, I've come here and told you, unlike the other cases you've mentioned, where there was nobody who came here and told you, there was no Director of Central Intelligence who came out and told you there's going to be an investigation. That's something." His attention to presence indicated a narrow participatory focus. Here and elsewhere, Deutch saw his task as addressing the charges of the "Dark Alliance" series and the agency's response. Though he expressed concern with the wider issues raised by audience members, Deutch directed his answers to the allegations that prompted the town hall meeting.

Whether hopeful or skeptical, community members discerned, perhaps better than Deutch, the power and tension in representation. They recognized that Deutch both manifested state authority and stood in for larger forces. They saw the "Dark Alliance" series as a precipitating event that drew the attention of those represented by Deutch. Community members believed that fundamental issues were at stake in the controversy that escaped the narrow focus of an agency investigation. Articulating the concerns of others, one woman asked Deutch "What can we do to make our city look like your city?" She appeared less interested in resurrecting past misdeeds than in constructing an alternative future. "We need a solution," she explained, "Nobody has spoken about a solution. We need jobs." Audience members understood that Deutch personally would not lead a jobs program. But they sought to convey their needs, interests, and capabilities to the larger forces he represented. Perhaps as the town hall meeting proceeded Deutch, too, recognized the fundamental tension in representation. As Millender-McDonald announced the end of the question-and-answer period, he asked her permission to make a closing remark. He stated: "I came here today to try and describe the approach that I'm taking to address these serious charges. But I go away with a better appreciation of what's on your mind and I go away with a conviction that we're going to do more to stop drugs from coming into this country."

* * *

Representing the state in South Central on 15 November 1996 in the Locke High School gymnasium produced a textured and polysemous encounter. Deutch's speech to community members represented the state as both a concerned and capable participant and a defensive, detached, and controlling power. This ambiguity invoked particular contexts of memory and experience to establish interpretations. These contexts themselves were potentially conflicting. Community members evidenced mistrust and suspicion as they reminded Deutch of a history of betrayal and oppression. Yet some audience members saw the presence of state authority as an opportunity for recognition. Others doubted that Deutch and those he represented could see community members except through the lens of negative stereotypes.

Recognition intimates successful negotiation of potential conflicts between a politics concerned with group identity and a politics oriented toward socioeconomic transformation. The increasing concern with identity from a range of groups has drawn criticism from commentators on the Left and Right. Todd Gitlin (1995) bemoans that "identity politics" has distracted the Left from more pressing issues and drained its energy in the process. From a conservative direction, Richard Bernstein rebukes attention to identity, manifested in celebrations of multiculturalism, as cultivating constant claims of victimization that make "people afraid to say what they think and feel" (1994, 8). Neither criticism addresses the complexity and content of interactions between counterpublics and the state. Rather than separating group identity from material redistribution, counterpublic and state interactions may engage both simultaneously. In this way, participants in the town hall meeting at Locke High School exemplified discursive practices that bridged the two aims. South Central community members linked recognition to a wider transformative politics. They sought societal recognition in ways that community members wished to be seen as a necessary step in ameliorating the socioeconomic ills that plagued their community.

Opportunities for recognition in this encounter arose from state participation in a counterpublic sphere. Active state participation reveals a lacuna in public sphere theory limiting the work of both Habermas and Schudson. Though they draw the line between the public sphere and the state differently, both theorists impute to the state an institutional existence that informs a context for public discourse. Neither considers the state as an active participant through its representatives. Yet the state does not enter into counterpublic spheres as one participant among others, but as a powerful participant that may affect discourse in counterpublic spheres and be affected in turn. State participation may undermine counterpublic spheres as sites that enable the invention of alternative discursive norms and practices. In this capacity, such participation may impose institutional rules on counterpublic spheres or co-opt counterpublic discourse to further the interests of more powerful participants in wider public spheres. More hopefully, state participation may extend the circulation of counterpublic discourse. State representatives' entry into counterpublic spheres may facilitate the expansion outward of counterpublic discourse beyond the reach of its regular advocates. Neither possibility excludes the other. Millender-McDonald's intersectional position as community member and state representative demonstrates that expansion and co-optation must be negotiated by participants in counterpublic and state interactions. The town meeting exhibited tendencies toward both potential outcomes. Whether one or the other eventually prevails depends on the continued efforts of South Central residents to uplift their community and the response of the state to help or hinder this project.

NOTES

1. The *San Jose Mercury News* published the series on-line and in print. All quotations in this chapter from the "Dark Alliance" series are excerpted from downloaded files of the on-line version.

2. Yet representations mask their constructed character. This reifying element has been noted by Frank Lentricchia, who describes the inherent claim of any representation as "an ontological claim, used like a hammer, that some part of the whole *really does* stand in for the whole" (1983, 153).

3. Perhaps in response to sustained media criticism, on 11 May 1997, *Mercury News* Executive Editor Jerry Ceppos published an open letter to readers that admitted errors in the "Dark Alliance" series. Ceppos (1997) asserted his belief that the newspaper had documented solidly that a drug ring associated with the Contras sold large quantities of cocaine in inner-city Los Angeles during the 1980s. Yet, he conceded that the series did not meet *Mercury News* standards in four areas: it presented one-sided interpretations of conflicting evidence; it did not label as estimates amounts of money involved in the trade; it oversimplified the growth of crack in the U.S.; and it presented imprecise language and graphics. Major newspapers regarded the letter as a retraction. In an editorial later that week, the *New York Times* praised Ceppos's admission as courageous. It cautioned that the incident ought not discourage investigative reporting: "Newspapers are among the few institutions in America with the resources and commitment needed to expose betrayals of public trust" (Mercury News 1997, A20). Similarly, the *Washington Post* commended Ceppos for taking the hard but right course of action. It explained that "newspapers are privileged in American society by law, tradition, and practice. In return, we owe readers as honest and full a version of a story like that one as we can produce" (Mercury's Hard 1997, A24).

4. All quotes from the town meeting are taken from a personal videotape of a C-SPAN broadcast of the event.

5. It is important to note that Turner's study approaches rumors as communicative acts that "often function as tools of resistance for many of the folk who share them" (1993, xvi). Turner rejects the position that explains rumors as reflecting "pathological preoccupations among African-Americans" (xvi). Her view differs starkly from the dismissive tone of mainstream news coverage of the "Dark Alliance" series recounted earlier. In mainstream news coverage of the series, references to African-American rumors and conspiracies connoted (and sometimes explicitly noted) baseless and irrational beliefs.

REFERENCES

Baker, Houston A., Jr. 1995. Critical memory and the black public sphere. In *The black public sphere*, edited by the Black Public Sphere Collective. Chicago: University of Chicago Press.

Bernstein, Richard. 1994. *Dictatorship of virtue: Multiculturalism and the battle for America's future.* New York: Alfred A. Knopf.

Ceppos, Jerry. 1997. To readers of our 'Dark Alliance' series. *San Jose Mercury News,* 11 May. http://www.sjmercury.com/drugs/column 051197.htm (19 October 1998).

CIA chief to attend town meeting on drug controversy. 1996. *Los Angeles Times,* 14 November, home edition.

Derrida, Jacques. 1982. Sending: On representation. *Social Research* 49:294–326.

Dyer, Richard. 1993. *The matter of images: Essays on representations.* New York: Routledge.

Fletcher, Michael A. 1996. Conspiracy theories can often ring true. *Washington Post,* 4 October, final edition.

Gitlin, Todd. 1995. *The twilight of common dreams: Why America is wracked by culture wars.* New York: Henry Holt.

Golden, Tim. 1996. Though evidence is thin, tale of CIA and drugs has a life of its own. *New York Times,* 21 October, late edition.

Habermas, Jürgen. 1996. *Between facts and norms: Contributions to a discourse theory of law and democracy.* Translated by William Rehg. Cambridge: Massachusetts Institute of Technology Press.

Hinz, Evelyn J. 1998. Introduction: The politics of representation. *Mosaic* 31:iii–vii.

Hutcheon, Linda. 1989. The politics of representation. *Signature* 1:23–44.

Katz, Jesse. 1996. Tracking the genesis of the crack trade. *Los Angeles Times,* 20 October, Sunday final edition.

Kornbluh, Peter. 1997. Crack, the contras, and the CIA: The storm over "Dark Alliance." *Columbia Journalism Review,* January/February, 33–39.

Lentricchia, Frank. 1983. *Criticism and social change.* Chicago: University of Chicago Press.

McCoy, Mary E. 2001. Dark Alliance: News repair and institutional authority in the age of the internet. *Journal of Communication* 51:164–193.

The Mercury's hard second look. 1997. *Washington Post,* 17 May, final edition.

The Mercury News comes clean. 1997. *New York Times,* 14 May, late edition.

Mitchell, John L., and Nora Zamichow. 1996. CIA head speaks in L.A. to counter crack claims. *Los Angeles Times,* 16 November, library edition.

Schudson, Michael. 1994. The 'public sphere' and its problems: Bringing the state (back) in. *Notre Dame Journal of Law, Ethics, & Public Policy* 8:529–546.

Stimpson, Catharine R. 1988. Nancy Reagan wears a hat: Feminism and its cultural consensus. *Critical Inquiry* 14:223–243.

Suro, Roberto, and Walter Pincus. 1996. The CIA and crack: Evidence is lacking of alleged plot. *Washington Post*, 4 October, final edition.

Taylor, Charles. 1995. *Philosophical arguments*. Cambridge, MA: Harvard University Press.

Turner, Patricia A. 1993. *I heard it through the grapevine: Rumor in African-American culture*. Berkeley: University of California Press.

Walzer, Michael. 1983. *Spheres of justice: A defense of pluralism and equality*. New York: Basic Books.

Webb, Gary. 1996a. America's 'crack' plague has roots in Nicaragua war. *San Jose Mercury News*, 18 August. http://www.sjmercury.com/drugs/day1main.htm (19 October 1998).

———. 1996b. Shadowy origins of 'crack' epidemic. *San Jose Mercury News*, 19 August. http://www.sjmercury.com/drugs/day2main.htm (19 October 1998).

———. 1996c. War on drugs has unequal impact on black Americans. *San Jose Mercury News*, 20 August. http://www.sjmercury.com/drugs/day3main.htm (19 October 1998).

Williams, Raymond. 1983. *Keywords: A vocabulary of culture and society*, rev. ed. New York: Oxford University Press.

Part II

New Communication Technologies and Globalization

6 Cyber-movements, New Social Movements, and Counterpublics

CATHERINE HELEN PALCZEWSKI

In the last decade, studies of public participation and social movements have recognized that assuming a multiplicity of publics is a more productive approach than operating with a singular opposition/state model of agitation and control. Jürgen Habermas's (1989) influential writings about the public sphere are premised on a distinction between the political public sphere, in which "the public discussions concern objects connected with the practice of the state," and the public sphere, which "mediat[es] between state and society, a sphere in which the public as the vehicle of public opinion is formed" (230–231). Building on and reacting to his concept of the public sphere, theorists such as Rita Felski (1989) and Nancy Fraser (1992) have argued that we need to theorize beyond the monolithic public sphere and recognize the existence of counterpublics as sites that develop critical oppositional discourses. Accordingly, in order to understand how social movements develop, scholars need to extend their focus beyond how movements appeal to the state for legitimacy. Absent an understanding of how counterpublics develop oppositional communication practices, a study of the relationship between counterpublics and the state becomes shallow. Ultimately, that relationship has as its precondition—and its directing force—the framework provided by the in-group discourse. Attention to both state-focused political activism as well as culturally driven discursive politics is necessary.[1]

Given the increasing role that emerging communication technologies are playing in activism, particular attention needs to be directed to how the Internet impacts counterpublic formation and public sphere activism. Because substantial scholarly attention has been given to Internet activities directed toward political institutions, this essay seeks to focus on the activities of cyber-movements that are necessary for, although not solely valued in relation to, interchange with the state. In fact, it may well be that the traditional theoretical approaches we take and the sharp distinctions we make are counterproductive when studying emerging communication technologies' interface with social activism. As Mark Poster (1997) notes in his discussion of cyber-democracy, the Internet institutes "new social functions" that "can only become intelligible if a framework is adopted that does not limit the discussion from the outset to modern patterns of interpretation" (202). He continues:

> For example, if one understands politics as the restriction or expansion of the existing executive, legislative and judicial branches of government, one will not be able even to broach the question of new types of participation in government. To ask, then, about the relation of the Internet to democracy is to challenge or to risk challenging our existing theoretical approaches to these questions. (202–223)

To ask about the relationship of cyber-movements to the state, we must first challenge our existing theoretical approaches to the questions we ask. Instead of focusing questions on counterpublics' relation to the state as it exists, perhaps we ought to examine how cyber-movements as counterpublics allow us to challenge the very conceptions of the state.

Unfortunately, as emerging communication technologies (such as the Internet) influence the function and form of participation (as seen in the December 1999 Seattle World Trade Organization protests and the April 2000 World Bank and International Monetary Fund protests), discussions of the Internet have not attended to developments in social movement and protest theory, particularly to counterpublic sphere theory. As a result, Internet studies replicate both traditional social movement studies' focus on the state and modernists' limited understandings of political participation.

Studies of cyber-activism have tended to focus on how the Internet can increase direct citizen participation in institutionalized politics (e.g., Browning 1996; Rash 1997; L. K. Grossman 1995; Selnow 1998; Hill and Hughes 1998; Tsagarousianou, Tambini, and Bryan 1998) and rarely speak of the potential for exclusively discursive politics offered by the Net. And, when the political functions of the Net are discussed, people tend to focus not on its interactive nature, but on its ability to transmit information (see W. M. Grossman 1997). Discussions of the democratic potential of the Internet, even when they recognize its interactive nature, still limit the form of interaction to political sphere participation (see L. K. Grossman 1995; Rheingold 1999a; Hill and Hughes 1998; Browning 1996; Sobchack 1996; Kinney 1996).

Perhaps the best representative of this approach is Wayne Rash's *Politics on the Net: Wiring the Political Process* (1997). When analyzing "political discussion" on the Net, he primarily is concerned with political parties (7). However, he does discuss the use of the Net by grassroots organizations, single-issue groups, and ad hoc committees, describing the Net as "an electronic life force that not only makes these groups function well but that may in fact make them possible" (10). However, Rash's explanation of this possibility is based not on the unique communicative function of the Internet but on its cost-effectiveness as a tool, as in his affirmation that "access to electronic communications can save money and time, increase flexibility, and provide a pathway for organization" (11). Rash highlights the utility of the Internet for "smaller, less traditional groups that do not have the membership numbers to get noticed . . . [and] instead, they must be able to communicate efficiently, act quickly, and use technology to substitute for people and money" (89).

Activist sites also limit themselves to modern modes of relation to the state. For example, the Activist's Oasis (matisse.net/politics/activist/activist.html) primarily has links to institutionalized politics' mailing lists. The Electronic Activist (berkshire.net/ifas/activist) is a state-by-state directory of the e-mail addresses of members of Congress, state legislators, and national and local media. Similarly, the 2MinuteActivist site (ccnet.com/zen&/Zen7.html) focuses on direct involvement in the traditional political process. Given the limits of many existing sites, it is easy to understand why theorizing also is limited.

Cyber-theory and cyber-activism's state focus would not be problematic if commentaries on cyber-activism treated it as distinct from traditional social activism. However, recent writings about citizen activism on the Net include myriad parallels between cyber-activism and social movements. Just as social movements seek to mobilize others of like mind, virtual communities are a way in which "the creative powers of controversy can spread beyond local communities" (Riley, Klumpp, and Hollihan 1995, 259). Riley, Hollihan, and Klumpp (1997) expand on this theme: "Internet communities redefine the concept of local concerns, however, as people can begin to form communities with like-minded individuals who share their interests even if they live in different states, cities, or even countries" (205). In fact, some sites manufacture a sense of virtual citizenship by using the rhetoric of nationality. One site offers the chance to join a virtual country simply by signing an environmental pledge (Dixon 1998), and Bastard Nation (bastards.org) uses the metaphor of national identity to create community between adoptees (Greiner 1997).

Popular press reports about cyber-activism also employ phrases typically linked to social movements. Phrases such as hacktivists (Farley 1999; 'Hacktivists' 1999; Harmon 1998), cyber-protest, the Billion Byte March (Kokmen 1998), virtual sit-ins (Harmon 1998), hacktivism, and electronic civil disobedience (Paquin 1998) provide evidence that connections between social movements and cyber-activism are emerging. One of the cofounders of the Electronic Disturbance Theater, Stefan Wray, describes his actions protesting Columbus Day celebrations as a way of "transferring the social-movement tactics of trespass and blockade to the Internet" (quoted in Harmon 1998). Not only are similarities between practices noted, but also sites themselves sometimes are described as movements (Rubens 1996, 5).

This brief review of literature on cyber-movements and cyber-democracy raises two interesting questions for those interested in emerging communication technologies, counterpublic spheres, and the state. First, are cyber-movements functioning as counterpublics in the same way as non-virtual social movements? Many of those engaged in cyber-activism seem to believe that it is the next stage of social movement development, that those things provided by the actual movements of the past can be provided by the virtual movements of the future. However, if we examine the function of movements through the lens of counterpublics, then there ought to be more wariness concerning the possibility that cyber-movements can generate counterpublics. Second, do existing examinations of cyber-democracy represent the range of communicative possibilities of the Internet? Much of the writing about the democratic potential of the Internet focuses on its ability to access the political sphere and tends to disregard the potential of cyber-activism to generate counterpublics. Given Poster's analysis, perhaps we should expand our assessments beyond the limits of traditional conceptions of the state.

At first glance, my two questions seem to pull in opposite directions—one urging caution regarding cyber-activism's potential to replace traditional social movements and the other chastising scholars for overly limiting the power of the Internet to the political sphere. However, these two questions stem from a common concern with the vitality of counterpublics. In those systems where a dominant public, often unfortunately coexistent with the state, marginalizes large segments of the population, how do we generate spaces in which dialogue may flourish? How can counterpublics develop discourses counter to the state, while not severing all potential for dialogue with it?

This chapter focuses precisely on these concerns. First, I argue that if social movements function as counterpublics when they develop oppositional discourses, then the present practices of cyber-activism fall short of constituting social movements. Second, I argue that we are not going to be able to envision the possibility of cyber-activism growing into cyber-movements unless we no longer limit our theories to merely discussing the ways in which cyber-activism can influence the political sphere. A full understanding of the democratic potential of the Net requires that we examine both how it facilitates contact with the state and whether it can provide communicative arenas free from the surveillance power of state and commercial interests. A full analysis of the interactions of counterpublics and the state requires that we explore the myriad and emerging ways in which counterpublics seek to maintain contact with the state even while they attempt to challenge it.

CYBER-MOVEMENTS AS COUNTERPUBLICS: THE (ALWAYS ALREADY CHANGED) REALITY

This section of the chapter briefly reviews existing counterpublic and social movement theory, recognizing how social movement theory has been advanced by recognition of the form and function of counterpublics. In particular, counterpublic theory encourages scholars to reconsider the role played by identity. Counterpublics, as temporal, discursive, and even physical spaces, are not exclusively defined by identity but, instead, aid in the definition of identity.

Social movement and counterpublic sphere theories have recognized the importance of identity creation and self-expression to the disempowered. While social movements originally were viewed as a violation of the smooth workings of society or as a form of deviation in need of explanation, scholars have come to understand the central role movements can play as a site for identity formation, which counters the state's designation and naming of identity (see Lake 1983, 1991, 1997; Flores 1996; Diani 1992; Habermas 1987; Melucci 1985; Scott and Smith 1969; Tucker 1989). In particular, recent work on new social movements (NSMs) as counterpublics has noted their ability to function outside the dominant public as a site of critical oppositional force, especially as the state and other mechanisms of control have come to colonize the lifeworld (e.g., Fraser 1992; Felski 1989).

NSMs as counterpublics are distinct because they no longer strive toward a universal understanding of the human condition but, instead, are "directed toward an affirmation of specificity in relation to gender, race, ethnicity, age, sexual preference, and so on" (Felski 1989, 166). The specificity allows one to develop and explore one's identity and to counter repressive characterizations of it (Flores 1996). But it is difficult to affirm that which is not present. Although I recognize the dangers of essentialism present in affirmation along the lines of physical and/or singular characteristics, I also recognize the utility of the necessary fiction of identity (see Butler 1993). One should not underestimate the energy generated by the comfort of being with others like you. Instead of guarding against the "spirit murder" associated with marginality (Wing 1997, 28), it becomes possible to feed one's spirit (hooks 1989; Lorde 1984).

As such, what happens within a movement in terms of identity creation may be as important as, if not more important than, the outward directed rhetoric. For example, Melucci (1985) argues: "The new institutional form of contemporary movements is not just 'instrumental' for their goals. It is a goal in itself. Since the action is focused on cultural codes, the form of the movement is a message, a symbolic challenge to the dominant patterns" (801). Thus, when creating one's own communicative norms, the issues addressed encompass who may speak, about what, to whom, in what way, and in what language. Instead of seeing a movement as a "unity, to which one attributes goals, choices, interests, decisions," Melucci argues we should examine these elements as results instead of as points of departure (793). Defining themselves as movements is one of the core actions of movements. And, in this very naming, Melucci argues, one may find a rejection of dominant patterns.

The power of the oppositional force relies on both an inward and outward trajectory to the group's rhetoric. Social movements seek both to convince the dominant social order to change (e.g., Griffin 1952, 1969; Bowers, Ochs, and Jensen 1993) and to validate group members' sense of identity and worth (Gregg 1971; Cathcart 1978; Scott and Smith 1969). Despite attention to in-group rhetoric, the scholarly focus long remained on in-group rhetoric's ability to reaffirm worth as in the case of consummatory or confrontational rhetoric, or to increase cohesion by distinguishing the group from the dominant public through the act of symbolic negation. Until recently, little to no attention was given to the power of in-group rhetoric to affirmatively construct its own discourse, its own standards for communication.[2]

Recent work on groups' ability to construct their own identity, counter to that fashioned by the state or the economy, is best represented by counterpublic theory. Fraser and Felski, two prominent counterpublic theorists, have enumerated several distinct qualities of counterpublics, particularly in relation to their ability to develop discourses relatively independent of a dominant public. Their writings indicate that counterpublics create safe spaces in which: (1) alternative validity claims may be developed; (2) alternative norms of public speech and styles of political behaviors can be elaborated; (3) oppositional interpretations of interests and needs can be formulated; (4) cultural identities can be constructed; and (5) activist energy to engage in political battles in the political and public spheres can be regenerated. Obviously, emerging communication technologies will affect, both stylistically and substantively, how these qualities are developed. By assessing present cyber-activism's ability to fulfill the functions of counterpublics, we may begin to answer whether it can function as a counterpublic sphere.

Alternative Validity Claims and Communicative Norms

Initially, it would seem quite plausible that cyber-movements can contest the basis of existing norms and develop alternative validity claims. Given that these activities primarily are discursive, the Internet's discursive format would seem amenable to this. However, it does not seem that the Internet is exploiting its dialogic potential.

The dialogic nature of chat groups and discussion lists would point toward the possibility of developing counterpublics. Rheingold (1999a), in his description of the "electronic democracy toolkit," recognizes the power of the Internet to provide space safe from the universalizing power of the mass media:

> Net technology makes possible a more democratic medium of expression than did previous communications technologies. A BBS-like public conversation is open to anyone who wants to join the discussion; it is not a "few-to-many" medium like television, talk radio, newspapers or magazines, but a "many-to-many" medium that gives large numbers of people access to large numbers of people. The power to persuade and educate— to influence people's beliefs and perceptions—is radically decentralized when people can communicate in this way: control is spread throughout the network. (n.p.)

Additionally, just as counterpublics often renegotiate the distinctions between the public and private, so may web sites. For example, Wood and Adams's (1998) study of Kathy Daliberti's web site (swanine.com/yellowribbon), which reacts to the imprisonment of her husband in Iraq, concludes that a home page can be considered "a space of rhetorical contest between human notions of public and private dimension" (219). In other words, just as Goodnight (1982) notes that the boundaries between the public and personal can be renegotiated through rhetoric, the Net may enable this as well.

Despite this potential, it seems as yet unrealized. Numerous examples exist of how social movements have developed new vocabulary, including the women's movements' development of the concepts of marital rape, sexism, sexual harassment, and acquaintance rape; the civil rights movement's development of the concept of environmental justice; and the women of color movement's development of the concept of reproductive freedom. Additionally, contemporary social movements also have challenged norms of public discourse, as when AIDS activists redefined medical issues into public health ones and translated technical data into public evidence (see Fabj and Sobnosky 1995). However, evidence of cyber-movements' ability to generate alternative validity claims is yet to be seen. Kathy Daliberti's web site, to be discussed in more detail later, is highly dialogic but does not really focus on challenging validity tests or the basis of existing norms. The only example of alternative validity claims I could find comes from cofounder of the Electronic Disturbance Theatre, Stephen Wray. He sees an inherent potential for cyber-activism to challenge dominant validity claims. He explains: "The entire notion of information warfare needs to be approached cautiously. Always remember who it is that is creating the language, rhetoric, discourse, definitions, etcetera, of infowar" (quoted in Paquin 1998). He would like to see his attempts at electronic civil disobedience redefine Infowar and make it a plausible form of activism because "we need to seriously question and abandon some of the language that the state uses to demonize genuine political protest and expression" (quoted in Paquin 1998).

The development of alternative validity claims requires a vibrant collection of previously silenced voices and their recognition of the Net as a venue in which to exercise their voices. Although the narrow-cast format of the Internet might enable it to affirm the ascriptive characteristics of gender, race, ethnicity, age, and sexual orientation, such a potential cannot be realized if those groups never make it onto the Net. As the next section details, those groups are the very groups who often are excluded from the Net. It is difficult to envision the possibility of expression about that which previously has been "buried alive" if you feel like roadkill along the side of the information superhighway.

Oppositional Interpretations and Constructions of Identity

Fraser (1992) includes women, workers, peoples of color, and gays and lesbians in her list of subaltern counterpublics. Given the central role counterpublics play for these traditionally marginalized groups, questions arise about the inherent inequalities built into the Internet. Counterpublics are praised because of their ability to open space for the marginalized to generate interpretations of their identities, interests, and needs. Counterpublics enable marginal groups to overcome the discursive barriers to participation because, by definition, they expand discursive space and provide discursive systems counter to those that exist.

Although the Net is theoretically as open as counterpublics, material barriers to open and full participation exist. If cyberspace is to generate alternative interpretations of identity, it needs to make sure it does not place structural barriers to access. Unfortunately, it appears that two conditions limit the ability of cyberspace to foster oppositional interpretations of identity. First, those most in need of an oppositional interpretation of identity are the very groups who most lack access. Second, existing sites actually discourage the formation of identity.

Despite the Internet's ability to bring together like people, it does not guarantee freedom from discrimination. Although some argue that the virtual world allows for the dissipation of the impact of discrimination linked to physical characteristics because of the lack of actual face-to-face communication, the reality is that discrimination continues, albeit in a masked form. Studies of the Internet contest its ability to function as the "great equalizer." Wolf (1998) argues: "At this point in its evolution it appears that the Internet serves only to equalize the differences among young, college-educated, middle-class, white males" (30).

The most comprehensive study to date, *Falling Through the Net*, supports this analysis (Lieberman 1999). The 1999 National Telecommunications and Information Administration report indicates, "Whites are more likely to have Internet access *at home* than Blacks or Hispanics are from any location." Not only that, the way in which one uses the Internet is determined by one's degree of subordination. For example, "demographic characteristics not only determine *whether* and *where* one uses the Internet. Income, education, race, and gender, among other characteristics, strongly influence what a person does online" (National Telecommunications and Information Administration 1999). Those belonging to subordinated demographic groups are more likely to use the Internet in public places, like at schools or community centers, and they are more likely to use it to take courses or conduct job searches. It is used as an instrument to enter the economic system of paid labor and is not used as a means to engage in the formation of public spheres. Shapiro (1999) echoes this concern when he notes that discrepancies between users will exist not only within countries but also on a global scale. Ross-Larson (1999) also worries about this, noting that 88 percent of users live in developed countries, which account for only 18 percent of the world's population. Despite falling computer prices, "the Internet revolution is largely bypassing the poor, minorities, and those who live in rural communities and inner cities" (Lieberman 1999, 1A).

The general differences in usage do not dissipate when one examines cyber-activism in particular. In their study of Internet activism,[3] Hill and Hughes (1998) find that Internet users are "considerably younger than the general public" and that "Internet activism is overwhelmingly male" (29). Specifically, "[n]on-political Internet users are divided about 60/40 between males and females, while Internet activists are 72 percent male" (29). They also find that the Internet is not likely to politicize someone who is not already political, explaining that people "are probably not converted from typical citizens to political junkies but are more likely to be political junkies to begin with" (72). The implication of this gap is made clear by Riley, Klumpp, and Hollihan (1995): "The use of electronic resources is heavily skewed toward current power groups and away from marginalized citizens" (259).

Not only do economic barriers limit the ability to challenge identity, but even in those cases where nondominant groups make it onto the Internet, they tend to limit their identity creation potential. For example, the Webgrrls site (webgrrls.com), which "aims to provide a non-competitive environment for women techno-heads to get together on the Internet in an industry dominated numerically by men," limits its transgressive potential when its creators make clear that it is "not a political or feminist organization but simply one for women in a male-dominated industry to make contacts, get ahead, and have some fun" (Rubens 1996, 5).

Some groups even go so far as to reject the notion of membership. For example, the PGA, the People's Global Action Against Free Trade and the WTO (agp.org), explains: "The PGA has no membership, and it does not and will not have a juridical personality. No organisation or person represents the PGA, nor does the PGA represent any organisation or person. The PGA will only facilitate coordination and information flow with the help of conferences and information tools" (PGA Bulletin 1997a). Despite its lack of willingness to recognize group identity, the PGA site does challenge dominant identity forms in other ways. In fact, the PGA urges people to think beyond national boundaries, explaining:

> We cannot confront transnational capitalism with the traditional tools used in the national context. In this new, globalized world, we need to invent new forms of struggle and solidarity, new objectives and strategies in our political work. We have to join forces to create diverse spaces of co-operation, equality, dignity, justice and freedom at a human scale, while attacking national and transnational capital, and the agreements and institutions that it creates to assert power. (PGA Bulletin 1997b)

Given the global scope of many problems, communication systems that are global in scope may also be necessary. Ironically, it may be the globalization of communication that enables activists to counter the economic globalization they find so troubling. Additionally, the way in which the Internet flattens time and space may create the time and space in which to fight problems of a global scale. The PGA recognizes this possibility when it writes: "These tools for co-ordination and empowerment provide spaces for putting into practice a diversity of local, small-scale strategies developed by people all over the world in the last decades, with the aim of delinking their communities, neighborhoods or small collectives from the global market" (PGA Bulletin 1997b).

Perhaps the cyber-activity that most resembles a full-fledged movement is the Blue Ribbon Campaign, which emerged in response to the Communications Decency Act (CDA) of 1996 and has been reactivated in response to the Internet School Filtering Act and the "Son of CDA" bill (Futrelle 1998). Inspired by the POW/MIA yellow ribbon and AIDS/HIV red ribbon, the campaign asks those who agree with its position to place a virtual blue ribbon on their web sites. Those who opposed the signing of the original CDA also engaged in a virtual protest, the Thousand Points of Darkness, in which they turned their web pages to a black background for forty-eight hours in order to mourn the death of the Internet after the CDA's passage. Perhaps most interesting about this protest is its thoroughly virtual nature: it protested a perceived assault on the Internet, using the Internet, contacting others through the Internet. Still, "whether the Net-based protest accomplished anything is a matter of opinion, but the answer is quite probably no" (Randall 1997, 271). Although the campaign mirrored many of the political activities of social movements, it does not seem to have created a counterpublic sphere. Instead, as might be predicted from the writings about cyber-democracy, it focused its activism not on countering the public sphere, but on engaging the political.

Ultimately, if marginalized groups are not represented on the Net, then oppositional interpretations of identity become impossible on the Net. Report after report indicates that those who most need access to counterpublics tend not to have access. If Fraser (1992) is correct that unless subordinated groups have "venues in which to undertake communicative processes that were not, as it were, under the supervision of the dominant groups . . . they would be less likely than otherwise 'to find the right voice or words to express their thoughts' and more likely than otherwise 'to keep their wants inchoate'" (123), then cyberspace is not expanding the discursive arena. Instead, it merely is replicating the "modes of deliberation that mask domination" as it absorbs the less powerful into a dominant cyber-we. In cyberspace, deliberation appears to emerge as folks are able to give feedback and interact. Yet, a series of monologues, or monetary bytes, traversing the web does not constitute critical engagement. The reason why inequitable Internet access should be troubling is not only because it mirrors other inequalities in society, but also because it can mask the very existence of those inequalities. It is difficult to recognize absences of some groups if you cannot even identify who is present.

Space Safe from Surveillance

Some potential for community and identity formation may be emerging on the Internet. However, even these sites tend to rely on existing identities, rather than on the critical formation of identity. Recently, a number of ethnic-identity based sites have appeared on the web (e.g., BlackPlanet.com, BlackVoices.com, Asia.com, Latino.com, and quepasa.com). In a 9 April 2000 episode of CNETnews.com, participants in these sites noted how they offered minorities a sense of community and allowed interaction in a functionally closed community. A number of independent grrl/gurl/gerl focused sites also have been developed (e.g., Tangy.net, Gerl.org, Plastique.org, and Narcissistic.org). However, recognizing the 275 billion dollars worth of purchasing power of young girls, a number of economically driven sites have begun to vie for attention (e.g., Alloy.com). The way in which commercial interests drive some sites clarifies that safe space issues are not resolved simply by group membership or a lack of state interference. Commercial and state interests can interfere with safety, states through tracking and naming and commercial interests through tracking and commodification (see hooks 1992).

Central to the ability to develop discourse counter to the dominant is the possibility of safe space. Space free from the surveillance by the dominant enables activists to regenerate energies, to be free from the small acts of discrimination that constitute spirit murder, and to be in a space where exploratory discourse is possible, where one is able to make mistakes knowing the opportunity to correct them exists. For the Internet, however, surveillance comes not only in the form of governmental patrol of usage, but also commercial tracking.

Researchers have recognized the way in which identity formation is central to contemporary social movements. For example, Randall Lake (1983) responds to others' declarations that the Red Power movement was unpersuasive by explaining that such assessments "are problematic because they misanalyze this rhetoric's primary audience" (128). Rather, "for the Indian audience, Red Power rhetoric is persuasive insofar as it serves consummatory purposes prescribed by traditional Indian religious/cultural precepts" (Lake 1983, 128). Writing about Chicana feminists, Lisa Flores (1996) offers a similar observation about the function of the "rhetoric of difference." Her essay notes the centrality of discursive space to Chicana feminist rhetoric, much as Fraser identifies the need to be free of the supervision of dominant groups. Flores explains: "By employing a rhetoric of difference, in which Chicana feminists construct an identity that runs counter to that created for them by either Anglos or Mexicans, Chicana feminists begin the process of carving out a space for themselves where they can break down constraints imposed by other cultures and groups" (143). Clearly, the actual form of a movement is central to its functioning, for in the form a space is opened—temporally, discursively, and sometimes physically—in which the movement exists.

In some ways, the Internet necessarily creates space for oppositional discourse and identity formation as it challenges our very understanding of space. For example, Wood and Adams (1998) argue: "the WWW creates a space for women to resist patriarchal constraints" (220) because the "WWW, by its nature, creates the space to interrogate gendered assumptions naturalized through architecture, such as the concept of home" (221). Unlike an actual home, a home page on the web can be "found" and "visited," yet "one can never open the door, for in reality, it doesn't exist" (223). Similarly, they argue that the WWW version of the AIDS quilt (aidsquilt.org/quilt) lessens feelings of isolation, the very things identity linked movements challenge: "In response to the potential for isolation, control, and violence, we argue that quilt and quilting (as product and process) merge to create an environment of community, liberation, and safety" (225).

Wood and Adams analyze the architecture of one page in particular: Kathy Daliberti's. In their evocative analysis of this page, they point out the potential power of a page to operate in ways central to the constitution of a counterpublic. They explain that "as with the physical process of quilts, Daliberti's page provides the means of communal expression. Unlike traditional uses of the electronic media, this use of computer technology empowers people who are otherwise unaffiliated with a power structure. Like the communal quilt, co-constructed in traditional 'bees,' Daliberti's web site provides the opportunity to add one's own panel" (225–226), making the goal "not individual consumption but a communal production of a response to a tragedy felt by people around the world" (226). In at least one instance, Daliberti's web site protesting the arrest of her husband in Iraq creates space for community: "Rather than attempt to command an isolated (and isolating) machine, Daliberti illustrates the power of technologically mediated interaction—the heart of the modern generation of computers—to liberate through the creation of community" (230–231). However, as Wood and Adams note, this web site is atypical in its community building focus.

Other web sites describe themselves as spaces in which people may come together as a community, even though they do not replicate the highly interactive nature of Daliberti's site. For example, Webgrrls International claims it "provides both a local and global community of women devoted to making technology a vital part of every woman's personal and professional life" (webgrrls.com/benefits/). However, it is not simply the site that provides community but also the meetings, classes, and events the group organizes. In many ways, this site recognizes its own virtual limits.

The Internet also offers ways to expand community by involving more people than might typically be involved in a group. Unique to the Internet is its ability to expand space and time, and include people in ways nonvirtual movements may not be able to. "[Net activist Jim] Warren says that because of the time-shifting ability of the nets that allows people to carry on conversations in something other than real time, the nets avoid sitting people out who work off shifts or spend long hours commuting" (Rash 1997, 94–95). Because the "nets are particularly well-suited for helping people who normally would not be able to participate in such political activities find a home and take part in the debate, even if they cannot do so personally," it means that the Internet's "organizational possibilities extend beyond just getting people to vote or attend rallies" (94). What is most interesting, however, is that left-oriented groups are the ones that tend to actively promote community expansion. Rash's (1997) analysis of politics on the Net notes that

> education and outreach . . . seems more prevalent in groups that classify themselves as being on the left politically. We found, for example, that some Web sites, notably the Institute for Global Communications (http://www.igc.org) in Palo Alto, California, provide links to dozens of organizations involved in issues from antinuclear protests to labor and women's issues. The list runs from Amnesty International to Zero Population Growth. We did not find a similar site that identifies itself as part of the far right. (92–93)

Theorists of the Internet also recognize the way in which new uses of the medium may enhance its community generating potential (see Foster 1996). Howard Rheingold, author of *The Virtual Community* (1999c) and owner of his own home page, highlights a few of the new techniques: "Conferencing systems structure discussions according to topic, making it easier for people to find others who share their interests. . . . By organizing information this way, i networks of people can serve as informal support systems for one another" (1999a). While the reenergizing that comes from safe spaces would be difficult in a totally computer-mediated world, there is evidence that computer contacts can lead to face-to-face communication. Rheingold describes how "The Brainstorms Community"—a project where people from around the world come together to talk about technology, the future, life on-line, and other things—is resulting in increasingly frequent face-to-face meetings. He explains that "the goal is to raise the bar for the level of discourse on-line—and not to forget to have fun" (1999b).

The question for researchers is whether we are using the new technologies to expand our ability to connect, communicate, and challenge, or whether we have limited ourselves to seeing the Internet as merely a tool, a mechanism through which to transmit information instead of a collective development of meaning. Other concerns about the space generating potential of the Internet arise when scholars attend to the privacy issues that emerge with a technology that is susceptible to surveillance.

Three challenges to safe space emerge within the Internet. First, the ability to track actions on the Internet interferes with the activities of some direct action groups. Second, the actual structure of the Internet, where the public and private is collapsed, begins to erode our own sense of interiority. Third, the anonymity enabled by the Net makes it difficult to develop trust between members of a group, trust that is essential if one is to feel free to be oneself.

The issues involved with the need for privacy cannot be underestimated. Simply because of the speed and scope of the Internet, privacy is undermined: "For all of the advantages of placing public data on the Net, it does have its downside. For example, it allows much faster and more efficient invasion of privacy" (W. M. Grossman 1997, 167). In fact, the emergence of search engines intensifies this problem, as personnel directors will soon be using them to check out prospective employees. As Wendy Grossman (1997) notes, "tomorrow's equivalent of today's failed urine test may be the discovery that you once posted a message to alt.drugs" (168). In particular, some groups face problems conducting direct action on the Internet; Enough!, Hunt Saboteurs, Reclaim the Streets, EarthFirst!, and Greenpeace all have voiced concerns about the ability of Internet activism to safely achieve their goals (Dixon 1998).

The collapse of spatiality further limits the ability of cyber-activism to create safe space outside of the realm of the public. Sobchack (1996) writes:

> Our sense of spatiality also has been transformed so that even to pose the notion of a 'public sphere'—as opposed to a 'private sphere'—is problematic in the age of electronic pervasion. . . .

While our personal access to the space of others has been appreciably amplified through television and computers, our privacy has been simultaneously reduced. Given to watching screens and what they display, our sense of surface and exteriority has been amplified, while our sense of depth (a function of bodily movement) and interiority has been reduced. (82)

In other words, if a group is attempting to develop an alternative sense of self, if it is attempting to develop "oppositional interpretations of their identities, interests, and needs" (Fraser 1992, 123), then a sense of "their" needs to be maintained. To the extent that the identity, the "I," of the members of a group is swallowed by a universal "we" as part of the process of political deliberation, their distinct needs are made inchoate. Thus, "[s]ubordinate groups sometimes cannot find the right voice or words to express their thoughts, and when they do, they discover they are not heard" (Mansbridge 1998, 143). If a total loss of the interior is one of the results of the collapse of space that seems to pervade the Internet, then the potential for safe space to emerge is limited. And all of this is complicated by the Commerce Department's study, which notes the different ways and places in which diverse peoples use the Net.

Safe space also involves issues of trust. The risks faced on the Internet are the development of false trust and the inability to develop trust. W. M. Grossman (1997, 183) notes that the feeling of intimacy created by the Internet may make users trust too quickly:

In a small community, online or real, you assume that everyone you meet is trustworthy unless proven otherwise, in a large one, you assume the reverse. The difficulty is that no matter how infinite and populated cyberspace becomes, it always feels small, partly because we experience it in the privacy of our own computers, and partly because everywhere you look people are dividing themselves up into small groups: newsgroups (which often split if they get too big), conferences, IRC channels and chat rooms, and now small online discussions on Web sites organized around those sites' official content.

If events make clear that the trust was unwarranted, then the risk is that as trust erodes, an additional level of mediators will emerge who can "sell our trust back to us. They will be the brokers in the new power structure that is already forming on and around the Net, however much people might like to think that all Netizens will always have an equal shot in the meritocracy of ideas" (Grossman 1997, 183).

Clearly, the medium of the Internet problematizes issues of space and time to such an extent that activists and theorists should attend to it. However, we cannot do this unless we are willing to entertain the possibility that the Internet is more than a quicker and easier way to access our political representatives. Theorizing about the counterpublic possibilities of the Internet becomes a prerequisite for removing ourselves from the web of state and corporate control.

CYBER-MOVEMENTS AS COUNTERPUBLICS: THE POSSIBILITY

Existing theoretical discussions of the possibility for cyber-democracy provide an overly limited role for the Net. Just as Fraser critiques those who would ignore the democratizing potential of counterpublics in highly stratified societies, I would challenge writers who limit the democratizing potential of the Net in their discussions of cyber-democracy. As noted in the introduction to this chapter, theorists need to expand their thinking beyond "modern patterns of interpretation" and consider "new types of participation." Earlier, I identified writings in which modern patterns of interpretation are visible. I now would like to identify possible locations on the Net where new types of participation are emerging. In particular, I challenge scholars to rethink the ways in which cyber-movements can function as counterpublics and, in so doing, redefine relations with the state.

Perhaps what is so discouraging about the focus on traditional politics is that it might short-circuit any liberatory potential that the Internet may hold. If Riley, Klumpp, and Hollihan (1995) are correct in their assessment that we are entering a "post-political age in which public life would need to exist in new institutional sites and with new argumentative forms" (254), then we should not dismiss the possible alternative site of cyberspace before its full potential has been explored. Thus, this section urges activists and theorists to focus not only on the way in which emerging communication technologies expedite access to the state, but also on the ways in which the unique elements of the Net can redefine relations to the state.

However, in the process of theorizing new types of participation, we must attend to the material realities that can limit it. If socioeconomic barriers to access exist, they must be remedied. If technology enables the collapse of space and time, then sites that account for this must be developed. Just as Habermas bemoans the encroachment of mechanisms of power and money into the public sphere, we must be wary of the encroachment of the state and corporations into cyberspace. Although cyberspace is theoretically limitless, the way in which that space is filled can create norms and expectations for use. If we are to embrace the Net's democratic potential, then we must actively engage it, theorize about it, recognize it.

Some sites and cyber-activism do challenge the limited uses of the Net described by theorists. In particular, several sites attempt to open space for the formation of publics and counterpublics. For example, the Institute for the Study of Civic Values (libertynet.org/edcivic/iscvhome. html) focuses on neighborhood empowerment, and the Political Participation Project (ai.mit.edu/projects/ppp/home.html) attempts to broaden civic participation in cyberspace. The What's New in Activism Online site (wnia.prognet. com/WNIA/) also has a more counterpublic-oriented function insofar as its primary goal is to offer activists access to the WWW to "find other organizations and individuals with similar values and interests." In many ways, it is seeking to create the space for safe discussion of ideas, for the development of alternative validity claims, and for the development of the vocabulary with which the subordinated can articulate their needs.

Activism on the Internet covers far more than presidential web sites and chat rooms about politics as usual. In fact, a number of revolutionary activities occur that fit within a broader interpretation of politics, activities that matter and contribute to the maintenance of counterpublics. While the Internet may not be able to generate counterpublics in the same way that social movements can, it can provide the means to open those counterpublics to others, to sustain counterpublics, and to encourage communication.

One example of how a movement's cyber-rhetoric can help maintain the movement can be found in the recent takeover of Reverend Phelps's "godhatesfags" web site (godhatesfags.com). According to those responsible, no illegal hacking was done. Instead, the domain for the site changed hands, and the new domain read "godlovesfags" (2600.com/hacked-philes/current/godlovesfags/hacked). Even though the domain was eventually returned to Phelps, the "godlovesfags" site continues to exist as it has since March 1999. Also noteworthy about the site is that the state was not the direct target of the protest, although the state's sanctioning of homophobia was indirectly challenged. As critical legal scholars have noted, "[g]utter racism, parlor racism, corporate racism, and government racism work in coordination reinforcing existing conditions of discrimination" (Matsuda 1993, 24). Drawing a parallel between racism and homophobia, one can infer from Matsuda's claim that an attack on gutter homophobia constitutes an attack on governmental homophobia as well.

Another intriguing example of where community may be defined and political action expanded is on the hacktivism.org web site. *Hacktivism*, as a term, is meant to cover more than government-oriented activities, although those are a central part. In a hacktivism.org report on the Legions of the Underground, which had declared an "electronic war" against China and Iraq and threatened to destroy those countries' computer systems in retaliation for human rights abuses, hacktivism is defined broadly. In the debate among hacktivist groups about the Legion's action, a discussion of hacktivism emerged. Many hacking groups condemned the planned war because undermining information infrastuctures was viewed as counter to the goal of political hackers, who try to expand access to information as a means of empowerment rather than limit it. As a result of this discussion, hacking groups concluded that hacktivism "covers everything from animal rights groups defacing the Web pages of fur companies to the use of computers by dissidents to promote democracy in totalitarian regimes" ('Hacktivists' 1999, 9E). In particular, a joint statement of hacker organizations on the hacktivism.org web site defines hacktivism as "using the skills and tools of hacking to advance progressive causes" (A Joint Statement). When faced with a challenge to their identity, hackers came together to develop an intersubjective understanding of their activities. They determined which were acceptable and which were not—and the decision was determined by how the group defined itself, as a group that sought to expand access to information. The contents of this debate can be seen on the hacktivism.org web site, where the statements of hacking groups such as 2600, Chaos Computer Club, Cult of the Dead Cow, LOpht Heavy Industries, and Phrack are posted. The "Joint Press Release of the International Hacker Coalition" indicated that the collaborative condemnation of the LoU attempt to destroy computer systems "may signal a turning point in the underground hacking community" (1999, n.p.).

Adding to the progressive potential of the Net are the emerging interconnections between electronic and physical activists. Quite simply: "The worlds of the hacker and the activist are interconnecting in ways that civil rights organizers and antiwar protesters of other eras could never have foreseen" ('Hacktivists' 1999, 9E). This interconnection may force us to rethink many of the theories that now guide our study of movements, of the Net, and of social change.

Despite the interconnections between activists and hackers and the emerging use of the Internet by activists to create counterpublics that challenge the dominant sphere, progressive politics are not guaranteed. For example, the 2600 (2600.com) site provides a list of recently hacked sites. Although I was encouraged to see that the kkklan.com site had been hacked, the method of hacking was anything but progressive insofar as the hackers wrote over the Klan site with claims that Klan members were all homosexuals.

Similarly, Sobchack's (1996) critique of the cyber-rhetoric of punks and hackers establishes that the cyber-sphere is not necessarily liberatory. Her assessment of the type of activism on the Net is not reassuring:

> [A]lthough our modes of perception and expression, our individual and social sense of time and space and embodied subjectivity, are being radically transformed by electronic mediation, the economic and political contexts in which this transformation is occurring (and which it will affect in a variety of ways over time) constrain its radical nature and put it to the service of familiar economic and political ends. (87)

The problem is that those who celebrate the new public sphere of the Internet ignore the marginalizations inherent in their visions. Sobchak continues:

> What is also revealing about the contradictions evident in the discourse around virtual reality and its focus on sexual activity at the expense of progressive social interaction is that it foregrounds the contradiction underlying the hacker's phenomenological relationship to electronic mediation and its possibilities. . . . [T]he hacker is less interested in these clearly-mediated—and thus hermeneutic—forms of public interactivity than he is in achieving complete transparency in his electronic interaction. (85)

CONCLUSION

Needless to say, we are at the beginning of the Internet, the beginning of our theorizing about it, and the beginning of activism on it. The concern that motivated me to undertake this project is one that is a concern for all teachers and activists: How can we assist in the development of public dialogue, civil society, change for the better? More particularly, I am interested in how to improve the ability of marginalized and subordinated groups to articulate their wants and needs. Given the unarguable impact of the Internet on contemporary communication, it is essential that we, as theorists and practitioners, begin both to question how it is being used and to envision how it could be used.

As of now, cyber-movements are not automatically functioning as counterpublics in the same way as nonvirtual social movements. The dialogic potential of the Internet is not being fully explored, although initial attempts are emerging. Material inequalities make Internet access difficult, if not impossible, for those who most need to make their needs heard. And the surveillance activities of state and quasi-state entities raise concerns about the possibility of safe space. Despite these problems, I do not think we should abandon cyber-movements as locations of activism. However, existing examinations of politics on the Net do not represent the range of communicative possibilities of cyber-movements. The focus on access to the modern political sphere and the disregard of cyber-activism's ability to generate counterpublics limit our understanding of cyber-activism and its potential.

The results of this chapter should provide some foundation from which to begin detailed studies of cyber-movements and cyber-activism. Up to now, scholars have had too much hope and have not allowed themselves enough hope when it comes to envisioning the ways cyber-activism can develop alternative validity claims, norms of public speech, and oppositional interpretations of identities. Presently, we are overstating what is happening on the Net and perhaps giving existing uses too much credit. If we are to generate cyber-movements that can function as counterpublics, activists need to be more attentive to the internal dynamics of their interaction. Space for dialogic discussion is necessary, and groups need to develop ways in which to guarantee the safety of their spaces. While lurkers may exist in reality and in virtual reality, at least in reality we have a chance to see them.

Similarly, scholars need to be willing to envision a function for the Internet beyond the ability to access political institutions. The Net is unique in the way it collapses space and time, suspends distinctions between public and private space, and opens issues and interactions to global influences. When theorizing the Net, just as when theorizing the public, scholars should be attentive to those issues, peoples, and forms of argument that exist counter to and within it. We need to look for the formation of electronic counterpublics on the Net in the same way we have begun to recognize counterpublics. The challenge that faces us, however, is that if the enclaved and subaltern are difficult to identify in reality, then they may be even more difficult to identify in cyber-reality.

Additionally, I have serious concerns about utopian visions of the Internet that ignore the actual exclusion of the very people who most need the oppositional functions of counterpublics. Just as we are on the verge of celebrating and recognizing the democratizing potential of counterpublics, a technology arises that creates the appearance of being open to all publics, yet this technology presents economic barriers that make it difficult for the ideal to be realized. My fear is that the appearance of equal access created by the Internet may mollify us into believing that we need not take affirmative actions to encourage democratic participation by all, and to praise participation in all the forms it may take. To account for the Net's potential power and its dangers, researchers might want to consider investigating specific instances of cyber-activism, as well as the usage patterns of those who most populate counterpublic spheres.

NOTES

1. In her study of feminism and the women's movement, Ryan (1992) notes that the women's movement engages in the mutually reinforcing strategies of political activism and discursive politics. Political activism tends to consist of national mass movements, led by top-down organizations, and aims to influence legislation rather than people. In contrast, "[d]iscursive political groups consist of small, sometimes temporary, feminist groups involved in direct action tactics" (92) and eschew hierarchical organization. Discursive action also has as its aim social, rather than political, change. My distinction between institutionally focused politics and discursive politics is influenced by Ryan's distinction.

2. Not until Lake's (1983, 1991) work on Native American rhetoric does one find in the field of communication studies detailed attention to social movement rhetoric independent of its agonistic relationship to the dominant.

3. Hill and Hughes define Internet activism as "posting a political message (political e-mail) or chatting about politics on-line" (37).

REFERENCES

Blue Ribbon Campaign. http://www.eff.org/blueribbon.html (13 February 1999).

———. http://www.lambda.net/blue.html (13 February 1999).

Bowers, John W., Donovan J. Ochs, and Richard J. Jensen. 1993. *The rhetoric of agitation and control*, rev. ed. Prospect Heights, IL: Waveland.

Browning, Graeme. 1996. *Electronic democracy: Using the Internet to influence American politics*. Wilton, CT: Pemberton Press.

Butler, Judith P. 1993. *Bodies that matter: On the discursive limits of "sex."* New York: Routledge.

Cathcart, Robert S. 1978. Movements: Confrontation as rhetorical form. *Southern Speech Communication Journal* 43:233–247.

Diani, Mario. 1992. The concept of social movement. *Sociological Review* 40:1–25.

Dixon, Katrina. 1998. The cyber warriors. *The Scotsman*, 25 February. http://web.lexis-nexis.com (13 February 1999).

Fabj, Valeria, and Matthew J. Sobnosky. 1995. AIDS activism and the rejuvenation of the public sphere. *Argumentation and Advocacy* 31:163–184.

Farley, Maggie. 1999. Dissidents hack holes in China's new wall. *Los Angeles Times*, 4 January. http://web.lexis-nexis.com (13 February 1999).

Felski, Rita._1989. *Beyond feminist aesthetics: Feminist literature and social change*. Cambridge, MA: Harvard University Press.

Flores, Lisa A. 1996. Creating discursive space through a rhetoric of difference: Chicana feminists craft a homeland. *Quarterly Journal of Speech* 82:142–156.

Foster, Derek. 1996. Community and identity in the electronic village. In *Internet culture*, edited by David Porter. New York: Routledge.

Fraser, Nancy. 1992. Rethinking the public sphere: A contribution to the critique of actually existing democracy. In *Habermas and the public sphere*, edited by Craig Calhoun. Cambridge: Massachusetts Institute of Technology Press.

Futrelle, David. 1998. Net.cetera/CDA II: Congress' new campaign to censor the net. *Newsday*, 5 January. http://web.lexis-nexis.com (13 February 1999).

Goodnight, G. Thomas. 1982. The personal, technical, and public spheres of argument: A speculative inquiry into the art of deliberation. *Journal of the American Forensic Association* 18:214–227.

Gregg, Richard B. 1971. The ego-function of the rhetoric of protest. *Philosophy & Rhetoric* 4:71–91.

Greiner, Marley E. 1997. Adoptees make progress in struggle to be heard. *Columbus Dispatch*, 7 March. http://web.lexis-nexis.com (13 February 1999).

Griffin, Leland M. 1952. The rhetoric of historical movements. *Quarterly Journal of Speech* 38:184–188.

———. 1969. A dramatistic theory of the rhetoric of movements. In *Critical responses to Kenneth Burke*, edited by William H. Reuckert. Minneapolis: University of Minnesota Press.

Grossman, Lawrence K. 1995. *The electronic republic: Reshaping democracy in the information age*. New York: Viking.

Grossman, Wendy M. 1997. *Net.wars*. New York: New York University Press.

Habermas, Jürgen. 1987. *The theory of communicative action, lifeworld and system: A critique of functionalist reason*, vol. 2. Translated by Thomas McCarthy. Boston: Beacon Press.

——. 1989. The public sphere. In *Jürgen Habermas on society and politics: A reader*, edited by Steven Seidman. Boston: Beacon Press.

——. 1992. Further reflections on the public sphere. In *Habermas and the public sphere*, edited by Craig Calhoun. Cambridge: Massachusetts Institute of Technology Press.

'Hacktivists' at center of controversy. 1999. *Star Tribune*, 8 February. http://web.lexis-nexis.com (13 February 1999).

Harmon, Amy. 1998. 'Hacktivists' of all persuasions take their struggle to the Web. *New York Times*, 31 October. http://search.nytimes.com/search/daily/bôgetdoc+site+site+59543+0+wAAA+hacktivist (13 February 1999).

Hill, Kevin A., and John E. Hughes. 1998. *Cyberpolitics: Citizen activism in the age of the Internet*. Lanham, MD: Rowman and Littlefield.

hooks, bell. 1989. *Talking back: Thinking feminist, thinking black*. Boston, MA: South End Press.

——. 1992. *Black looks*. Boston: South End Press.

A joint statement by 2600, the Chaos Computer Club, the Cult of the Dead Cow, !Hispahack, L0oht Heavy Industries, Phrack, and Pulhas. http://www.hacktivism.org (13 February 1999).

Kinney, Jay. 1996. Is there a new political paradigm lurking in cyberspace? In *Cyberfutures: Culture and politics on the information superhighway*, edited by Ziauddin Sardar and Jerome R. Ravetz. New York: New York University Press.

Kokmen, Leyla. 1998. "Byte me" is slogan for cyber-protest. *Denver Post*, 26 October. http://web.lexis-nexis.com (13 February 1999).

Lake, Randall A. 1983. Enacting Red Power. *Quarterly Journal of Speech* 69:127–142.

——. 1991. Between myth and history. *Quarterly Journal of Speech* 77:125–151.

——. 1997. Argumentation and self: The enactment of identity in *Dances with Wolves*. *Argumentation and Advocacy* 34:66–89.

Lieberman, David. 1999. Internet gap widening. *USA Today*, 9–11 July, weekend edition.

Lorde, Audre. 1984. *Sister outsider: Essays and speeches*. Trumansburg, NY: Crossing Press.

LoU strikes out. http://www.hacktivism.org (30 August 1999).

Mansbridge, Jane. 1998. Feminism and democracy. In *Feminism and Politics*, edited by Anne Phillips. New York: Oxford University Press.

Matsuda, Mari J. 1993. Public responses to racist speech: Considering the victim's story. In *Words that wound*. Boulder, CO: Westview Press.

Melucci, Alberto. 1985. The symbolic challenge of contemporary movements. *Social Research* 52:789–815.

National Telecommunications and Information Administration (NTIA). 1999. *Falling through the Net: Defining the digital divide.* http://www.ntia.doc.gov/ntiahome/fttn99 (28 July 1999).

Paquin, Bob. 1998. Hacktivism: Attack of the e-guerillas! *The Straits Times (Singapore)*, 13 December. http://web.lexis-nexis.com (13 February 1999).

PGA Bulletin. 1997a. November-December. http://www.agp.org/agp/en/PGAInfos/bulletin0.html (30 August 1999).

———. 1997b. March. http://www.agp.org/agp/en/PGAInfos/bulletin1.html (30 August 1999).

Poster, Mark. 1997. Cyberdemocracy: Internet and the public sphere. In *Internet culture*, edited by David Porter. New York: Routledge.

Randall, Neil. 1997. *The soul of the internet: Net gods, netizens and the wiring of the world.* New York: International Thomson Computer Press.

Rash, Wayne, Jr. 1997. *Politics on the net: Wiring the political process.* New York: W. H. Freeman.

Rheingold, Howard. Electronic democracy toolkit. http://www.well.com/user/hlr/electrondemoc.html (2 February 1999a).

———. Rheingold's brainstorms. http://www.rheingold.com/ (3 February 1999b).

———. The virtual community. http://www.rheingold.com/vc/book (3 February 1999c).

Riley, Patricia, James F. Klumpp, and Thomas A. Hollihan. 1995. Democratizing the lifeworld of the twenty-first century: Evaluating new democratic sites for argument. In *Argument and values*, edited by Sally Jackson. Annandale, VA: National Communication Association.

Riley, Patricia, Thomas A. Hollihan, and James F. Klumpp. 1997. The dark side of community and democracy: Militias, patriots and angry white guys. In *Argument in a time of change: Definitions, frameworks, and critiques*, edited by James F. Klumpp. Annandale, VA: National Communication Association.

Ross-Larson, Bruce. 1999. A human face for globalization. http://www.undp.org/hdro/E1.html (1 September 1999).

Rubens, Paul. 1996. Cyber-movement for women opens Wellington chapter. *The Dominion (Wellington)*, 29 January. http://web.lexis-nexis.com (17 February 1999).

Ryan, Barbara. 1992. *Feminism and the women's movement: Dynamics of change in social movement ideology, and activism.* New York: Routledge.

Scott, Robert L., and Donald K. Smith. 1969. The rhetoric of confrontation. *Quarterly Journal of Speech* 50:1–8.

Selnow, Gary W. 1998. *Electronic whistle-stops: The impact of the Internet on American politics.* Westport, CT: Praegar.

Shapiro, Andrew. L. 1999. The internet. *Foreign Policy* 115:14–27.

Sobchack, Vivian. 1996. Democratic franchise and the electronic frontier. In *Cyberfutures: Culture and politics on the information superhighway,* edited by Ziauddin Sardar and Jerome R. Ravetz. New York: New York University Press.

Tsagarousianou, Roza, Damian Tambini, and Cathy Bryan, eds. 1998. *Cyberdemocracy: Technology, cities and civic networks.* New York: Routledge.

Tucker, Kenneth H., Jr. 1989. Ideology and social movements: The contributions of Habermas. *Sociological Inquiry* 59:30–45.

Wing, Adrien Katherine, ed. 1997. *Critical race feminism: A reader.* New York: New York University Press.

Wolf, Alecia. 1998. Exposing the great equalizer: Demythologizing internet equity. In *Cyberghetto or cyberutopia?: Race, class, and gender on the Internet,* edited by Bosah Ebo. Westport, CT: Praeger.

Wood, Andrew F., and Tyrone L. Adams. 1998. Embracing the machine: Quilt and quilting as community-building architecture. In *Cyberghetto or cyberutopia?: Race, class, and gender on the Internet,* edited by Bosah Ebo. Westport, CT: Praeger.

7 Crafting a Virtual Counterpublic

Right-to-Die Advocates on the Internet

TODD F. McDORMAN

In 1998, Michigan, the home state of noted suicide doctor Jack Kevorkian, considered a measure to legalize physician-assisted death. The emotional campaign waged between advocates and opponents of what was known as Proposition B not only underscored the right to die as an issue of great dispute, but also as one that raises important questions for how private citizens can best obtain a public voice in political decision making. The controversy of physician-assisted death demonstrates that crises emerge as ideas once considered "private," such as one's death, become almost entirely "public"—and yet are often beyond the control of the individual. With its ultimate resolution predicated on whether the body is defined as a private or public possession, euthanasia provides an intriguing case of the challenges counterpublic agents present to the state in negotiating public space.

Scholars recently have demonstrated the need for reflection on the meaning, contours, and accessibility of the public sphere. Pretensions that status in the public sphere is irrelevant and access is equal have been discarded, and the public often appears to resemble more a battlefield on which those who can speak the loudest or the longest prevail. In the case of the right to die, the once heated but balanced public discussion largely has given way to, or been appropriated by, sensationalized media coverage, the Jack Kevorkian side-show, and state protocols in the form of legislation and judicial opinions. However, these considerable obstacles to meaningful participation also are being countered by the phenomenal growth of a medium that optimistically avows the attainability of a mass public: the Internet. Thus, my purpose is not so much to glorify or reminisce about what no longer exists, but rather to explore the potential of the Internet as a counterpublic tool for revitalizing the role of the public sphere in mass reform of public policy and private action. To that end, this essay explores the use of New Communication Technologies (NCTs) by right-to-die advocates as a case study in how the Internet may prove beneficial to counterpublic mobilization.

A topic of great discussion since John Dewey ([1927] 1954) and Walter Lippmann (1925), the dimensions of public and private space and the resultant rights and responsibilities of those spaces are central to understanding the options and influence of various discourse communities. For instance, in *The Structural Transformation of the Public Sphere*, Jürgen Habermas (1989) argues that the expansion of the public sphere has diluted its strength and effectiveness in contributing to real decision-making. Habermas's historical investigation of the rise and demise of the public questions its continued ability to serve a valuable role in negotiating social policy. Contrary to the imagined design of the public sphere, the state has greatly infringed on the private domain while private organizations have seized an expanding segment of public power. The intermingling is to such an extent that we occasionally lose sight that the public sphere is, as Nancy Fraser argues, "conceptually distinct from the state" (1992, 110). Public space, as Seyla Benhabib laments, is not intended or understood as the locale of the elite but "as the creation of procedures whereby those affected by general social norms and by collective political decisions can have a say in their formulation, stipulation, and adoption" (1992, 87). The "affected," however, have lacked an effective means of response in the altered public.

The exponential growth and resultant power of an intrusive media is one explanation for the weakened position of public challenges to state power. Robert W. McChesney's (1999) insightful *Rich Media, Poor Democracy* laments that while the explosion of media megaconglomerates offers a mass of information, society is increasingly depoliticized and possesses a minimal understanding of relevant social and political affairs. The megaconglomerates, forming the basis of a "political media complex" linking politics, government, and the media, have developed a system that privileges the powerful elite who make immense decisions in isolation from public participation (McChesney 1999, 281; Swanson 1992). This new media oligopoly, McChesney concludes, is an "antidemocratic force" darkening the promise of democracy while eliminating social thought, suffocating social movements, and discouraging participation in public life (2, 7).

Combining with this powerlessness is growing public apathy. Richard Sennett ([1976] 1992) contends that the population-at-large has withdrawn from public discussion, primarily because of a pacifying media, which publicizes but makes readers, listeners, and viewers mere spectators. Television, criticizes Sennett, promotes passivity as one is capable only of turning it off and cannot "talk back" to it as such, making any effort at protest nothing more than "an invisible act" (283). W. Lance Bennett adds that the expansion of television media spectacles into the primary source of political information threatens the vitality of democracy by marginalizing the public's participation and encouraging passivity (1992, 403). Such developments force G. Thomas Goodnight to conclude that the power of the individual is seriously compromised by a "mass media industry" that "works to remove the process of crafting communication from the public sphere" and "exists in a parasitic relationship to human communication" (1990, 185). The net result is a gap between information and interaction, making mobilization a less enticing adventure.

Despite these obstacles, most scholars view the importance of maintaining a viable public sphere as indisputable. The task of how to maintain its utility is a more daunting challenge. By placing the focus on counterpublics and exploring means by which they can thwart media control, promote critical reason, and allow broad participation, one may locate an avenue for reinvigorating a vital public sphere. Specifically, right-to-die groups exemplify the nature of counterpublic challenges by bringing attention to their cause while expanding their membership base and challenging the legal and moral control imposed by the state. In exploring these groups, I argue that in an age of mass media dominance, the Internet offers the possible rejuvenation of the public by nurturing strong counterpublic challenges to state power. I critique the possibilities offered by the Internet for bolstering insurgent counterpublics through an analysis of how right-to-die advocates are utilizing NCTs in pursuit of legalized assisted dying. Specifically I explore how the Internet is strengthening counterpublics, how NCTs can increase public sphere discussion, and how these developments can positively impact counterpublic mobilization.

CAN COUNTERPUBLICS SUCCEED?
RIGHT-TO-DIE ADVOCATES ON THE INTERNET

Recent research on the emergence of World Wide Web (WWW) communities acknowledges a growing role for cyberspace in a variety of communication contexts. From newsgroups to e-commerce, the Internet is becoming "a more mature forum for communication." While the manner in which the Internet currently is being utilized is deserving of extended study, evaluations must also recognize that the Internet has not reached adulthood, making steadfast conclusions difficult (Mitra 1997, 162). The rapidity with which the Internet is changing communications makes any prediction of its ultimate effect "nearly impossible" (McChesney 1999, 121). This is an equally important observation for both those who, because of present deficiencies, casually dismiss the potential of NCTs in the work of counterpublic resistance and those who, without qualification, valorize the counterpublic possibilities of the Internet.

Those who believe the potential impact of NCTs is either negligible or almost entirely negative offer a variety of interesting and, often, sound arguments. Four of the primary objections to the Internet are that commercialization will ruin its potential, access is limited to the elite, reflective interaction among participants is rare, and it fails to produce truly deliberative democracy. That commercial forces will overwhelm the idealized free space of the Internet is among the most common concerns of Internet detractors (Barber 1997; Buchstein 1997; McChesney 1999). While the spread of commercialization cannot be denied, the decentralized nature of the Internet makes commercialization a less powerful threat than in the centralized media. Unlike radio and television, there is no limit to the number of channels or frequencies available, ruling out corporate monopoly. Thus, despite the existence of commercial forces in other segments of the Web, the Internet provides space for dissent through independent web sites and chat rooms. Even McChesney reflects that if the Internet becomes primarily a commercial medium, it still "will have all sorts of interactive activities that never existed in the past. It can, at the very least, be . . . open to a plethora of voices to speak, and be heard, worldwide at relatively minimal expense" (1999, 175).

Second, critics rightly charge that today cyberspace is not representative of the world at large. While some individuals purposefully choose to remain low-tech, an even greater concern is that the poor and less educated have less access to the Internet or e-mail and thus may be disproportionately excluded from this type of participation (Barber 1997; Streck 1998). Timothy Luke, for instance, argues that "getting 'access to' the global infostructure's material infrastructures is a real issue, and it is a life chance which is still very unequally distributed" (1998, 128). However, these problems do not deny the future potential of the Internet or its rapid growth. The National Telecommunications and Information Administration has found that personal computer (PC) ownership in the United States increased 74.7 percent over the past five years to 42.1 percent nationwide. Similarly, from 1997 to 1998 home Internet access jumped by 40.9 percent (1999, 3). The "digital divide" based on income, education, and race continues to be problematic but on the whole access is quickly rising. The expected growth in WebTV and digital television in the next decade, the possible development of a new, less expensive "network" computer, and continued computer rebate promotions coupled with Internet service signups will also bring more people on-line (McChesney 1999, 162, 147). Of greatest note is that regardless of inequalities, *more* individuals have access to e-mail and the Internet than have the opportunity to voice their opinion in other media forums. The number and extent of the opportunities are greater, even if the access is not, at this point, equitable. Universal connectivity is certainly a goal toward which the United States should strive, but its absence is not a broad indictment of the potential of the Internet for mobilization.

The final two objections worthy of note are interrelated: the Internet is not truly interactive, and it does not produce the type of deliberation inherent to a healthy democracy. Critics contend that communication in chat rooms, on bulletin boards, and over listservs is dominated by reactionary ad hominem attacks that voice polarized and extreme positions (Buchstein 1997). "On a day to day basis," John Streck claims, cyberspace "is about as interactive as a shouting match." Rather than serving as "an environment for rational discussion," it is "a soapbox for extreme opinions which would not be entertained anywhere else" (1998, 45). Such charges are undoubtedly true of some forums, but all should not be judged on the basis of these generalizations. Academics should place more faith in the intellect of net surfers to sort through the rubbish in arriving at sites that are more reflective and reasoned. As I demonstrate in my analysis of right-to-die groups on the Internet, this sort of blanket accusation is an inaccurate summary for all Internet activity.

Finally, Internet dystopians contend that the instantaneous nature of the Internet discourages critical democratic reflection and instead encourages reactionary decision-making (Barber 1997; Buchstein 1997). As McChesney summarizes the concern: "the notion that the Internet is a democratic medium—that it will remain or become available to the public on anything close to egalitarian terms—seems dubious at best" (1999, 183–184). I suggest that while such assessments may be accurate, they are also shortsighted. First, they fail to take into account the ongoing nature of many political discussions on the Internet. If a message or brief exchange is viewed in isolation, such a conclusion is understandable. However, observing an organization devoted to activism, as opposed to a chat room where visitors air individual grievances, might produce much different conclusions. Second, and perhaps what is most at issue, unrealistic expectations are placed on the Internet. The Internet should not be condemned because it is unable to "save" democracy. If that is the expectation, it will undoubtedly be a disappointment and a failure. Rather, it would be better to view the Internet as an advocacy tool, as a means of supplementing current efforts. One of the contributions of the Internet and this case study is to highlight the benefit of virtual efforts for the extension, development, and revitalization of more traditional nonvirtual social movements and strategies.

Even accepting much of this criticism at face value, the expansion of the Internet presents conditions favorable to a broad range of counterpublics and social movements. In an analysis of how Indian immigrants use NCTs, Mitra claims that "increasingly, the Internet and the WWW is playing a role in the production of a virtually connected community of people who are producing a cyberidentity" (1997, 159). David Resnick optimistically notes that "the Internet might facilitate the particular style of democratic politics favored by activists" (1998, 64), while Douglas Kellner enthusiastically claims that "cyberactivists have been attempting to carry out globalization from below, developing networks of solidarity and circulating struggle throughout the globe" (1998, 185). Cynical evaluations are challenged by Anna Sampaio and Janni Aragon, who argue that NCTs challenge traditional notions of language and social construction, "disrupt[ing] the production of more traditional subjectivities" and "allow[ing] for the production of alternate subject positions, and by extension alternate political practices" (1998, 145). Laura J. Gurak adds, "Communication technologies provide a potential means to span the physical boundaries of local communities and . . . provide potential forums for citizen participation" (1997, 7). For counterpublic resistance, expanded forums mean valuable discursive spaces from which to challenge state power.

To this point, however, little scholarly work, particularly from the field of communication, has attempted to analyze concretely how this technology is actually being used (Bettig 1997, 154; Mitra 1997, 162). Such work can explore the potential advantages of cyberspace while investigating significant questions such as how virtual space changes the operation of the public sphere and whether it truly offers new opportunities or merely presents the same obstacles in new forms without any real potential for the advancement of resistance. My analysis of right-to-die advocates' use of computer technologies provides some initial answers to these inquiries while highlighting several interesting issues. One issue concerns the vitality of the Internet in promoting increased political activism of groups that have had a prolonged physical existence. A related issue addresses the extent to which such virtual activism allows these groups to circumvent limitations imposed by traditional media. A third issue highlights the possibilities of NCTs to increase participation in social movements and facilitate different forms and styles of discursive exchange. Finally, a more sobering issue, which recalls a popular criticism of the Internet, involves the extent to which a group wishing to establish an on-line presence must be populated with members who possess a high degree of technological competence.

As a result of these inquiries, I argue that while not an unqualified success, right-to-die advocates' use of the Internet offers potential for counterpublic resistance to state control. Three interconnected points of analysis provide the basis of my optimism. First, the WWW alters the influence, function, and use of media. The new format, in turn, provides the possibility for and encourages not only more meaningful individual participation but also a more egalitarian dialogue. Third, increased participation and dialogue enhance the prospects of successful mobilization against the state.

STAKING OUT THE NET:
USING THE INTERNET TO BOLSTER COUNTERPUBLICS

The ability of the WWW to function as an alternative to mainstream media is an important feature in revitalizing public and counterpublic spheres. As a flexible user-friendly medium where information is available with a click of the mouse, the Web restructures the traditional individual-media relationship in ways that promote the empowerment of group and individual resistance. The Web provides an independent media outlet that changes the dynamic between media producer and consumer while promoting participation and interaction. I will explore this development by first discussing the importance of the change in format and second focusing on how right-to-die advocates are actually using the Web to nurture and encourage the formation of counterpublics.

The difference in texture between cyberspace and traditional media makes the Internet a more inviting forum, providing benefits to the stimulation of counterpublics. While some theorists espousing reader-response criticism praise the polysemeous nature of television in allowing audiences to actively construct meaning (Carpignano et al. 1993; Fiske 1986), the possibilities of NCTs seem much greater. In contrast to television and other media, "the Web is a 'pull' media—consumers can decide for themselves whether they want to call up what the publishers are offering" (Toulouse 1998, 4). And while Sennett criticizes television for its unidirectional nature, "computer communication is often two-way, or even omnidirectional. . . . [C]omputer involvement can be interactive and participatory" (Kellner 1998, 180).

A reader's selection of web site links that are most relevant to him or her is an extension of the "negotiation that takes place between the text and its socially situated viewers," as observed by Carpignano et al. (1993, 112). Perhaps the better comparison is to deconstruction as the multiple options of the Web deny, as deconstruction theorists argue, "the possibility of preferred meaning be[ing] structured into the text with any degree" of certainty (Fiske 1986, 400). Instead, it is a more free-floating text with meaning constructed based on the pathways selected by the electronic visitor. The pieces allow the reader to weave the text out of the multitude of fragments (McGee 1990).

Through the use of the Web, as well as discussion lists, groups can directly post news releases of events, rallies, and protests, bypassing traditional media and presenting the story from their own perspective. Broadcast via web pages and listservs, releases are received by those with the greatest interest while larger media outlets may also pick them up. This way, the counterpublic message is broadcast without being filtered by the media and reduced to a thirty-second sound bite or three inches of news space. Moreover, this capability can both provide a voice for counterpublics that lack sustained media attention and, perhaps more important, partially compensate for financial shortcomings. Because operating on-line is relatively inexpensive, Resnick (1998) argues, groups can more efficiently "spread their message, recruit new members, raise funds, lobby politicians, mount petition drives and the like. Many of these familiar political strategies and activities would have been impossible even to attempt without the Web" (66). Kevin A. Hill and John E. Hughes concur, arguing that "it is actually far cheaper to get your political message to 100,000 people over the Web than it was in 1930 to get that same message to 1,000 people via long distance telephone calling" (1998, 134). Hill and Hughes further explain that for just a few thousand dollars an interested group could construct a "super deluxe" web site, purchase a powerful computer, and obtain a fast Internet connection. A more frugal organization could purchase space on a commercial server for as little as fifty dollars per month.

Death and dying advocates at DeathNET (2000a), the Euthanasia Research & Guidance Organization (ERGO! Euthanasia World Directory 2000a), and the Hemlock Society (2000) are capitalizing on these possibilities to varying degrees of effectiveness. Formed in January 1995 by John Hofsess, Executive Director of the Right to Die Society of Canada, DeathNET claims to be the first web site to specialize in death and dying. Its intended purpose is "to be not only an uniquely valuable resource on the Internet but a state-of-the-art web-based information service: easy to use and a pleasure to visit" (DeathNET 2000c). DeathNET claims to offer "the world's largest collection of 'right to die' materials and services on the Internet" with an impressive collection of more than 950 different files and 200 links to medical and health resources (2000c). Those interested can read significant court cases as well as find information on hospice care, end-of-life options, and discussion lists for a variety of terminal illnesses. It is a virtual encyclopedia referencing all aspects of the right to die. The site demonstrates the appeal of the web as a "pull" media, allowing a visitor to navigate through and around whatever is of interest.

Working almost as a parallel in the United States, ERGO provides much of the same information, although it lacks the extensive links to medical resources. The ERGO! Euthanasia World Directory (2000a) specifically claims that it is working to "create a better America—electronically." The embrace of computer technologies is deliberate and important in sustaining this virtual group. ERGO binds a conglomeration of advocates around the world through its web site and is able to provide a home base for right-to-die advocates to convene. It provides potential advocates with multiple contact points, such as Internet addresses and fax numbers, to U.S. representatives, senators, and government committees. The demand for this information has increased precipitously. Previously, technical consultant John David Duncan (1999) reported a daily average of nearly 3,000 hits; during the first eight months of 2000, the site claimed an average of 417,000 visits per month and more than five million hits to the site (ERGO staff 2000a).

Although its web site has lacked the depth of information of the other sites, the Hemlock Society (2000), the largest membership based right-to-die organization in the United States, has also taken steps to capitalize on the possibilities of cyberspace. Acknowledging the shortcomings of its site, the Hemlock Society has engaged in a technological overhaul that extends well beyond a more pronounced presence on the WWW. Clark W. Trammell, Director of Operations at the Hemlock Society, explains that recent efforts have focused on strengthening the structure of the organization and making it more technologically advanced. Trammell (1999) feels recent changes in technology at the Hemlock Society have created "a state of the art operation" that allows its staff of ten "to do the job of twenty people."

Of particular importance for Hemlock's current improvements is their web page. Trammell is excited about the communication potential of an enhanced web site and its ability to allow near-instantaneous exchanges. However, Trammell laments that currently the page is not at a level to optimize the usefulness of the site for the nearly 130,000 hits the Hemlock Society home page gets per month (Girsh 1999). When the overhaul is complete, "we will be able to capture and maximize someone's visit to the page." Hemlock's possible plans include organizing chat rooms on its web site, merchandising materials more extensively, and covering organizational efforts better. "We can be more timely with our message," Trammell says, "and just the enhancement of that [the web page] makes this dynamic move up the ladder."

Developing a presence on the WWW presents counterpublic organizations with a way to take control of the information from the media. By crafting their message, providing extensive resources, and operating outside the constraints of traditional channels, organizations using the WWW may stimulate and nurture interest. While this in itself does not constitute the existence of an active dynamic counterpublic, by providing individuals with important information critical of state controls it will encourage interested parties to consider becoming advocates. Moreover, the development of a web site, a cyberspace location for the meeting of those with a common cause, creates other avenues for the development of resistance. The posting of messages on web-based bulletin boards and the development of e-mail discussion lists for interested activists may stimulate dialogue, are more egalitarian, and can be utilized to promote political action.

EXPANDING THE DIALOGUE: USING NCTS
TO INCREASE PUBLIC SPHERE COMMUNICATION

Through the use of e-mail, discussion listservs, and web displays the Internet may revitalize the public's participation and reform the mobilization of counterpublics. On DeathNET, for example, the "Garden of Remembrance" invites visitors to contribute to the site by submitting on-line obituaries and memorials for deceased loved ones, creating a tapestry of sharing (2000b). Through the ERGO web site those supportive of the right to die can sign up for an e-mail listserv that distributes information on new right-to-die developments while also serving as a source of public information. And at various locations across cyberspace, from lists moderated by the *Detroit Free Press* to those of various search engines, individuals can post their views on nearly any aspect of the issue.[1]

Such locations are important for the right to die as well as for understanding the meaning of counterpublics to the public sphere. First, the broad communication network of sharing provided on the Internet enhances the creation of what I call an agency-saving resistant identity of right-to-die advocates more easily than in mass-mediated physical space. That is, rather than quietly allowing the status quo to rob individuals of power over end-of-life decisions, this network fosters the crafting of a collective identity that empowers personal and political action through shared energy. Second, the absence of material boundaries in virtual space demonstrates the fluidity of modern public communication and the public sphere. Third, the rapid expansion of the Internet facilitates an increasing number of voices participating in the discussion.

The broad communication network of sharing fostered by the Internet allows right-to-die advocates to craft more expansively and emotionally an agency-saving resistant identity. Whether it is in praise of an advocate who has controlled her own death, the sharing of personal stories critical of the state's intervention into death and dying, or the announcement of the presence of a new member of the death and dying community, virtual forums demonstrate the resolve of euthanasia advocates to continue struggling against the state and provide an emotional outlet and confessional space that unites the group in shared compassion and pain.

The most prominent and intellectually rich outlet is the ERGO listserv. Populated by more than 700 individuals, including attorneys, authors, educators, lobbyists, and persons in the midst of end-of-life decisions, the interaction of the list discloses an independent and politically active community (ERGO Staff 2000b). Not only does it offer participants the latest information on aid in dying, ranging from court cases and legal initiatives to the latest books on the topic, but the forum, by providing contact with others who have similar concerns, builds an international network of knowledgeable advocates who have the capability of leading challenges against the state. Moreover, interaction between the "public" and high-profile activists permitted by such lists breaks down barriers and promotes more equal participation. The opportunity to exchange messages with Derek Humphry—the most visible advocate other than Jack Kevorkian—and the leadership of right-to-die organizations not only crosses organizational boundaries but also avoids a rigid hierarchy and gives a grassroots, communitarian feel to the discussion. List contributors pose and answer pressing questions while debating controversial aspects of euthanasia and assisted dying. The interaction promotes introspection and reflection and provides individuals with important reinforcement and encouragement for their positions. In addition to consistently criticizing the state's opposition to the right-to-die, members have considered substantive and philosophical issues such as how living wills could be modified to protect choice in dying, raised questions concerning the potential actions of HMOs in end-of-life care, and engaged in debates over the religious implications of the right to die.[2] Such acts of participation strengthen the movement by developing thoughtful positions on the various issues and furthering the unity of the group. In turn, this strengthens the foundation of the counterpublic.

The August 1997 passing of Janet Good, founder of the Michigan chapter of the Hemlock Society, demonstrates the community-building function of the list as well as the implicit connection between participation and mobilization of resistance. Good, a longtime Kevorkian associate, died with the assistance of the suicide doctor after battling pancreatic cancer. The instant access provided by the Internet created a virtual forum (or funeral home) for right-to-die advocates to mourn and pay tribute to Good. List contributors praised Good's accomplishments while using her death as a source of inspiration for future advocacy. Derek Humphry (1997) described Janet Good as "a brave and hard-working woman who dedicated herself to two things: the principle of individual civil liberties and helping others. People of her calibre come rarely." A certified hospice nurse contributed a message urging right-to-die advocates to "not let her passion to help the terminally ill pass along with her. . . . Let us band together even closer than we have ever been. Janet helped put in motion the right to die movement, lets [sic] not let it fail" (Allison 1997). Other messages praising Good, as well as obituaries from across the nation, were posted for the benefit of ERGO's electronic subscribers. Here we begin to glimpse the potential of this technology to optimize counterpublic resistance. The sharing promotes a bonding that motivates action against the state.

Finally, the ERGO list provides a forum for sharing personal stories and conditions. It serves an almost therapeutic purpose since contributors are not drawn out by the media or displayed for the public at large, but instead can both seek compassion from those in similar situations with similar ideals and spur others to act. Both ideas are captured in one emotional post in which a woman questioned, "How many politicians have had to witness a loved one die from a terminal illness? If only my father had had the option to die with assistance," she says, "it would have been a blessing." Instead, the daughter explains, "His death . . . was gruesome . . . he drowned in his own fluids. . . . [D]ying must have been horrific for him." Like many who share on the list, she closes with an appeal for a change in policy: "Our greatest gift we can give to the dying is our compassion and if they choose to end their suffering before it becomes too great we should as a society be able to let them choose" (Brand 1997). Those battling illness also join and write to the list on occasion. As an Iowa man announced: "I'm a new member of the Right-to-Die community. (I have leukemia and have been told I have about a year to live)." The individual expressed his thanks to advocates like Derek Humphry who had increased his "chances of having a dignified death when the time comes" (Caminiti 1997). Another contributor, an elderly gentleman, expressed his frustration with the law: "For God's sake when we want to die and have given it over a year's consideration then why can't we die with dignity? We're senior citizens and have earned the right to die in our own time" (Dawson 1997). These posts, note Michael J. Hyde and Kenneth Rufo in their analysis of interactions between ERGO members and Not Dead Yet, a disability rights organization, are among "the most down-to-earth and moving discourse" distributed on the list (2000, 8). This opportunity for expression not only demonstrates the resolve of euthanasia advocates but provides people with an emotional outlet, a coping mechanism that allows for confession to strangers while receiving compassion from those who have experienced similar hardship.

That sick and dying individuals, dispersed throughout the world, can overcome material boundaries in this virtual space demonstrates the fluidity of modern public communication and the public sphere. Ironically, the virtual nature of the Internet allows those who cannot mobilize physically to participate virtually. Those terminally ill and elderly who are limited in the physical world are offered new possibilities in the virtual forum. The electronic medium gives voice to the absent body while providing a community of strangers with the ability to stay connected—at their own pace and in their own time. It is a forum where access is open, authorship can be anonymous, and the structure is less hierarchical, more fluid, and fundamentally altered by the next e-mail message or update to a web page. Thus, the public space is constantly reconfigured by a community of individuals in search of the right tools to challenge state authority.

By using NCTs these individuals are united as a political and social entity with strength beyond their numbers. The ability to meet virtually multiplies the possibilities for advocacy and sharing. The Hemlock Society wants to capitalize on this by linking its local chapters across the Internet. When accomplished, Trammell (1999) argues that this will "keep chapters vibrant longer" and help fill the transition from one leader to the next. If a new chapter leader does not immediately emerge after the retirement or death of a predecessor, the computer network can help hold the chapter together until a new local leader emerges. "We don't have to close the chapter" because of the ability provided by computer communication. Additionally, electronic communication can provide the illusion of stronger numbers. As Trammell explains, "a strong volunteer who is bright, capable, and confident" and has "a computer with email [can] create a virtual chapter and in the eyes of the public that chapter can be as large as what I want you to think it is and it can be as dynamic with one person as with ten."

As more and more people go on-line, the number of voices in the chorus will continue to grow. Increased use of the Internet, discussion groups, and listservs provides new outlets for a more egalitarian dialogue and the reinsertion of private individuals into social deliberation. With ideas in the foreground and identifying markers such as title, gender, race, and appearance in the background, cyberspace can put the private citizen on more equal footing (Streck 1998, 35). This dynamic of disparate individuals connected through the Internet via modems, as right-to-die advocates demonstrate, "make[s] possible a new type of public communication. . . . This constitutes a new form of public dialogue and interaction" (Kellner 1998, 180). This new dialogue raises new prospects for mobilizing against the state.

MOBILIZING THE VOICES: ARTICULATION INTO ACTION

The virtual realm can overcome distance, encourage community formation, and empower action through virtual, in addition to physical, mobilization. Utilizing these NCTs to organize and lead campaigns to secure choice in dying bolsters movements by allowing more individuated independent participation. And while the virtual forum does not supplant physical mobilization, the virtual does complement the physical. Activist networks expand as technology reaches into more homes across the nation, providing stronger lines of communication and the ability to align a national strategy that is more adept at reflection and revision.

The ERGO listserv provides multiple examples of how electronic communications can assist counterpublic mobilization against the state. Beyond the regular contributions that challenge state philosophy and make calls for broad action, specific means of contributing to the cause are presented. For instance, in late July 1999, ERGO subscribers were presented with the opportunity to support a candidate for the Virginia legislature who is sympathetic to the right to die, participate in an electronic letter-writing campaign, and organize against a Senate bill that put Oregon's physician-assisted death law in jeopardy (Brickman 1999; Harris 1999; Humphry 1999). In the appeal opposing the Pain Relief Promotion Act, which would overturn the Oregon legislation, list moderator Derek Humphry urged the use of electronic media to voice displeasure. In an appeal to "ERGO subscribers" he encouraged: "Please make your voice known to your senator or representative. This is urgent." Humphry included information that would allow subscribers to contact their elected representatives, before closing with an appeal emphasizing the threat presented by the bill: "PLEASE ACT NOW. . . . . . . THIS HYDE-NICHOLS

ACT IS THEIR WAY TO KILL THE UNIQUE OREGON LAW" [double ellipses in original].[3] Subsequent invitations to participate have included writing to the imprisoned Jack Kevorkian, whom a poster described as "very grateful for the encouragement he gets from his supporters through the mail" (Poenisch 1999), and contributing to the Hemlock Foundation efforts for the Kevorkian Legal Defense Fund (Girsh 2000).

Similarly, the Merian's Friends campaign, organized in Michigan in 1998, utilized several means of electronic advocacy in attempting to form a counterpublic capable of changing Michigan law. Merian's Friends used the ERGO list for national and international support, developed a web page, and attempted internal email communications to assist their campaign. On collecting enough signatures to get Proposition B on the November 1998 ballot in Michigan, campaign chair Robert Moreillon (1998a) used the ERGO listserv to publicize the campaign's progress. The press release, intended for news services, educated right-to-die advocates on the basis of the proposition by explaining that Merian's Friends was formed after Merian Frederick, a victim of Lou Gehrig's Disease (ALS), had to end her life with Jack Kevorkian's help. The press release stated: "She refused to become a mind trapped in a suffocating body, and wished to end her life and suffering." The release closed with information on how people could join, phone, and write the campaign—information useful to both those in Michigan and those interested in assisting with the issue nationwide.

The use of the ERGO network continued throughout the campaign. In coordinating the press and public relations for Merian's Friends, Davi Napoleon (1998) used the ERGO listserv to ask members to take advantage of a *Detroit Free Press* invitation for readers to "share experiences with death or dying that shapes their views on the proposal. If we think about it, most of us know someone whose last days were very painful—this is the time to fax those stories . . . or mail them . . . or E-mail." Another e-mail posted by Mr. Moreillon (1998b), only a month before the November election, was prefaced with: "FOLLOWING IS A 496–WORD GENERAL STATEMENT AND DESCRIPTION OF PROPOSAL B FOR YOUR EDITORIAL AND BACKGROUND INFORMATION USE." As indicated, the e-mail provided advocates with a simple and direct way to get information about Merian's Friends out to the public.

Despite the ultimate landslide defeat of Proposition B, ERGO list members were able to use the experience to perform maintenance on the right-to-die movement. That is, the failure of the initiative did not signal the ineffectiveness of activists' electronic advocacy. Prodded by Olli Pentilla (1998) of the World Federation for the Right-to-Die in Israel, subscribers sought an explanation for "the disastrous voting results."

Numerous subsequent responses such as Ken Shapiro's (1998) gleaned "important lessons to be learned from Michigan that can and should be used in the future to help guide other states that are thinking of trying to pass a law legalizing and regulating the issue." Lessons for the future included the need for better organization, better internal and external circulation of critical information, and improved understanding of the overpowering financial superiority and tactics of the state and organized religion. More recently, groups such as Mainers for Death with Dignity (2000) and California's Friends of Dying Patients (2000) employed on-line resources in their support of state initiatives.

While ultimately unsuccessful, the Merian's Friends campaign, just like the varied examples from the ERGO listserv, demonstrates the growing utility of NCTs in encouraging and organizing resistance. The world is changing and social activists must, and generally are, changing with it. While not fully integrated into the actions of social movements or society, new communications, from the WWW to e-mail, can make important contributions if activists utilize them. As one Merian's Friends insider notes of their campaign, "For those of us using email it helped a great deal in keeping in touch and finding out what was happening." The difficulty, however, was that some key leaders either "did not have access to email or were unwilling to use it" (Everham 1999). As the technology becomes more commonplace these shortcomings should become less prevalent. In the meantime, the public sphere—and counterpublic resistance—should be reenergized by the growing network of individuals, participating on more equal ground, using this communication technology to assist their challenges to the state.

THE PROBLEMS AND PROMISES OF
INTERNET ACTIVISM IN THE PUBLIC SPHERE

The shape of the public sphere is a complicated issue, growing ever more so as communication outlets expand and potential voices multiply. This study of the use of NCTs in the right-to-die controversy not only exposes the nature of public argument on this emotional and timely issue, but on several levels adds to the understanding of the changing nature of the public sphere and the possible impact of the Internet on the identity formation and mobilization of counterpublics.

In light of criticisms that focus on limitations of the Internet as an exclusive means of mobilization, this analysis offers insights into the relationship between virtual and nonvirtual advocacy. This case study suggests an alternative model that integrates traditional and on-line efforts. By using its web site to supplement its existing infrastructure, the Hemlock Society is able to extend its presence and fortify its efforts. Similarly, through its online operation, ERGO is able to link advocates across the world, providing a unifying thread among advocate efforts as varied as Maine's ballot initiative and Dr. Philip Nitschke's work in Australia. Such efforts underscore that the Internet, as Calhoun argues, "figures in primary relationships mainly as a useful supplement" (1998, 379). It is "most empowering when it adds to the capacities of people organized outside it, not when an attempt is made to substitute 'virtual community' for the real thing" (382). If scholars and advocates approach the Internet in such terms its merits and applications will be most fruitfully realized.

This analysis also highlights the means by which NCTs enable accurate, sustained, and broad transmission of an organization's message. As the media have become an almost oppressive force, parceling out coverage of social movements on their own terms, NCTs offer the possibility of reclaiming a degree of organizational autonomy. These technologies allow groups to generate complete messages that are readily and continually available for public consumption, regardless of whether media coverage of a movement is limited or nonexistent. The web-based operations of DeathNet, ERGO, and the Hemlock Society provide for a virtual presence that can temporarily sustain movements in times of depleted public interest, allowing a movement to better seize the opportunity for a new initiative on short notice. This ability is not only demonstrated in the medical archives of DeathNet, the legal archives of ERGO, and the ongoing initiatives of Hemlock, but also through the ability of the ERGO listserv to rally support when an issue is suddenly thrust back into the public consciousness, as occurred with the introduction of the Pain Relief Promotion Act.

We should not underestimate the potential of NCTs to bring new and unique voices to public discussion. This analysis should make clear that virtual participation allows for a level of sharing that often is unavailable in traditional outlets. The personal exchanges and disclosures found on ERGO and DeathNet's "Garden of Remembrance" are two critical examples of the emotional exchange allowed for and promoted by the use of NCTs. While this is not to suggest that traditional organizations lack such disclosure, it is to say that the extent of the sharing in terms of the potential number of participants is much greater when NCTs are utilized. Additionally, NCTs allow for the inclusion of individuals who might not otherwise be able to participate in the movement. That is, the virtual forums allow the disabled and the ill, some of the most persuasive advocates for the right to die, to participate. While the ability to give voice to the absent body is particularly important in an issue such as the right to die, it is an opportunity that could benefit almost any burgeoning movement.

Yet technological access and competence will remain important obstacles for Internet advocacy for the immediate future. As virtual advocacy groups continue to emerge, the access, use, and development of NCTs should be monitored closely. Despite a lack of universal access, the Internet provides *more* access for a broader base of people, which is important in itself. And as the use of these technologies expands, their potential impact will grow. As more and more elementary school children learn computer basics, and more and more adults use computers as part of their employment, cyberspace will become more familiar territory. Such evolution allows Clark W. Trammell (1999), the Hemlock Society Director of Operations, to be optimistic about growing technological competence. The current generation of Hemlock leaders, by nature a more elderly group, were not "brought up with computers . . . so they are afraid to try something new or they just don't have the desire or it's frustrating and mind-boggling. The group underneath them are [sic] computer literate." While complete computerization may be more than a generation away, the huge expansion of school and workplace computers along with the technology-driven stocks of Wall Street seem to indicate that this transition is underway, making issues of access and competence of slightly diminishing concern.

Cyber successes provide encouraging signs forecasting the long-term viability of on-line efforts such as those launched by the right-to-die community. "This is indeed a communication revolution," says McChesney, "and one that is being taken advantage of by countless social and political organizations that heretofore were marginalized" (1999, 175). As long ago as 1991, activists using e-mail and the Internet dissuaded the Lotus Development Corporation from releasing Lotus MarketPlace, a database designed to give small businesses access to direct-mailing lists and personal information about consumers (Gurak 1997). Similarly, in March 1999, a flood of more than 200,000 e-mail messages prompted federal bank regulators to withdraw a proposed plan to monitor individuals' bank transactions in the detection of money laundering. Federal Deposit Insurance Company chairperson Donna Tanoue directly credits the deluge of e-mail with the decision. "It was the nature and the volume" of the e-mail, she said. "When consumers can get excited about an esoteric bank regulation, we have to pay attention" (Raney 1999b). Less esoteric issues, including the right to die, are also clearly making an impact as "flash campaigns . . . are erupting on the Internet" (Raney 1999a). In the case of physician-assisted dying, from on-line memorials to newsgroups to listservs, people are coming together to talk about the issue. This dialogue is important to the health of the individuals and the creation of an extensive virtual community. Finally, activists orient themselves and their arguments toward wider publics, including the state.

It remains uncertain whether a less sensationalized and more partici-patory community and a reinvigorated public sphere can be crafted if forced to deal with a medium that works largely at cross-purposes to indi-vidual concerns and a state that often overwhelms the individual. How-ever, with more open channels of communication able to exist outside the bounds of traditional media, the Internet offers advocates a more realistic opportunity to participate in the negotiation of social policy, thus invigo-rating the public sphere. If a viable public sphere is to be preserved—and even strengthened through strong counterpublic challenges to the state—then activists will be well advised to nurture the development of NCTs and maximize the advantageous possibilities examined in this analysis of right-to-die advocates on the Internet.

NOTES

1. These sites range from the *Detroit Free Press*, where visitors can participate in the "Kevorkian Forum," to Usenet groups such as talk.euthanasia.

2. These sorts of discussions are ongoing. I have not quoted from specific e-mail messages in order to protect the privacy of the individuals who use this discussion. Subsequent references to "private" e-mail—that is, e-mail by individuals who are not advocates in the public eye or who have requested that I protect their privacy—use aliases.

3. Neither this version of the bill nor the one passed by the House of Representatives in 2000 secured final passage from the Senate. Passage at the end of the 2000 session appeared imminent, despite threats of a fili-buster by Oregon Senator Ron Wyden, before the Senate found itself immersed in the presidential election recount. The future of the Oregon measure remains uncertain as President George W. Bush has indicated his opposition to the right to die and could place federal restrictions on the distribution of narcotics in a manner that would in effect nullify the Oregon law.

REFERENCES

Allison, Deborah. [pseud.]. Re: Death of Mrs. Janet Good. right_to_die @efn.org (26 August 1997).

Barber, Benjamin R. 1997. The new telecommunications technology: End-less frontier or the end of democracy? *Constellations* 4:208–228.

Benhabib, Seyla. 1992. *Situating the self: Gender, community, and post-modernism in contemporary ethics.* New York: Routledge.

Bennett, W. Lance. 1992. White noise: The perils of mass mediated democracy. *Communication Monographs* 59:401–406.

Bettig, Ronald. 1997. The enclosure of cyberspace. *Critical Studies in Mass Communication* 14:138–157.

Brand, Mary. [pseud.]. Re: Charles Hall: Question: Health care proxy/durable power of attorney. right_to_die@efn.org (28 April 1997).

Brickman, Myrtle. Hugh Finn case—How you can help promote death with dignity in Virginia. right_to_die@efn.org (24 July 1999).

Buchstein, Hubertus. 1997. Bytes that bite: The Internet and deliberative democracy. *Constellations* 4:248–263.

Calhoun, Craig. 1998. Community without propinquity revisited: Com-munications technology and the transformation of the urban public sphere. *Sociological Inquiry* 68:373–397.

Caminiti, Michael. [pseud.]. Re: About Derek. right_to_die@efn.org (20 June 1997).

Carpignano, Paolo, Robin Anderson, Stanley Aronowitz, and William DiFazio. 1993. Chatter in the age of electronic reproduction: Talk television and the "public mind." In *The phantom public sphere*, edited by Bruce Robbins. Minneapolis: University of Minnesota Press.

Dawson, Rick. [pseud.]. Re: Reuters: End of life care & pain. right_to_die @efn.org (19 August 1997).

DeathNET. http://www.rights.org/deathnet/ (27 September 2000a).

———. Garden of Remembrance. http://www.rights.org/deathnet/gate.html (29 September 2000b).

———. What is DeathNET? http://www.rights.org/death/about_death-net.html (29 September 2000c).

Dewey, John. [1927] 1954. *The public and its problems.* Reprint, Athens, OH: Swallow Press.

Duncan, John David. Re: ERGO web page. [personal e-mail]. (21 July 1999).

ERGO! Euthanasia World Directory. http://www.finalexit.org/ (29 Sep-tember 2000a).

———. Subscribe to the right_to_die Internet Mailing List. http://www.finalexit.org/subscribe.html (29 September 2000b).

ERGO Staff. Not in the big Internet league, but . . . right_to_die@efn.org (28 August 2000a).

———. Statistic. right_to_die@efn.org (11 January 2000b).

Everham, Raymond. [pseud.]. Comments on Merian's Friends. [personal e-mail]. (19 July 1999).

Fiske, John. 1986. Television: Polysemy and popularity. *Critical Studies in Mass Communication* 3:391–408.

Fraser, Nancy. 1992. Rethinking the public sphere: A contribution to the critique of actually existing democracy. In *Habermas and the public sphere*, edited by Craig Calhoun. Cambridge: Massachusetts Institute of Technology Press.

Friends of Dying Patients. http://www.fodp.org/fodp.htm (6 January 2000).

Girsh, Faye. 1999. Interview by author. Denver CO, 27 July.

———. Kevorkian legal defense. right_to_die@efn.org (5 January 2000).

Goodnight, G. Thomas. 1990. The rhetorical tradition, modern communication, and the grounds of justified assent. In *Argumentation theory and the rhetoric of assent*, edited by David Cratis Williams and Michael David Hazen. Tuscaloosa: University of Alabama Press.

Gurak, Laura J. 1997. *Persuasion and privacy in cyberspace: The online protests over Lotus Marketplace and the Clipper chip*. New Haven, CT: Yale University Press.

Habermas, Jürgen. 1989. *The structural transformation of the public sphere: An inquiry into a category of bourgeois society*, translated by Thomas Burger and Frederick Lawrence. Cambridge: Massachusetts Institute of Technology Press.

Harris, Jim. Rule re patients rights. right_to_die@efn.org (27 July 1999).

Hemlock Society. http://www.hemlock.org/hemlock/ (29 September 2000).

Hill, Kevin A., and John E. Hughes. 1998. *Cyperpolitics: Citizen activism in the age of the Internet*. Oxford: Rowman & Littlefield.

Humphry, Derek. Death of Mrs. Janet Good. right_to_die@efn.org (26 August 1997).

———. Re: Patients' rights (fwd). right_to_die@efn.org (26 July 1999).

Hyde, Michael J., and Ken Rufo. 2000. The call of conscience, rhetorical interruptions, and the euthanasia controversy. *Journal of Applied Communication Research* 28: 1–23.

Kellner, Douglas. 1998. Intellectuals, the new public spheres, and technopolitics. In *The politics of cyberspace*, edited by Chris Toulouse and Timothy W. Luke. New York: Routledge.

Lippmann, Walter. 1925. *The phantom public*. New York: Harcourt, Brace.

Luke, Timothy W. 1998. The politics of digital inequality: Access, capability and distribution in cyberspace. In *The politics of cyberspace*, edited by Chris Toulouse and Timothy W. Luke. New York: Routledge.

Mainers for Death with Dignity. http://www.mdwd.org/ (29 September 2000).

McChesney, Robert W. 1999. *Rich media, poor democracy: Communication politics in dubious times.* Urbana: University of Illinois Press.

McGee, Michael Calvin. 1990. Text, context, and the fragmentation of contemporary culture. *Western Journal of Speech Communication* 54:274–289.

Mitra, Ananda. 1997. Diasporic web sites: Ingroup and outgroup discourse. *Critical Studies in Mass Communication* 14:158–181.

Moreillon, Robert. Gen. descrip. Prop. B. right_to_die@efn.org (8 October 1998b).

———. We made it in Michigan. right_to_die@efn.org (26 May 1998a).

Napoleon, Davi. hello from Merian's Friends. right_to_die@efn.org (4 September 1998).

National Telecommunications and Information Administration (NTIA). 1999. *Falling through the Net: Defining the digital divide.* http://www.ntia.doc.gov/ntiahome/fttn99 (2 January 2000).

Pentilla, Ollie. Any analysis on Michigan? right_to_die@efn.org (4 November 1998).

Poenisch, Carol. Write to Jack. right_to_die@efn.org (3 November 1999).

Raney, Rebecca Farley. 1999a. Flash campaigns: Online activism at warp speed. *New York Times,* 3 June. http://www.nytimes.com/library/tech/99/06/cyber/articles/03campaign.html (14 September 1999).

———. 1999b. Flood of e-mail credited with halting U.S. bank plan. *New York Times,* 24 March. http://www.nytimes.com/library/tech/99/03/cyber/articles/24email.html (14 September 1999).

Resnick, David. 1998. Politics on the Internet: The normalization of cyberspace. In *The politics of cyberspace,* edited by Chris Toulouse and Timothy W. Luke. New York: Routledge.

Sampaio, Anna. and Janni Aragon. 1998. "To boldly go (where no man has gone before)": Women and politics in cyberspace. In *The politics of cyberspace,* edited by Chris Toulouse and Timothy W. Luke, 144–166. New York: Routledge.

Sennett, Richard. [1976] 1992. *The fall of public man.* New York: W. W. Norton.

Shapiro, Ken. Michigan Prop. B. right_to_die@efn.org (5 November 1998).

Streck, John. 1998. Pulling the plug on electronic town meetings: Participatory democracy and the reality of the Usenet. In *The politics of cyberspace,* edited by Chris Toulouse and Timothy W. Luke. New York: Routledge.

Swanson, David L. 1992. The political-media complex. *Communication Monographs* 59: 397–400.

Toulouse, Chris. 1998. Introduction to *The politics of cyberspace*, edited by Chris Toulouse and Timothy W. Luke. New York: Routledge.

Trammell, Clark W. 1999. Interview by author. Denver, 27 July.

8 A Structural Transformation for a Global Public Sphere?

The Use of New Communication Technologies by
Nongovernmental Organizations and the United Nations

MARIE A. MATER

In April 1997, Jon Katz (1997a) declared the "Birth of a Digital Nation" in *Wired*, a magazine that examines the politics and culture surrounding New Communication Technologies (NCTs).[1] His announcement was based on the new type of political public opinion that he discovered on the Internet during the 1996 United States election campaign period. In the article, Katz described a new process of constructing digital political opinion:

> I watched people learn new ways to communicate politically. I watched information travel great distances, then return home bearing imprints of engaged and committed people from all over the world. I saw positions soften and change when people were suddenly able to talk directly to one another, rather than through journalists, politicians, or ideological mercenaries. I saw the primordial stirrings of a new kind of nation—the Digital Nation—and the formation of a new postpolitical philosophy. (n.p.)

Several months later, Katz's observations were tested by the Wired/Merrill Lynch Forum Digital Citizen Survey in which 1,444 randomly selected Americans were polled to explore their opinions on society and technology. The results defied the conventional wisdom on digital politics: "The

Internet, it turns out, is not a breeding ground for disconnection, fragmentation, paranoia, and apathy. Digital Citizens are not alienated, either from people or from civic institutions. . . . [They are] the most informed and participatory citizens we have ever had or are likely to have" (Katz 1997b, 71). Although the survey was small and limited to citizens from the United States, it did illustrate that new digital political spaces with lively actors are emerging as a result of NCTs. Moreover, Katz (1997a) asserted that the social actors in these new digital political spaces had the potential to create a more civil society:

> Of all the prospects raised by the evolution of digital culture, the most tantalizing is the possibility that technology could fuse with politics to create a more civil society. It's the possibility that we could end up with a media and political culture in which people could amass factual material, voice their perspectives, confront other points of view, and discuss issues in a rational way. (n.p.)

If this fusion of technology and politics is indeed occurring, then public sphere scholars must be prepared to examine critically the consequences of such a development.

The potential of NCTs to transform political public spaces and the public opinion that is produced within them increasingly is being discussed by theorists in many disciplines. Some theorists (e.g., Braman 1996; Fernback 1997; Rheingold 1995; Simonsen 1996) believe that NCTs could have positive implications for political public spaces. A positive aspect of this fusion of technology and politics includes increased opportunities for people to gather information about important issues and then discuss this information with others in order to form their own opinions about it. As a result, the mass media's current domination of the construction of public opinion is challenged. NCTs also enable those actors who have traditionally lacked communicative power to have a voice and, theoretically at least, to become involved in political decision-making processes. In contrast to such optimism, most scholars (e.g., Breslow 1997; Jones 1995, 1997, 1998; Poster 1995, 1997, 1998; Tsagarousianou 1998; Verstraeten 1996) are more ambivalent; and of course, there are those (e.g., Haywood 1998; Kinney 1996; Sardar 1996; Sobchack 1996) who believe that NCTs will have an extremely negative impact on the production of public opinion in political public spaces. Limited access to NCTs because of economic, geographic, or educational inequalities certainly exists, and the dominant use of the English language is also a serious concern. Additionally, there is the potential for intrusiveness through the control of electronic political public spaces by economic actors, political actors, or both. As will become apparent, however, I find in recent structural innovations by nongovernmental organizations (NGOs) and the United Nations (UN) reasons to be optimistic about the cultivation of a global public sphere.

Unfortunately, there have been few, if any, theorists to examine thoroughly the *global* nature of the digital political spaces created by NCTs, and to investigate how various actors can influence the construction of *global* political public opinion and be involved in the *global* decision-making processes present within these digital political spaces. Most theorists have instead focused on the communicative potential of NCTs for smaller publics at the local, regional, or national levels. While these are, indeed, important theoretical contributions, they fail to take into consideration the unique potential of NCTs for *global* communication. It is my contention that NCTs are playing an important role in the emergence of a global public sphere because of their use by NGOs and the UN. Increasingly, NGOs are effectively using NCTs to network with like-minded organizations around the globe, increase worldwide public awareness of their concerns, and question the accountability of nation-states' responses to the issues that they address. At the same time, the UN has begun to experiment with NCTs as a way to increase significantly the participation of NGOs within its own decision-making activities that, as yet, have involved only nation-state representatives.

The very idea of a global public sphere is complicated, however, by the multiplicity of voices and issues circulating within contemporary channels of political discourse. As Dewey noted even in 1927,

> the machine age has so enormously expanded, multiplied, intensified and complicated the scope of the indirect consequences . . . that the resultant public cannot identify and distinguish itself. . . . There are too many publics and too much of public concern for our existing resources to cope with. ([1927] 1954, 126)

Although he was writing about the United States, Dewey's concern certainly applies in a global context. In a truly global public sphere, the threat of "information overload" exists. Too much information coming from too many places could so overwhelm the public that there would be no time or desire to have an opinion.

Jürgen Habermas has famously addressed formations of publics within nation-states. However, he has also laid the theoretical groundwork for thinking about global publics. Thus, in this chapter, I begin by examining Habermas's suggestive comments on the possibility of a global public sphere and by conceptualizing the global political spaces that have been created by NGOs and the UN. I then go on to examine the use of NCTs by NGOs and the UN at important global conferences such as the United Nations Conference on Environment and Development (UNCED), the United Nations Fourth World Conference on Women (UNFWCW), Earth Summit+5, and Beijing+5. Finally, I conclude with an optimistic view of the potential future role of NCTs based on the notion of a "real communication community within a planetary civilisation" presented by Karl-Otto Apel (1991), Habermas's colleague and collaborator.

HABERMAS ON THE POSSIBILITY
OF A GLOBAL PUBLIC SPHERE

While Habermas's theoretical work has tended to focus on public spheres that occur in Northern liberal democratic societies, he has also suggested the existence of a global public sphere for almost forty years (Habermas 1979, 1989, 1996, 1998). The notion of a global public sphere first emerges in Habermas's original rendering of the public sphere in 1962. In *The Structural Transformation of the Public Sphere*, Habermas (1989) comments on Kant's "cosmopolitan society" and goes on to argue that "the as yet unconquered state of nature in international relations has become so threatening for everybody that its specific negation articulates the universal interest with great precision" (233). Habermas (1989) examines the specific nature of international relations in a global public sphere in a thought-provoking, but limited footnote:

> The functions of the public sphere were the same for the legal relationships between states as for the legal order inside a state. Ever since Wilson attached high-flown hopes to international public opinion as a sanction at the disposal of the League of Nations, governments have actually been increasingly forced to have at least a propagandistic regard for the world public. (295–296, n. 133)

Although warning of the cultivation of a vacant, *pro forma* commitment to global public opinion, this brief footnote is significant because it acknowledges that global bodies like the League of Nations and its successor, the UN, have created a type of global public sphere in which the decisions made by nation-states regarding international relations must be justified to world citizens.

Habermas's most recent and thorough consideration of such a public sphere has been in the book, *The Inclusion of the Other: Studies in Political Theory*. Here, Habermas discusses very briefly the impacts of the UN, NGOs, and the Internet on the emergence of a global public sphere. In the essay, "Kant's Idea of Perpetual Peace: At Two Hundred Years' Historical Remove," Habermas (1998) describes the global political spaces created by the UN:

> It was only recently that the UN organized in quick success a series of conferences on global issues. . . . These "global summits" can be interpreted as so many attempts to bring at least some political pressure to bear on governments simply by thematizing problems important for human survival for the global public, that is, by an appeal to world opinion. (176–177)

Throughout its history, the UN has been responsible for creating global political spaces in which important political, economic, and social issues have been discussed. Traditionally, these global political spaces have been the meetings of the UN General Assembly in which nation-state actors have had almost exclusive participation. Beginning with the 1972 Stockholm Conference on the Environment, however, it has become common for the UN to sponsor "global conferences" in which there are two parallel global political spaces—a formal one for nation-state actors and an informal one for NGOs.

NGOs have a crucial role to play in these informal global political spaces, Habermas (1998) maintains, because they influence nation-states through their construction of global public opinion:

> the central role played by a new type of organization—namely, nongovernmental organizations such as Greenpeace or Amnesty International—not only in these conferences but more generally in the creation and mobilization of transnational public spheres is at least an indication of the growing impact on the press and media of actors who confront states from within the network of an international civil society. (177)

In what Toulmin (1999) has described as a "post-Westphalian" world,[2] the nation-state no longer dominates global politics and must now compete with NGOs. Indeed, it seems that we have begun to enter into a new realm of global politics in which nation-states must justify their actions to a global public because of the discourse produced by NGOs. NGOs attempt to hold nation-states accountable through their construction of global public opinion about political, economic, and social issues at both global conference venues and local crisis sites. But how is NGO discourse communicated to the global public and the nation-states?

Habermas (1996) contends that the mass media control communication in the general public sphere. However, although mass media actors may perform a "gate-keeping" role in the general public sphere, Habermas believes that "it is by no means clear how the mass media intervene in the diffuse circuits of communication in the political [regulated] public sphere" (377–378). In the ideal case, he believes that "the mass media ought to understand themselves as the mandatary of an enlightened public. . . . They ought to be receptive to the public's concerns and proposals, take up these issues and contributions impartially, augment criticisms, and confront the political process with articulate demands for legitimation" (378).

Greater uncertainty attends the role of mass media actors within the global public sphere created at UN conferences. Habermas (1998) argues that

> one should not overlook the fact that this temporary, issue-specific public attention [achieved by UN conferences] is still channeled through established structures of national public spheres. Supporting structures are needed to institute permanent communication between geographically distant participants who simultaneously exchange contributions on the same themes with the same relevance. (177)

Although it is technically feasible for NCTs to link geographically dispersed actors through permanent communication structures, Habermas does not see them as fulfilling this role socially. In another essay, "The European Nation-State: On the Past and Future of Sovereignty and Citizenship," Habermas (1998) claims, for example, that "the publics produced by the internet remain closed off from one another like global villages" (121). Habermas fails to provide evidence for his pessimism, however, leaving open both empirical and theoretical verification of an emergent global public sphere.

In the remaining portions of this chapter, I articulate the structural foundations of a global public sphere and examine the use of NCTs by NGOs and the UN within such a global public sphere. I hope to provide a framework for understanding the different political spaces created by the UN for both nation-state and NGO actors. By examining specific structural innovations, I aim to test and extend Habermas's theory on global politics.

TOWARD A THEORY OF A GLOBAL
PUBLIC SPHERE: THE UN AND NGOS

At the global level, I would argue that Habermas's "two-track" theory of the public sphere has currency. Although Habermas has not specifically identified it as such, a global procedurally regulated public sphere is emerging in the form of the UN. Established on 26 June 1945, at the end of World War II, the UN brings together the representatives of the world's nation-states in an attempt to produce cooperative solutions to international problems. The purposes of the UN as set out in Chapter 1, Article 1 of "The Charter of the UN" illustrate this:

- To maintain international peace and security;
- To develop friendly relations among nations based on respect for the principle of equal rights and self-determination of peoples;
- To achieve international cooperation in solving international problems of an economic, social, cultural, or humanitarian character, and in promoting and encouraging respect for human rights and for fundamental freedoms; and
- To be a centre for harmonizing the actions of nations in the attainment of these common ends. (Power 1995, 290)

In order to achieve these purposes, the UN has six main organs: the General Assembly, the Security Council, the Economic and Social Council, the Trusteeship Council, the International Court of Justice, and the Secretariat. Additionally, it has fifteen agencies and many other programs and bodies.[3]

The General Assembly is the main deliberative body. All of the member nation-states are represented in it, and each has one vote. Decisions on ordinary matters are taken by a simple majority vote, but important questions require a two-third's majority vote. The Assembly has the right to discuss and make recommendations on all matters within the scope of the UN Charter. This charter institutionalizes a global communication community in which communicative action, not strategic action, is the ideal form of decision-making for global political, economic, and social problems. The goal, as enshrined in the charter, is to reach an agreement, or in some cases, a rational dissent based on the "force of the better argument" and not military might.[4]

The idea that the UN could become a global procedurally regulated public sphere is complicated by several factors. First, there has been a history of the outright exclusion of potential nation-state participants and all NGOs in the General Assembly and the Security Council. Second, NGOs must follow strict procedures for communicating their recommendations within the UN system. These procedures are based on the categorization of the NGO.[5] Third, the UN is generally considered to be more of a "weak public" than a "strong public" in Fraser's (1992) terms because it has no institutionalized power to compel action by any nation-state. Unlike the legislation passed by nation-states, the international law produced by the UN has historically lacked enforcement mechanisms. This has been a direct result of the Westphalian notion that a nation-state has absolute sovereignty.

Despite these complications, my optimism about the UN's ability to foster and sustain a global public is justified on several counts. First, there has been a gradual broadening of inclusion of nation-state actors within the General Assembly and of NGOs within the UN system. In fact, the current Secretary-General, Kofi Annan (2000) has made calls for an "intensified NGO revolution." Second, although the UN lacks extensive enforcement mechanisms, it is generally acknowledged that its recommendations carry the weight of global public opinion. Moreover, as can be seen in the areas of human rights and the law of the sea, the principle of absolute sovereignty is increasingly being challenged by the creation of international laws with enforcement mechanisms.[6] Another important development has been the build-up of transnational agreements in areas of international relations such as trade that result in "international regimes" (Bohman 1994). These developments seem to support Toulmin's (1999) diagnosis that we are moving into a "post-Westphalian" state of global politics in which nation-states are losing their absolute sovereignty.

The most important development of this transitional period, I believe, has been the increasing power of global public opinion. This global public opinion is being generated by NGOs in the peripheral and spontaneously developing "general public spheres" that resist the legitimacy of the actions of the UN's member nation-states. As Habermas has pointed out, NGOs are increasingly being organized by individuals and groups as a channel for involvement in the international discussion of political, economic, and social issues at the global level. In fact, the number of NGOs has greatly expanded over the past few decades.[7]

Like contemporary social movements, NGOs raise the necessary "crisis consciousness" in the general public spheres that have the power to make political, economic, and social problems into salient issues. Once picked up and carried by the mass media, these issues must be dealt with by nation-states in the regulated public sphere of the UN. Clark (1995) explains how this process occurs:

> With increasingly dense networks of communications and informational exchange in the twentieth century, international

NGOs now also pursue concerns with other NGOs in self-created international arenas. In this respect, the interaction of NGOs might be said to form a nascent international civil society, which is independent of government policy making paths but brings individuals and grassroots groups together for informational exchange and political action. (514)

This informational exchange detects, identifies, thematizes, and dramatizes problems in order to produce "bundles" of public opinion which, through the mass media, have the power to define and determine the political, economic, and social issues that are dealt with by the nation-states in the UN. Clark (1995) argues that "popular opinion thus plays a role in allowing NGOs the influence both nationally and internationally to capitalize on their memberships' purchase on representation before particular governments" (518). Some of the most effective examples of this NGO-produced public opinion have been in the areas where the most extensive legislation has been passed: human rights and the environment.

Traditionally, the UN and its nation-state members have looked on NGOs with some suspicion. This is because NGOs are deemed to suffer from the "tunnel vision" that results from their exclusive focus on their special interest (Matthews 1997, 64). Unlike nation-state actors, they are private organizations that represent no one but themselves. Many also have a negative stereotype because of their insensitive behavior toward the constraints of the UN system and toward diplomatic etiquette (Riddell-Dixon 1995, 300). Consequently, these groups have lacked the credibility necessary to influence UN and nation-state actors. This situation of distrust has begun to change, however.

For example, the United Nations Conference on Environment and Development (UNCED) in 1992 represented "a landmark in the UN-NGO relationship" (Power 1995, 185). At the UNCED, 17,000 people attended the informal gathering of the Global Forum to consider global environmental problems and development issues and to influence the nation-state representatives at the formal UNCED site. The NGOs in attendance ranged from well-known Northern NGOs like Greenpeace International and Friends of the Earth International to lesser-known Southern NGOs such as Third World Network and the Green Earth Organization. Together, the NGOs produced more than 30,000 pages of persuasive texts for the UNCED, Global Forum, and the 10,000 on-site mass media representatives in the form of special publications, serials, press packs, and press releases. In addition, the very first use of NCTs at a UN global conference occurred.

Consequently, it does appear that a two-track global public sphere may be emerging because of the increasing institutionalized communicative action present in the UN and the increasing discursive power of NGOs in general public spheres throughout the world. As we will see, NCTs have been used by NGOs to connect and interact with other NGOs and to pressure nation-states. They also have been used to communicate directly with a global public. NCTs also create new communicative links between the NGO community and the UN. I believe that the use of NCTs by NGOs and the UN to create permanent global communication links is an important development that deserves further examination.

FORGING GLOBAL COMMUNICATION LINKS:
THE APC, NGOS, AND THE UN

While the global public debate of important political, economic, and social issues will continue to increase in the current "two-track" global public sphere, the emergence of a truly global sphere could come about because of the communication links among the various political, economic, social, and mass media actors that are made possible through the use of NCTs. I concur with Poster's (1998) position on the communicative potential of NCTs:

> But Habermas clearly has got things wrong. Whereas peasant villages were isolated in time and space, Internet communities, embedded in a web-like electronic structure, are no more distant from one another than a keyboard stroke or a mouse click. The communications logic of the Internet is interconnectedness not autochthony. (12)

In fact, the use of NCTs in the "two-track" global public sphere is multiplying dramatically precisely because of this capability for communicative interconnectedness. Increasingly, electronic bulletin boards, electronic conferences, electronic databases, electronic mail, and interactive World Wide Web (WWW) sites are being used by NGOs in the general public spheres to network with other NGOs, to communicate directly with nation-states, and to produce global public opinion. These electronic media are also employed by the regulated public sphere of the UN to attempt to involve NGOs more in its decision-making processes.

Although one of the major criticisms of NCTs is the lack of access to them by less powerful social actors (e.g., Ebo 1998; Loader 1998), it is important to note that the Association for Progressive Communications (APC) has been providing NGOs with NCTs since 1987. The APC was initiated in that year when GreenNet in England began cooperating with

PeaceNet/EcoNet in the United States. In 1989, these two networks were joined by networks in Sweden (NordNet), Canada (Web), Brazil (AlterNex), Nicaragua (Nicarao), and Australia (Pegasus); together in 1990, they founded the APC to coordinate their operations and development (APC 1999a). Most of these networks were established because people contributed their personal equipment, phone lines, and free time to provide access to their colleagues in the NGO community.

The APC is now the world's most extensive provider network of NCTs dedicated to serving NGOs by offering fast, reliable, easy-to-use communication tools, training, and support. Specifically, the APC member networks provide NGOs with Internet access, training, and support; WWW site development; mailing lists and newsgroups; and databases and search engines (APC 1999c). The APC's stated mission is: "to build strategic communities and initiatives for the purpose of making meaningful contributions to equitable human development, social justice, participatory political processes and environmental sustainability" (APC 1999b). Its main goal is to empower and support the NGOs that are working for environmental, social, and economic justice—especially those in the South that traditionally have little access to NCTs. According to Matthews (1997), "The nonprofit Association for Progressive Communications provides 50,000 NGOs . . . access to tens of millions of Internet users for the price of a local phone call" (54). As an NGO with consultative status to the Economic and Social Council of the UN, the APC has also been particularly effective in forging communication links between NGOs and the UN. Since 1990, it has also served as the primary telecommunications provider for both NGOs and UN delegates before and during global conferences. Having explained the emergence of the APC, I now examine the use of its networks at global conferences such as the UNCED, UNFWCW, Earth Summit +5, and Beijing +5. This examination reveals a history of structural innovations initiated by NGOs and the UN in conjunction with UN-sponsored global conferences.

The United Nations Conference on
Environment and Development (UNCED)

As mentioned previously, the first use of NCTs by NGOs and the UN was during the Preparatory Committee Meetings for the UNCED in 1990. At that time, the APC could only offer electronic mail and electronic conferences. Electronic mail, on the one hand, provided the unprecedented opportunity for NGOs to share ideas with other NGOs privately, quickly, and cheaply. The electronic conferences, on the other hand, created the first electronic public spaces for UN representatives to communicate directly with NGOs in geographically dispersed locations. The electronic conferences created especially for the preparatory process were considered "official" by the UN, and important documents were posted for NGOs to download and read (TWI, IDRC, and CCOHS 1993). Although the documents were "read-only," the NGOs could access them in a timely manner.

Other electronic conferences were created by and for NGOs for use before, during, and after the UNCED. These conferences were more inter-active because they were not "read-only" and actually allowed NGO actors from around the world to post public messages on selected topics (TWI, IDRC, and CCOHS 1993). The topics covered within each confer-ence varied, but all actors who posted messages within the conference were encouraged to communicate with each other with respect and a sense of equality. For most conferences, the postings on topics were unrestricted and unmoderated so that a wide variety of opinions could be heard from a wide variety of actors.

During the formal UNCED at Rio, the UN provided all conference participants with access to the Earth Summit Information System (ESIS) that was set up through a donation by the Digital Equipment Corporation (UN 1993).[8] The ESIS enabled both UN and NGO representatives to send electronic messages to each other. The ESIS did not, however, allow for electronic mail to be sent to anyone outside of the official UNCED set-tings. The ESIS also provided access to a number of on-line Videotex (VTX) databases. These databases included an itinerary of daily events at both the formal UNCED and the informal Global Forum and a structured presentation of "Agenda 21."

Although their first use was quite limited at the UNCED, NCTs did provide an unprecedented communicative opportunity for an emerging global public sphere. First, they created the communicative structures necessary for NGO actors to communicate directly with other NGO actors. This led to more information-sharing and information-gathering among NGOs in the general public spheres of the Prepatory Committee Meetings and the Global Forum. Second, NCTs also provided NGOs with direct communicative links to UN actors and nation-state actors in the regulated public sphere of the UNCED. These communicative struc-tures decreased the need for mass media actors to provide a "bridge" between the general public spheres and the regulated public sphere. Con-sequently, NGOs were able to influence the agenda-setting of the UN actors and contribute to the nation-state discussion and debate on the "Rio Declaration" and "Agenda 21."

The United Nations Fourth World
Conference on Women (UNFWCW)

Three years later, at the UNFWCW in Beijing, the use of NCTs increased considerably. In addition to electronic mail and electronic conferencing, technological advances allowed "real time" WWW sites to be set up by the APC through its United States member network, the Institute for Global Communications (IGC). The *Beijing '95: Women, Power & Change* WWW site was complex and communicated a great deal of information (IGC 1995). Some of the most important information provided was the draft "Platform for Action," the critical areas of concern for women's groups, and a summary of women's lobbying strategies. The site also included a link to news, information, and updates from NGO, UN, and alternative media actors. Additionally, the WWW site provided Internet mailing list addresses and contact information for official nation-state delegations, NGOs, and other attendees.

The *Beijing '95: Women, Power & Change* WWW site gave NGOs several powerful communicative advantages. First, it provided the global public with comprehensive information about events happening in Beijing at the informal NGO forum and the formal UNFWCW in "real-time" without it first being communicated through mass media actors. The WWW site also allowed geographically dispersed NGO actors who were unable to go to Beijing to participate through electronic conferences and electronic mail.

An official "real-time" WWW site was also created by the UN through the United Nations Development Programme for the formal UNFWCW. Like the *Beijing '95: Women, Power & Change* WWW site, the formal *Fourth World Conference on Women* WWW site communicated a large amount of information (FWCW Secretariat and UNDP 1995). It provided access to most of the official UN documents that were discussed at the conference, including the official "Beijing Declaration" and "Platform for Action." Furthermore, the WWW site furnished the official press releases that were issued by the UN Department of Public Information for use by the alternative and mass media actors. The WWW site also offered the full texts of the statements made by nation-state, NGO, and UN actors while at the conference.

Like the *Beijing '95: Women, Power & Change* WWW site, the *Fourth World Conference on Women* WWW site also provided NGOs and the global public with comprehensive information about events happening in Beijing at the informal NGO forum and the formal UNFWCW in "real-time," without the involvement of mass media actors. It was not as effective, however, at encouraging non-nation-state participation in the official

UNFWCW decision-making process. Unlike its unofficial counterpart, the *Fourth World Conference on Women* WWW site did not allow geographically dispersed actors to participate through electronic conferences and electronic mail.

The use of NCTs at the UNFWCW was significant for several reasons. First, information-sharing and information-gathering increased dramatically in the NGO general public sphere. More opinions were heard, especially the opinions of absent actors. Additionally, they created some of the first communicative structures that enabled NGO actors in the general public sphere and nation-state actors in the regulated public sphere to communicate directly with a geographically dispersed global public without the assistance of mass media actors. Although this global public was limited to those individuals who had access to the NCTs, it was still an important step in the emergence of a global public sphere because the discourse produced by NGO actors and nation-state actors could be judged by the global public in its own right.

While the use of NCTs at the UNFWCW facilitated opinion formation, the lack of electronic conferences and electronic mail links on the official UN WWW site indicated that there were still barriers to non-nation-state actors. These actors' voices were kept in the NGO general public sphere and not permitted in the UN regulated public sphere, where the discussion and debate of the "Beijing Declaration" and "Platform for Action" occurred. This situation of outright exclusion of non-nation-state actors in this part of the decision-making process indicates that the UN and nation-state actors wanted to maintain their exclusive power in the regulated public sphere.

Earth Summit +5

In 1997, Earth Summit +5 was held. It was a special session of the UN General Assembly established to review and appraise the implementation of the UNCED's Agenda 21. WWW sites were used for this global conference as well. The APC member the Institute for Global Communications set up the WWW site for NGOs for the Earth Summit +5 preparatory process. This informal WWW site, *Towards Earth Summit Two*, was strictly text-based in order to communicate significant amounts of information (IGC 1997). For example, it provided UN and NGO documents on the special session of the General Assembly, the Earth Summit Two preparatory meetings, and the NGO Global Gathering/Expo. It also posted editions of the NGO community newsletter on the Commission on Sustainable Development and a "synthesis paper" on NGO priorities and concerns.

The *Towards Earth Summit Two* WWW site appears to be one of the first attempts to use a WWW site extensively in a UN preparatory process. This WWW site was hosted on behalf of the NGO Steering Committee for the Commission on Sustainable Development as a "clearing house" for collecting and distributing information. Comments, questions, or both regarding the documents that were available on the WWW site were able to be sent back to the steering committee. This enabled official documents to be presented, discussed, and revised on-line. The WWW site also listed the address for an electronic conference where more extensive discussion could take place.

The UN (through the Department of Economic and Social Affairs) set up an official "real-time" WWW site for the UN community, NGOs, and the general public. This *Earth Summit +5: Special Session of the General Assembly to Review and Appraise the Implementation of Agenda 21* WWW site was quite innovative (Department of Economic and Social Affairs 1997). One of the most interesting links on the WWW site was the "Earth Summit +5 Coverage" link, which provided the statements by delegates, a daily journal of speakers and events, the United Nations television coverage from the General Assembly hall, the United Nations press releases, and a link to an independent webcast coverage. In addition, the stories of successful, sustainable development activities undertaken by nation-states, NGOs, and UN agencies were included. There was also an "Information for the Media" link that provided a fact sheet, press releases, backgrounders, and other key documents for the alternative and mass media actors.

Although the *Earth Summit +5: Special Session of the General Assembly to Review and Appraise the Implementation of Agenda 21* WWW site directly provided a great deal of information to NGOs and the global public in "real-time," it still did not allow much non-nation-state participation in the review and appraisal of "Agenda 21." It did, however, provide the opportunity for NGOs to submit their own "Agenda 21 Success Stories" to the UN. The WWW site also provided unprecedented alternative mass media involvement with its link to the independent webcast coverage by OneSoft and WETV. This WWW site provided the global public with an introduction to the issues, major participants, success stories, and resources related to sustainable development. The OneSoft and WETV WWW site also provided limited, "real-time" coverage of key events at the Earth Summit +5.

The use of NCTs at Earth Summit +5 had important implications for the emergence of a global public sphere. By using NCTs extensively during the preparatory process, NGOs extended the electronic communicative links that were established among NGO actors, nation-state actors, and UN actors at the UNCED five years before. This again improved the information-sharing and information-gathering processes significantly. Moreover, it enabled the NGO actors to influence the agenda-setting process directly. By participating in the creation of the agenda for the regulated public sphere, NGO actors influenced the nation-state actors.

The UN WWW site, on the other hand, seems to have been an attempt to bring the mass media actors back into the communicative process with its inclusion of the webcast coverage by OneSoft and WETV. Although they are considered "alternative" mass media actors by the UN actors, I would argue that they are more like traditional mass media actors because OneSoft is a corporation that provides software and services for global Internet commerce and WETV is an international television network which currently has thirty-eight broadcasting partners in approximately thirty countries. Consequently, the electronic communicative links that originally enabled NGO actors and nation-state actors to communicate directly with a global public at the UNFWCW in 1995 were replaced with the mass media webcast coverage at Earth Summit +5.

Beijing +5

Another important global conference, Beijing +5 (the special session of the UN General Assembly to review the "Beijing Platform for Action" adopted at the UNFWCW) was held in June 2000. In preparation for Beijing +5, the APC coordinated the *WomenAction 2000* WWW site that enabled NGOs to participate in the UN review of the "Beijing Platform for Action" (WomenAction 2000). The most unique aspect of this WWW site was the "How to Get Involved" link, which enabled NGOs to participate in twelve on-line working groups and to contribute to the "Women and Media Review." Recommendations from those global and regional on-line consultations were submitted to the regional NGO and UN preparatory meetings and also to the forty-fourth session of the Commission of the Status of Women and the PrepCom II for Beijing +5. Comments on the "Alternative Global Report on Section J: Women and Media Review" and examples for the "Best Practice Models in the Area of Women and Media" were also submitted through the WWW site and then compiled for use in NGO lobbying efforts.

The *WomenAction 2000* WWW site aimed to build on existing networks and collaborative partnerships with other important UN and NGO networks. Its strategy was to develop a communications network that allowed women in every region of the globe to participate in the five-year review of the implementation of the 1995 "Beijing Platform for Action." It attempted to do this by establishing a global network of regional and subregional focal points so that women could share information and experiences and discuss key issues in global and regional electronic conferences.

The UN (through the UN Development Fund for Women and the UN International Research and Training Institute for the Advancement of Women) also developed the *Beijing +5 Women 2000: Gender Equality, Development and Peace for the 21st Century* WWW site (UN 2000). This official WWW site had a "Review and Appraisal" link providing the original "Questionnaire to Governments on the Implementation of the Beijing Platform for Action" and, at later stages, the nation-states' responses to the questionnaire. Moreover, the site presented links to the twelve on-line NGO working groups when they were active and also to the archives of the groups when they ended. In addition, the site made available an advance unedited version of the final report.

The *Beijing +5 Women 2000: Gender Equality, Development and Peace for the 21st Century* WWW site was remarkable because it represented one of the first attempts by the UN to use NCTs for actual input into the review process. For example, nation-state actors could download and complete the "Questionnaire to Governments on Implementation of the Beijing Platform for Action," and NGOs could participate in the twelve "Online Working Groups." The information gained from the questionnaire and the discussion occurring in the on-line groups was then incorporated into the General Assembly's assessment of progress and the recommendations that it made for further actions.

The use of NCTs at Beijing +5 was a noteworthy episode in the move toward a global public sphere because it enabled more than 120 nation-state actors and 10,000 NGO actors to be directly involved in the information-sharing, information-gathering, agenda-setting, and deliberating that constitute the UN review process. Despite their geographical dispersion, these actors presented their opinions in the same public digital spaces at the same time. Moreover, most of the discussions taking place in these digital spaces could be accessed by interested members of the global public without the assistance of any mass media actors. These discussions, while not the actual deliberations on international law and international regimes that we might find at an actual UN conference or a General Assembly meeting, were at least a first step in that direction.

As we have seen in this review of the history of the structural innovations initiated by NGOs and the UN in conjunction with UN-sponsored global conferences, the emergence of a global public sphere has been slow but steady. Certainly, NGO use of NCTs in the general public sphere has been the most innovative. It has increased access to information significantly, allowed geographically dispersed and absent actors to participate, and decreased the reliance on the mass media actors to communicate NGO positions to nation-state actors and a global public. The UN, it seems, has tried to keep up with NGO innovations in most respects. At times, however, the UN deliberately did *not* use NCTs to include NGOs in its regulated public sphere activities. This indicates that the UN favored the traditional power structure of nation-state actors within the UN system. However, the fact that the UN chose to use NCTs as a way to include NGOs at Beijing +5 justifies a more positive overall assessment of UN use of NCTs.

TOWARD A REAL COMMUNICATION COMMUNITY?

The increasing use of NCTs by NGOs and the UN could result in two very different types of global public spheres. The first type would be the globalization of the current two-track public sphere model outlined by Habermas. In this case, the use of NCTs by NGOs would maintain their current role in the general public spheres at the periphery where they influence the UN and nation-state actors through the production of global public opinion carried by traditional mass media actors. In this situation, the current movement of the UN toward a "stronger" public sphere that produces international law and international regimes would have to continue.

The second type, however, would be the emergence of a truly global public sphere involving all interested actors in the discussions of actions that need to be taken with regard to important global political, economic, and social problems. This might lead to the realization of Apel's "real communication community within a planetary civilization." As Apel (1991) explains, the dialogues that currently occur at on-site global conferences attempt to be practical discourses:

> For, in my opinion, every serious question that is asked in this context shows that by asking questions we implicitly take coresponsibility, in principle, for the progressive solutions of all those problems of the lifeworld that can be posed and possibly solved by cooperation on the level of practical discourses . . . [in] the hundreds of dialogues and conferences on vitally important questions which take place every day on all political, economic and cultural levels. . . . [T]hese conferences and dia-

logues at least *pretend* in most cases to be something like practical discourses, striving for solutions that are acceptable for all affected human beings. (275)

Although Apel never discusses the role of NCTs in global conferences, I believe that they provide an opportunity to go beyond the level of *pretending to produce* practical discourse to the level of *actually producing* practical discourse. This possibility arises from the potential of NCTs to provide NGOs with access to a truly global public sphere in which they could be directly involved in the UN's decision-making processes through electronic conferences and IRC chat rooms. Instead of relying on the mass media to publicize NGO positions to nation-state actors involved in UN decision-making, NGO actors could present their positions to nation-state actors directly. The nation-state actors could then discuss these positions with the NGO actors directly, again without the mass media actors having to be involved. Consequently, there is the possibility that truly critical rational debate about political, economic, and social issues of global public importance could occur. This process might spur UN reforms such as a creative restructuring of relations among its members in response to new global forces.

This development would be in line with Katz's belief that technology has the capacity to fuse with politics to form a more civil society in which informed citizens actively participate in digital political spaces. In fact, this has been the UN Department for Policy Coordination and Sustainable Development's (DPCSD) goal since 1995: "Through a combination of World Wide Web, Internet gopher and electronic mail access, the DPCSD takes the intergovernmental negotiating process . . . to the desktops of Member States . . . international organizations, nongovernmental organizations, academia and the public-at-large" (DPCSD 1995).

In my opinion, NCTs could continue to help the UN to achieve these goals. Limited access and language problems are serious concerns, but the APC and the UN have begun to address them. In addition, the credibility of NGO actors within the UN system has historically been a problem, but this has begun to change. The structural innovations initiated by NGOs and the UN in conjunction with UN-sponsored global conferences reviewed in this chapter indicate that NCTs *are* providing the effective permanent communication structures that would allow nation-state actors and NGO actors to confer and cooperate with each other within the UN system. Incorporation of NCTs into the UN decision-making process at global conferences and at meetings of the General Assembly may lead to the creation of a truly global public sphere involving all interested actors in critical rational debate on political, economic, and social issues. It only requires, as Habermas (1998, 188) claims, the "institutional imagination."

NOTES

1. In this chapter, I am limiting NCTs to the following technologies: electronic bulletin boards, electronic conferences, electronic databases, electronic mail, Internet Relay Chat (IRC) rooms, and World Wide Web (WWW) sites.

2. In 1648, the Peace of Westphalia ended the religious wars in Europe and created the institution of the "nation-state," in which social order is maintained within territorial boundaries and is embodied with absolute sovereignty.

3. The agencies include, for example, the World Health Organization (WHO) and the International Monetary Fund (IMF). Examples of UN programs include the United Nations Environment Programme (UNEP) and the United Nations Children's Fund (UNICEF).

4. Here, I am incorporating Miller's (1992) idea that in the case of some social conflicts, there can be no agreement on a solution to a particular problem, only a rational dissent in which the parties agree only on the identification of the source of the disagreement. This is the case, for example, with the continuing conflict in Northern Ireland.

5. Category I includes big international groups and Category II includes smaller organizations that have internationally recognized competence. Roster status is given to groups that make "occasional and useful contributions" (Power 1995, 193).

6. For human rights, the most recent mechanism to be put into place is the United Nations High Commissioner for Human Rights, whose office can take preventative and punitive action (UN 1998, 217). For the law of the sea, three bodies (the International Seabed Authority, the International Tribunal for the Law of the Sea, and the Commission on the Limits of the Continental Shelf) enforce the law and settle disputes between nation-states (UN 1998, 265).

7. In 1945, there were only 41 NGOs; and in 1993, there were more than 1,500 according to UN figures (Power 1995, 193). Matthews (1997) claims that published figures are inaccurate and that the true number is in the millions.

8. Unfortunately, none of the ESIS material is archived on *The Earth Summit CD-ROM* (IDRC, UN, and CCOHS 1993), so examples of electronic mail and electronic database material were unavailable for analysis.

REFERENCES

Annan, Kofi. 2000, May 22. Secretary-General, addressing participants at Millennium Forum, calls for intensified "NGO revolution." In *Millen-*

nium assembly. http://www.un.org/News/Press/docs/2000/20000522. sgsm7411.doc.html (30 September 2000).

Apel, Karl-Otto. 1991. A planetary macroethics for humankind: The need, the apparent difficulty, and the eventual possibility. In *Culture and modernity: East-West philosophic perspectives*, edited by Eliot Deutsch. Honolulu: University of Hawaii Press.

Association for Progressive Communications (APC). 1999a. About APC—A brief history of the APC. In *Association for Progressive Communications' global internet community for environment, human rights, development & peace.* http://www.apc.org/english/history.html (12 February 1999).

———. 1999b. About APC—Mission statement. In *Association for Progressive Communications' Global Internet Community for Environment, Human Rights, Development & Peace.* http://www.apc. org/english/mission.html (12 February 1999).

———. 1999c. Members & services—APC services. In *Association for Progressive Communications' Global Internet Community for Environment, Human Rights, Development & Peace.* http://www.apc. org/english/services.html (12 February 1999).

Bohman, James. 1994. Complexity, pluralism, and the constitutional state: On Habermas's *Faktizitat und geltung. Law & Society Review* 28:897–930.

Braman, Sandra. 1996. Interpenetrated globalization: Scaling, power, and the public sphere. In *Globalization, communication and transnational civil society*, edited by Sandra Braman and Annabelle Sreberny-Mohammadi. Cresskill, NJ: Hampton Press.

Breslow, Harris. 1997. Civil society, political economy, and the Internet. In *Virtual culture: Identity and communication in cybersociety*, edited by Steven G. Jones. London: Sage.

Clark, Ann Marie. 1995. Non-governmental organizations and their influence on international society. *Journal of International Affairs* 48:507–525.

Department for Policy Coordination and Sustainable Development (DPCSD). 1995. United Nations advances global development through world of internet [Press release]. In *United Nations.* http://www.un.org/plweb-cgi/idoc.pl?463+unix+_free_user_+www. un.org.80+un+un+pr1995++internet (14 May 1998).

Department of Economic and Social Affairs. 1997. *Earth Summit +5: Special session of the General Assembly to review and appraise the implementation of Agenda 21.* http://www.un.org/esa/earthsummit/ (15 January 2000).

Dewey, John. [1927] 1954. *The public and its problems.* Reprint, Athens, OH: Swallow Press.

Ebo, Bosah. 1998. Internet or outernet? In *Cyberghetto or cybertopia? Race, class, and gender on the Internet,* edited by Bosah Ebo. Westport, CT: Praeger.

Fernback, Jan. 1997. The individual within the collective: Virtual ideology and the realization of collective principles. In *Virtual culture: Identity and communication in cybersociety,* edited by Steven G. Jones. London: Sage.

Fourth World Conference on Women Secretariat (FWCW Secretariat) and United Nations Development Programme (UNDP). 1995. *Fourth World Conference on Women.* http://www.undp.org/fwcw/dawfwcw. htm (12 January 2000).

Fraser, Nancy. 1992. Rethinking the public sphere: A contribution to the critique of actually existing democracy. In *Habermas and the public sphere,* edited by Craig Calhoun. Cambridge: Massachusetts Institute of Technology Press.

Habermas, Jürgen. 1979. *Communication and the evolution of society.* Translated by Thomas McCarthy. Boston: Beacon Press.

———. 1989. *The structural transformation of the public sphere: An inquiry into a category of bourgeois society.* Translated by Thomas Burger and Frederick Lawrence. Cambridge: Massachusetts Institute of Technology Press.

———. 1996. *Between facts and norms: Contributions to a discourse theory of law and democracy.* Translated by William Rehg. Cambridge: Massachusetts Institute of Technology Press.

———. 1998. *The inclusion of the other: Studies in political theory.* Edited by Ciaran Cronin and Pablo De Greiff. Cambridge: Massachusetts Institute of Technology Press.

Haywood, Trevor. 1998. Global networks and the myth of equality: Trickle down or trickle away? In *Cyberspace divide: Equality, agency and policy in the information society,* edited by Brian D. Loader. London: Routledge.

Institute for Global Communications (IGC). 1995. *Beijing '95: Women, power & change.* http://www.igc.apc.org/beijing/beijing.html (12 January 2000).

———. 1997. *Towards Earth Summit two.* http://www.igc.apc.org/habitat/csd-97/ (12 January 2000).

International Development Research Centre (IDRC), United Nations (UN), and Canadian Centre for Occupational Health and Safety (CCOHS). 1993. *The Earth Summit CD-ROM.* Ottawa, Canada: International Development Research Centre, United Nations, and Canadian Centre for Occupational Health and Safety.

Jones, Steven. 1995. Understanding community in the information age. In *CyberSociety: Computer-mediated communication and community*, edited by Steven Jones. Thousand Oaks, CA: Sage.

——. 1997. The Internet and its social landscape. In *Virtual culture: Identity and communication in cybersociety*, edited by Steven Jones. London: Sage.

——. 1998. Information, internet, and community: Notes toward an understanding of community in the information age. In *CyberSociety 2.0: Revisiting computer-mediated communication and technology*, edited by Steven Jones. Thousand Oaks, CA: Sage.

Katz, Jon. 1997a. Birth of a digital nation. *Wired* [On-line edition], 5.04. http://www.wired.com/wired/5.04/netizen.html (2 April 1998).

——. 1997b. The digital citizen. *Wired*, December, 68–82, 274–275.

Kinney, Jay. 1996. Is there a new political paradigm lurking in cyberspace? In *Cyberfutures: Culture and politics on the information superhighway*, edited by Ziauddin Sardar and Jerome R. Ravetz. New York: New York University Press.

Loader, Brian D. 1998. Cyberspace divide: Equality, agency and policy in the information society. In *Cyberspace divide: Equality, agency and policy in the information society*, edited by Brian D. Loader. London: Routledge.

Matthews, Jessica Tuchman. 1997. Power shift. *Foreign Affairs* 76:50–66.

Miller, Max. 1992. Discourse and morality: Two case studies of social conflicts in a sedimentary and a functionally differentiated society. *Archives Européennes de Sociologie* 33:3–38.

Poster, Mark. 1995. *The second media age*. Cambridge, UK: Polity Press.

——. 1997. Cyberdemocracy: Internet and the public sphere. In *Internet culture*, edited by David Porter. New York: Routledge.

——. 1998. Nations, identities and global technologies. Paper read at the forty-eighth Annual Conference of the International Communication Association, 20–24 July, Jerusalem, Israel.

Power, Jonathan. 1995. *A vision of hope: The fiftieth anniversary of the United Nations*. London: Regency.

Rheingold, Howard. 1995. *The virtual community: Finding connection in a computerized world*. London: Minerva.

Riddell-Dixon, Elizabeth. 1995. Social movements and the United Nations. *International Social Science Journal* 47 (2): 289–303.

Sardar, Ziauddin. 1996. alt.civilizations.faq: Cyberspace as the darker side of the West. In *Cyberfutures: Culture and politics on the information superhighway*, edited by Ziauddin Sardar and Jerome R. Ravetz. London: Pluto Press.

Simonsen, Kristian Mailand. 1996. Expanding public sphere: Foundations for accountability and responsibility in cyberspace. In *Mailand.* http://dorit.ihi.ku.dk/~mailand/skrifter/004.html (2 April 1998).

Sobchack, Vivian. 1996. Democratic franchise and the electronic frontier. In *Cyberfutures: Culture and politics on the information superhighway*, edited by Ziauddin Sardar and Jerome R. Ravetz. New York: New York University Press.

Third World Institute (TWI), International Development Research Centre (IDRC), and Canadian Centre for Occupational Health and Safety (CCOHS). 1993. *The Earth Summit NGO CD-ROM.* Ottawa, Canada: Third World Institute, International Development Research Centre and Canadian Centre for Occupational Health and Safety.

Toulmin, Stephen. 1999. The ambiguities of globalization. *Futures* 31:905–912.

Tsagarousianou, Roza. 1998. Electronic democracy and the public sphere. In *Cyberdemocracy: Technology, cities and civic networks*, edited by Roza Tsagarousianou, Damian Tambini and Cathy Bryan. London: Routledge.

United Nations (UN). 1993. Information for participants. In *The Earth Summit CD-ROM.* Ottawa, Canada: International Development Research Centre, United Nations, and Canadian Centre for Occupational Health and Safety.

———. 1998. *Basic facts about the United Nations.* New York: United Nations.

———. 2000. *Beijing +5 Women 2000: Gender equality, development and peace for the 21st century.* http://www.un.org/womenwatch/followup/beijing5/index.html (20 January 2000 and 15 March 2000).

Verstraeten, Hans. 1996. The media and the transformation of the public sphere: A contribution for a critical political economy of the public sphere. *European Journal of Communication* 11:347–370.

WomenAction 2000. 2000. *WomenAction 2000 frontdoor.* http://www.womenaction.org/ (20 January 2000 and 15 March 2000).

9 Doing Away with Suharto— and the Twin Myths of Globalization and New Social Movements

DANA L. CLOUD

"The need of a constantly expanding market for its products chases the bourgeoisie over the whole surface of the globe. It must nestle everywhere, settle everywhere, establish connections everywhere. . . . In place of the old local and national seclusion and self-sufficiency, we have intercourse in every direction, universal interdependence of nations." (Marx and Engels [1848] 1998, 7–8)

"Modern bourgeois society with its relations of production, of exchange and of property, a society that has conjured up such gigantic means of production and of exchange, is like the sorcerer, who is no longer able to control the powers of the nether world whom he has called up by his spells." (Marx and Engels [1848] 1998, 11)

The first passage above from the *Communist Manifesto*, penned more than 150 years ago, indicates the long-standing recognition in Marxism of the tendency of capitalism to seek global resources and markets. This tendency is not new to our era. In the words of social theorist Immanuel Wallerstein, "in the nineteenth and twentieth centuries there has been only one world-system in existence, the capitalist world economy" (1979, 5). The second quotation from Marx and Engels, however, represents another side to this continuity that is perhaps too-often forgotten today: namely, that while the reach of capital is wide and strong, the capacity of ordinary people to mobilize against it also has been an ever-present reality.

That there was a revolution in Indonesia in 1998 is testament to the reality of effective resistance against the workings of global capital.[1] In a series of unexpected events, large numbers of students, workers, and the urban poor took to the streets to demand an end to the harsh austerity of the 1997–1998 Asian economic crisis. Their revolution ended with the deposing of thirty-two-year dictator Thojib Suharto and with the installation of a new, if not profoundly more democratic, regime. It also included as an intertwining development the independence from Indonesia of the republic of East Timor.

The reality of the 1998 Indonesian Revolution challenges some current theories regarding the capacity of ordinary people around the world to challenge the power of nation-states embedded in the relations of global capitalism. This chapter examines events in Indonesia in 1998 in order to argue against one such commonly held "globalization hypothesis": the contention that economic and political forces have generated a rupture or break away from modern capitalist relations among the state, the economy, and counterpublics.[2] Proponents of this idea suggest that the centrality of the nation-state as a site of political agency and transformation for subaltern counterpublics has waned and that social movement agents should look elsewhere to demand something less than wholesale redress (DuBoff and Herman 1997; Sivanandan 1997). New Social Movement theory is tied to the globalization hypothesis; its adherents argue that modernist modes of organizing—the conjoining of student, labor, and other interested groups in mass protest aimed at taking economic and state power—are no longer proper to either organizing or studying contemporary social movements.

In assuming that the forces of globalization have so empowered capital in our era that mass struggle among laborers for economic justice is unfeasible, some iterations of the globalization hypothesis are profoundly pessimistic. As Ellen Wood writes, "the concept of globalization as it is commonly understood is the heaviest albatross around the neck of the Left today. In the conventional wisdom about globalization, the Left now occupies the same ground as the neo-liberal right, in a historically unprecedented kind of ideological alliance. . . . In the current conception of globalization, left joins right in accepting that 'There Is No Alternative' [Margaret Thatcher's phrase]" (Wood 1997a, 20; see also Moody 1997; Wood 1997b; Tabb 1997a). Events in Indonesia fly in the face of the idea that "there is no alternative," even as the same events point toward the ways in which alternatives are limited by certain social movement choices and strategies. On the basis of the Indonesian Revolution, this chapter contests the assumption of a reigning, unassailable, globalized capital and reasserts the importance of nation-states to the project of social change. Indeed, I regard New Social Movements theory (NSM) and a set of pessimistic globalization theories as twin harbingers of unnecessary doom.

The chapter is organized as follows. First, the chapter summarizes and contests the "doomsday" version of globalization theory in the context of other, more persuasive accounts of the shape of global capitalism. Second, the chapter argues that a rejection of the doomsday globalization theory (hereafter referred to as DGT) also calls into question the assumptions of New Social Movements theory. Third, the chapter narrates a history of the Indonesian Revolution and argues that its development supports the viability of a more traditional, modernist social movements model. Fourth, following an elaboration of some criteria based on a history of revolutionary movements, I assess the weaknesses and strengths of the activities and strategies of the Indonesian Revolution.

The chapter concludes that social movement activity has targeted and should continue to target both economy and state as interdependent sites of social change. As an alternative to either micropolitical struggles for recognition or contained liberal reforms that leave fundamental, unequal economic relations unaltered, I offer a set of criteria for revolutionary social movements aimed at redistributive justice and seizure of state power by and for ordinary people. We ought not regard these criteria as archaic or irrelevant to the workings of Left counterpublics today.

THE IDEOLOGY OF GLOBALIZATION

To make the argument that globalization theory in its doomsday incarnations has reactionary ideological consequences is not the same thing as to deny the (ongoing since the last century) reality of global capitalism. Nor do I mean to suggest that nothing has changed in the 150-year tenure of industrial capitalism with regard to its international reach or reliance on the protective forces of the nation-state. Along with some socialist scholars associated with the publication *Socialist Register*, I am suggesting that the Left should account for shifts in the epiphenomena of global capitalism without losing sight of its fundamental characteristics, which include the expropriation of the labor of the many for the wealth of the few and the involvement of nation-states in that process (see Panitch and Leys 1999; Miliband and Panitch 1994). The changes in global capitalism to which the Left must adapt, furthermore, are more shifts in degree than in kind. Marx and Engels described the tendency of capital to spread its reach around the globe in search of raw materials, labor, and markets. Global capitalism today represents an intensification of this process rather than a break with it.

Arguments insisting on the continuity of contemporary capitalism with its previous incarnations often meet such questions as, how can Marxist theory account for "new" phenomena such as Nike Corporation's business, which is based in Portland, manufactures shoes in Asia, is traded on the New York Stock Exchange, has as its chief spokesperson a famous Chicago athlete, and markets its products in the United States, Europe, and elsewhere? On its face, the question suggests a giddy swirl of novelty and complexity unknown to critics of capitalism in 1848 or in 1917. In 1848, however, under the relations of colonialism, very similar situations pertained: the East India Company having its base in England, gathering resources and operating plants in India, and returning profits and goods to the company's home country. In terms of degree, today's Nike Corporation may be different, but I would suggest that the differences have been overestimated.

Likewise, I am skeptical with regard to claims that regional trade alliances such as the General Agreement on Tariffs and Trade (GATT), the European Union (EU), or the North American Free Trade Agreement (NAFTA) represent a break with prior modern global economic relations. The history of the capitalist world has been one in which nation-states band together for periods of time when their interests converge (either militarily or economically) and break apart again in warfare or indifference when they do not. In 1848 or in 1998, trade agreements among elites of various nations rarely have represented the interests of ordinary people in the countries involved, and in both eras, popular responses to the agreements of elites have been outright rebellion.[3]

However, there are two neocolonial developments in global capitalism that I wish to cover here.[4] The first is the emergence out of the two world wars of organizations and international bodies whose mission is to regulate and moderate world trade and to decide the terms of globalization. These organizations, whose mandates since World War II have been to protect U.S. capitalism in an unstable world market, include the United Nations (UN), the International Monetary Fund (IMF), the World Bank (WB), and the more recent World Trade Organization (WTO), among others. These agencies do not represent a break with modern relations of capitalist exploitation and imperialism. The World Bank funded the despotic Suharto regime beginning in 1968 and in 1969 funded population relocation programs with devastating effects on the environment and cultures of indigenous people. During the 1997 to 1998 economic crisis in Southeast Asia, the International Monetary Fund offered loan packages in exchange for the privatization and deregulation of enterprises, elimination of millions of jobs, cutbacks in social spending, and the elimination of price subsidies on basic food and energy. The goal of the loans was not to help starving people but to "recapitalize banking systems that were on the verge of collapse in order to protect depositors and foreign lenders" (Geier 2000, 20). Across the developing world, the IMF and World Bank have offered funds for "structural adjustment programs" that led not to an increased standard of living for ordinary people but to hunger, malnutrition, poverty, disease, and death.[5]

A second set of developments hailed as "new" to late capitalism has to do with the ways in which, after the end of outright colonial rule, leaders of nation-states in the developing world serve as proxies for the interests of capitalists in other, industrially advanced, countries.[6] This second situation has pertained in Indonesia, where Suharto and his successors have provided American and other firms with cheap labor, access to raw materials such as metals, and military support in defense of corporate installations. In such a situation, national rulers and a thin layer of a national policy elite profit from foreign investment while the foreign corporations plunder the environment and exploit local labor. These modern developments do not entail a rejection of the state or the economy as sites of social antagonism. Especially in the economies of the developing world, which depend heavily on foreign investment and trade, the ruling elites of states take on an increasingly repressive role in defending capitalist enterprises, either native or foreign (Panitch 1994; Radice 1999; Sassen 1998; Tsoukalas 1999).

In short, the position I am taking is that while global capitalism is real, some versions of globalization theory actually both mystify and sustain that reality by promoting some ideological myths with regard to the state and social movements. The range of positions on globalization is marked by divergent understandings of globalization's *reality, vulnerability*, and *valence*:

Globalization is real and represents a new and virtually unassailable form of capitalism—and this is good. This is basically the neo-liberal, "capitalism has won," "end of history" position adopted by free-market proponents such as Thomas Friedman (1999), who sees a loss of local tradition as the primary downside to an inevitable global prosperity. This category also includes authors of "how-to" handbooks for managers of transnational corporations (Marquardt 1998; Ohmae 1999).

Globalization is real and represents a new and virtually unassailable form of capitalism—and this is lamentable. This is the doomsday (DGT) "mourn, don't organize" position that I will be criticizing at some length below as unwittingly complicit with contemporary capitalism and as warranting a turn away from system-oriented social movements.

Globalization is real and represents a new but not necessarily unas-sailable form of capitalism to which the Left should adapt its strategies. This is the position of the *Socialist Register* scholars cited above along with several others including Amin (1997) and Sassen (1998). In this camp I include scholars who argue for localized urban politics as opposed to mass-national confrontations with state power (e.g., Cox 1997). This position risks overestimating the extent to which globalization represents a break with former capitalist social relations. As Hirsch notes, the posi-tion retains the centrality of class struggle but argues that "class theory needs new categories and perspectives" (1999, 279).

The idea of globalization understood as a break with prior capital-ist social relations is an ideological fiction that underestimates the ongo-ing capacity for nation-states and international regulatory agencies to mitigate against capitalism's worst effects. This reformist perspective, adopted by Hirst and Thompson (1996; see also Reich 1992) can be regarded as a "head-in-the-sand" approach that has *always* overesti-mated the willingness and capacity of governments to ameliorate the effects of capitalism. What we have seen in recent years in the rise of what is called neoliberalism is the defeat of Keynesian intervention into economies in favor of deregulation and the erosion of social welfare. This defeat is not new but is like a return to the laissez-faire era of rampant industrialization and capitalist expansion of the turn of the twentieth century. This reformist position offers a thorough and astute critique of corporate rule but suggests, implausibly, that we look to corporations or governments themselves to reform their behavior in line with a more humane ideal (Korten 1995).

The idea of globalization understood as a break with prior capitalist social relations is an ideological fiction that, in telling ordinary people not to struggle at the site of the state and economy, mystifies and sustains the capitalist world system. Predictably to be sure, this is the position to which I am most drawn, despite some caveats to the "new categories and perspectives" position above. This "globalization-as-fiction" position emphasizes the continuity of the capitalist world system in order to retain the visibility of class and state power; it does not necessarily deny shifts in the shape of this system around these central features. To my mind the most significant advantage of this position is that it encourages a critical reflexivity about the truth claims of scholarly discourse about globaliza-tion. The critics operating within this camp are to globalization what the work of Fredric Jameson (1992, 1998) is to postmodernism. As Jameson manages to describe postmodernism as the cultural logic of late capitalism without embracing either postmodernism or capitalism, it behooves us to understand "globalization" as a theoretical logic of late capitalism.

DISPELLING THE DISCOURSE OF DOOM

Unfortunately, the DGT version of globalization theory has gained persuasive momentum across social theory and the humanities. Socialist scholar Chris Harman has summarized this prevailing globalization theory as follows: "Everywhere it is used to mean the world economy has reached a new stage, which governments and workers alike are virtually powerless to withstand" (1996, 4). The writings of doomsday globalization theorists bear out this summary. For example, Sivanandan has written that globalization has resulted in the destruction and complete impotence of the working-class movement (1997, 20). Theorists such as Horsman (1994), Ohmae (1999), and Reich (1992) have contended that world market forces and the will of transnational corporations have become stronger than nation-states and nearly invulnerable to national politics and social movements. On this argument, the global system is governed and can be governed only by the logic of market competition, which allegedly has rendered virtually impotent the activities of governments, international regulatory bodies, and social movement actors to make large-scale social change.

This would, indeed, be a bleak picture for ordinary working people, pro-democracy activists, and their movements, if the picture were an accurate one. However, there is ample evidence to challenge the assumptions of this version of globalization theory. The protests in November and December 1999 at the meeting of the World Trade Organization in Seattle gave voice to a series of critiques of a world governed by market logics and priorities. The protests, involving tens of thousands of unionists, students, and environmentalists, forced the delegates to suspend their business. In addition, the protests brought the issue of international governance and the role of capital in dictating the standard of living of millions of people around the globe to the forefront of public consciousness worldwide. These events are evidence of the potential power held by ordinary people to confront the rule of the global market (Tabb 2000).[7]

Despite the claims of DGT, capital is actually more centrally organized than ever in its history, concentrated into three regions dominated by the United States, the European Union, and Japan. Moody takes note of the following economic statistics: Only 20 percent of foreign direct investment, a key statistic for globalization theorists, flows from the industrialized global North to the developing South. Ninety-seven percent of all fixed capital (plant and equipment, which is very difficult to relocate on a whim) is nationally planted, and over 70 percent of all fixed capital investment occurs within the twenty-five industrial nations of the North (1996, 55–59). Moody suggests, therefore, that theorists of the international economy look not only to the movement of money but also to its final resting place. Moody concludes: "Today's hierarchical production chains are commanded from corporate headquarters mostly in a dozen or so of the major industrial powers of the North" (1996, 78).

While a number of corporations have embraced a decentralized model of internationalized production, the greater number of major firms in major industries remain firmly tied to their national bases. Socialist and other scholars have pointed out that production has not been universally internationalized, that capital is not as mobile as globalization theorists would have it, and that the vast majority of production still takes place in nationally based companies, with profits returning, on the whole, to the home nation-state (Moody 1997; Tabb 1997a, 1997b; Wood 1997a, 1997b).[8]

This is not to say that today's international capital is the same as that of 1848. The nation-state today works as the main agent of international capital, keeping social costs low, keeping social conflict in check, enforcing austerity on ordinary people, and keeping labor immobilized while capital moves freely across national boundaries (Moody 1997, 12–13). The governments of nation-states are often in the position of defending enterprises whose home base is in another nation-state. This relationship has obtained in Indonesia, where Suharto and his family were amply rewarded for providing access to land, resources, labor, and the armed forces of the Indonesian state by American, British, and Australian firms, including Mattel, Nike, Boeing, the mining company Freeport-McMoran, and many others. Even in this context, relations of power are still overwhelmingly determined by the imperatives of international capitalism as they were described by Marx and Engels 150 years ago. As Boris Kagarlitsky writes, while "it is clear that the left needs to have its own international economic strategy . . . the instrument and starting-point of this new cooperation can only be a national state" (1999, 294). Organizing against this system on a modern model that takes on state and corporate power is not only feasible; it is absolutely necessary if we who are committed to social justice are to win more than symbolic gains against the austerity and misery that confront the vast majority of the world's population.

Critics of DGT have mobilized evidence toward different, modernist political ends that could all loosely be described as belonging to the traditions of pragmatic reformism and "old" social movements.[9] Moody (1997; see also Gordon 1988) argues for a renewed effort to build social movement unions that link economic demands with political demands on the part of ordinary people. Hirst and Thompson (1996) argue for the continuing relevance and necessity of state and international governance—

by the G3, the World Trade Organization, the European Union, and NAFTA—of corporate power. Harman (1996) criticizes Hirst and Thompson's faith in the organizations of international governance, seeing them not as watchdogs but as lapdogs of international capital. However, all of these critics of globalization theory wonder why, if the situation of world capital is not so "new" or different from its modern industrial manifestation as much as it is just ever more so, do we need "new" social movements? The concern is that the argument for New Social Movements represents a retreat from the kinds of reformist and revolutionary struggle that have driven social change throughout capitalism's history.

DISPELLING THE GLAMOUR OF NEW SOCIAL MOVEMENTS

Several recent works have attempted to put into the background issues of state power, economic class, and the forces of labor in favor of attention to "New Social Movements."[10] Such movements, it is argued, form around shared identities as women, African-Americans, and other social categories, and mark a qualitative shift in movement strategy and goals, away from mass-movement demands for direct and immediate economic redress and toward a micropolitics of identity and consumption. New Social Movements scholars often support such political projects as correctives to "old" (either liberal, legislation-oriented or socialist, labor-oriented) models of organization (see Aronowitz 1992; Certeau 1984; Escobar 1992; Eyerman and Jamison 1991; Giddens 1991; Habermas 1981; Laclau and Mouffe 1986; Melucci 1988, 1992; Touraine 1984).[11] Most prominently, Alberto Melucci (1996) has suggested that we abandon any notion of totality or materiality in social movement organizing. He argues instead that the micropolitical work of contemporary social movements in what he calls (without distinguishing it theoretically or empirically from any prior "age") "the information age" should be to construct group identities in public spaces in order to challenge codes—as if commodities were no longer produced in sweatshops and as if Indonesians, reduced to eating bark during the economic crisis that has lasted from 1997 up until the time of this writing, could satisfy themselves with codes or concern themselves primarily with the discursive construction of their shared identity.

The designation of identity movements as "New Social Movements" predated our current obsession with theories of globalization. However, one can regard the emergence of these theories as belonging to roughly the same historical moment. They are twin manifestations of the poststructuralist impulse to make discourses and subjectivities the Alpha and

Omega of social theory. In addition, both theories emerged from a sense of defeat among the scholarly Left in the 1980s and 1990s. As the pairing of title and subtitle of Anthony King's collection of essays *Culture, Globalization and the World System: Contemporary Conditions for the Representation of Identity* (1997) indicates, there is a theoretical link between theories of globalization and the focus on the representation of identity as the goal of counterpublics.

Indeed, there seems to be a completely unwarranted consensus among New Social Movement theorists that real social change is no longer possible in the allegedly "globalized" "information age." This move risks covering over despair and resignation to marginality and austerity with the gloss of the "new." For example, James Scott (1990) has suggested that scholars turn their attention to the "infrapolitics" of subordinate groups, in which the critic discovers "hidden transcripts" of resistance in the offstage activities and conversations of the powerless. Following Scott's lead, Robin Kelley (1994) describes the infrapolitics of Black subaltern counterpublics in American culture. Although both Scott and Kelley insist that they do not mean to suggest that "infrapolitics"— the strategic, small-scale survival strategies and makings of subversive meaning on the microlevel by social actors without access to institutional power—replace politics more traditionally understood, their works can be read as a reflection of the problematic "settling" for cultural raids and the microstrategies of sheer survival when there is no reason, in fact, not to think that large-scale, redistributive social change can be achieved. I do not mean to attribute malign intent to scholars working within New Social Movement and globalization paradigms. Rather, I mean to suggest that theories have political and ideological implications whether we intend them to or not.

While Scott and Kelley are scholars aligned with the Left critique of racism and imperialism, the rhetoric of New Social Movements can be appropriated by the right. This is evident in an essay by Richard Flacks called, in an instance of wishful thinking about the demise of the Left, "The Party's Over." In this essay, Flacks openly adorns arguments against the most basic provisions of access and social welfare in American society with the language of supporting "new" social movements, which he defines as the enabling of "people to find power in and through communities" (1994, 348). The harmony of this vision of a smaller federal state and inactive mass movements (especially those demanding material redress) with the "compassionate conservatism/I feel your pain centrism" of contemporary Republicans and Democrats should not go unnoticed.

Nancy Fraser has offered an incisive critique of the decoupling of struggles for cultural recognition (now known as "new" social movements) from the old social movement project of redistribution. She writes that since 1989, which she sees as marking the beginning of a "postsocial-ist" condition,[12]

> claims for the recognition of group difference have become intensely salient in the recent period, at times eclipsing claims for social equality. This phenomenon can be observed at two levels. Empirically, of course, we have seen the rise of 'identity politics,' the decentering of class, and, until very recently, the correspond-ing decline of social democracy. More deeply, however, we are witnessing an apparent shift in the political imaginary, especially in the terms in which justice is imagined. Many actors appear to be moving away from a socialist political imaginary, in which the central problem of justice is redistribution, to a 'postsocialist' political imaginary, in which the central problem of justice is recognition. With this shift, the most salient social movements are no longer economically defined 'classes' who are struggling to defend their 'interests,' end 'exploitation,' and win 'redistribu-tion.' Instead, they are culturally defined 'groups' or 'communi-ties of value' who are struggling to defend their 'identities,' end 'cultural domination,' and win 'recognition.' The result is a decoupling of cultural politics from social politics, and the rela-tive eclipse of the latter by the former. (1997, 2)

While Fraser argues—and I agree—that justice requires both redistribu-tion and recognition, she also argues that scholars must question their ten-dency to privilege the latter as an ideologically troubling move. Revolutionary transformation, she suggests, requires redistribution in the form of socialism, or a deep restructuring of the relations of production, and recognition in the form of deconstruction, which destabilizes the processes of group differentiation. Such a dual emphasis incorporates struggles to end injustices of class, race, gender, and sexuality and at the same time ties the material realm to the cultural-ideological in a way that can understand their interrelationship. As Michael Denning (1997) has recently argued with regard to the explosion of proletarian culture in the 1930s United States, agitation from below can produce new spaces and identities at the level of culture; but rarely have interventions exclusively on a cultural stage produced fundamental material and institutional change. At its best, symbolic work can accomplish consciousness-raising in an already politicized context.

An exclusive politics of recognition disconnected from materialist pro-jects emerges from three politically and empirically flawed premises. The first flawed assumption is that movements aimed at winning economic gains and material improvements for ordinary people have already established an adequately egalitarian material terrain. Another version of this idea is that whether or not the terrain is adequately egalitarian, it is as good as it is going to get. Either way, the implication is that all we can fight for now is the recognition of multiple identities on a cultural stage. This assumption and the theories that rest on it risk imposing the perspective of Western scholars on movements and peoples of developing nations. In Indonesia in 1998, the vast majority of the population was unemployed and living in poverty. The country was and remains dependent on trade with and investment by corporations housed in more wealthy nations. To the many displaced urban workers forced to flee the cities to scavenge for roots, bark, and beetles as sources of nutrition, the idea that one should seek recognition of one's identity as an outcome of a social movement would be ludicrous.[13]

Therefore, the second flawed premise has to do with locating the starting point of globalization theory in the advanced industrial world. From the vantage of one of the nation-states in control of international trade (the G7 nations), it is perhaps too easy to embrace the first assumption of adequate economic parity and opportunity around the world. In such a context the relevance of "new" social movement theories heralding a politics of recognition must be questioned.

Finally, the third and most important premise of NSM and DGT scholars is that revolutionary change is no longer possible and perhaps not even desirable in what is described, inaccurately, as a new "age" of globalized capitalism and impotent nation-states. Indonesian workers and students proved otherwise in challenging not only an entrenched dictator but also the IMF and World Bank as agents of transnational capital. As David McNally (1998) has argued, we ought to look to resistance and revolt in Asia to witness the possibilities of a fighting back against globalization. In Fraser's terms, the Indonesian Revolution brought together demands for redistribution and recognition. Interwoven with the revolutionary struggle that deposed Suharto and demanded an end to state-imposed austerity was the movement of independence activists in East Timor for recognition of their separate nation.

TALK AND ACTION IN INDONESIA, 1998–1999

A Brief Historical Account

In 1945, Indonesia won its independence from Dutch colonial rule. Nationalist leader Achmed Sukarno became president, backed by the

Indonesian Communist Party (PKI). In 1965, Thojib Suharto came to power in a coup backed (perhaps planned) by the U.S. Central Intelligence Agency (CIA) and with British and Australian backing. Suharto destroyed the PKI in a massacre that also targeted all other radical elements in Indonesian society. From 1965 until 1998, the United States and Britain supported Suharto with arms and money in exchange for Suharto's provision of low-cost production facilities and labor and access to resources on the part of foreign firms. In 1975, the Indonesian army invaded and annexed East Timor, killing two hundred thousand people, or one-third of the republic's population. It should be noted that despite Suharto's iron-fisted rule, millions of students and workers protested living conditions and state repression throughout the 1970s and 1980s. In response to bleak economic conditions in the 1990s, unions such as the Indonesian Prosperous Trade Union (SBSI) and the Center for Indonesia Working Class Struggle (PPBI) were formed and led thousands of strikes in spite of the murder and imprisonment of their leaders.

In 1997, rigged parliamentary elections provoked a surge of protests, rioting, and demonstrations by urban poor and youth. Then, the 1997–1998 Asian economic crisis hit Indonesia with tremendous force. The rupiah lost 80 percent of its value, all banks failed, and the nation's foreign debt topped 137 billion dollars. Food prices soared even as wages were frozen. The International Monetary Fund offered a 43-billion-dollar "rescue" package that depended on enforced austerity. Meanwhile, Suharto was "elected" for the seventh time, provoking massive protests at universities. Throughout 1998, huge strikes and student protests called for the smashing of state power. In May, U.S. and other foreign companies shut down the majority of their offices and some plants in Indonesia. On 21 May, under pressure from the military which could not control the unrest, Suharto stepped down, and Vice-President B. J. Habibie, regarded as a Suharto crony, took over. Students and workers immediately called for his resignation.

Under pressure from the growing revolutionary movement during the fall of 1998 and spring of 1999, Habibie freed a number of jailed unionists and other activists even as Indonesian military and paramilitary organizations attempted to quell the ongoing unrest. Many of these attacks focused on the East Timorese resistance. In August 1999, East Timor voted for independence after Habibie called for a referendum on the question, leading to a wave of militia violence against the East Timorese that lasted into 1999 and prompted the deployment of a UN peacekeeping force in the area. Meanwhile, tens of thousands of antigovernment demonstrators continued to protest against Habibie in the lead up to the October 1999 election. In this election, an unknown underdog, Abdurrahman Wahid, was elected by the 700–member People's Consultative Assembly and chose Megawati Sukarno as his vice president. Megawati had distanced herself from the revolutionary movement and called for peace and calm. Activists resigned themselves to this new situation with some difficulty.

Strong Hunger, Weak Counterpublics

Thus, the 1998 Indonesian Revolution mobilized thousands of ordinary people across sectors of Indonesian society to demand a radical change. The movement targeted the Indonesian state and won significant, if not total, reforms. The example is in itself enough to challenge the broad strokes of the dominant tendencies in globalization theory. Yet the revolution falls short of satisfying a set of criteria invested in the winning of substantial economic and political democracy and a better material life for ordinary people.

Direct action in response to coercive state power and material inequity requires communicative activity on the part of movement leaders who aim to mobilize, organize, and sustain the commitment of large numbers of people. A number of organizations played these roles. Prominent among them were the unofficial "Fighting" Indonesian Democratic Party, headed by Megawati Sukarno, who made an unsuccessful bid for the presidency after the revolution; Muslim organizations headed by Amien Rais; a range of nongovernmental organizations organized around labor, women's and human rights, and the environment; the Indonesian United Democratic Party, whose leader was jailed under Suharto; and the Indonesian Prosperous Trade Union (SBSI) led by Muchtar Pakpahan, the largest independent union in Indonesia.

In addition, one of the most important organizations in the revolution was the People's Democratic Party (PRD), a small but important Left organization that called for the overthrow of Suharto and for the nationalization of major industries to provide basic necessities for the people. Mirah Mahardika, one of the PRD's leaders, noted that these goals required "mobilizing masses on a large scale." He described in an interview how the actions of the PRD aimed to demystify Suharto's reign. "Our actions are not aimed to cause panic, but to spread awareness so that people don't continue to be deceived by the dictator. The people are living in misery, prices are soaring, there are sackings everywhere swelling unemployment, and the people are supposed to be silent and accept it. That's false consciousness. Well, the PRD intends to shatter that false consciousness" (Workers' Representatives and Socialists [WRS] 1998, 11).

While recognizing the importance of public communication in the lead-up to the revolution, Mahardika emphasizes the economic crisis of 1997–1998 as a galvanizing factor in the Indonesian Revolution. Likewise, SBSI member Rekson Silaban suggested in an interview that government inaction in the face of devastating economic crisis was the goad for the revolutionary activity:

> There has been a real increase in poverty. . . . Now there are 150 million below the poverty line—and this with a population of 200 million. There has been a massive increase in workers' unemployment. People have lost confidence in the government. They are waiting for political reforms, but these are not coming. . . . The people are now thinking we must have a revolution because there is no chance of the existing government stopping the suffering.
>
> During the last election there was no political party that spoke about change. Now the PRD has been suppressed because it wanted political change. People are really very outspoken now about the government in the press and they have taken to the streets. During the recent election there was an order from the military to suppress the demonstrations and send the organisers to prison, but the people don't listen and they demonstrate more and more. Recently there have been quite a number of student demonstrations. . . . The struggle today is much bigger now than it has ever been because it has spread throughout the country. (WRS 1998, 11)

The remarks of these leaders indicate two cautions regarding the role of communication in making revolution. The first caution comes from noticing how in these accounts, economic crisis itself galvanized street protest; demonstrations were organized but there is a sense in which the movement simply spread out of desperation and despair. Silaban comments: "Today people need food—they are hungry, and if they can't get food they will go out onto the streets. A lot of people now try and force open the shops and take food. It is the first time I think that there is a possibility of a revolution. The situation is getting out of control" (WRS 1998, 11). In this remark, there is a direct tie between hunger and activity; the role of social movement organizations is backgrounded even by their own leaders. The implication is that very little persuasion is necessary to spark activity in such a materially grievous situation, even if, as I would argue, leadership and persuasion become essential in giving a movement coherent shape and direction.

The second theme about communication arising from these firsthand accounts is that open organizing before and during the revolution were subject to forceful repression on the part of the state. The PRD's activities were suppressed, and many movement leaders were jailed until well into Habibie's interim presidency. Silaban notes in the interview quoted above that "the police have arrested eight of our members. They were worried about the alliance between workers and students. The government clearly fears this solidarity" (WRS 1998, 11). In large part the SBSI and other organizations were forced underground, but masses of people revolted almost spontaneously despite these repressive conditions. A possible interpretation of these two features of the interviews—brutal state repression of organizing alongside spontaneous rebellion—is that in the Indonesian Revolution the role of communication was constrained. However, if Left organizations had been able to take the lead and enact more careful public strategies of propaganda, recruitment, and mobilization, the revolution might have gone farther than it did. Today the organizations listed above are attempting to build their numbers to continue to press for a higher standard of living for Indonesian people.

Assessing the Indonesian Revolution is difficult because, by all accounts, it is an unfinished project. If one took a snapshot of the situation today, the new guard of Wahid and Megawati seems unlikely to break fundamentally with the policies of the old regime. However, the weaknesses of the Indonesian revolutionary movement have emerged not from anything like an overdependence on "old" Left strategies but rather from the very lack of connection to the revolutionary Left in that country. Even by the 1990s, the Indonesian Left had not recovered from the systematic annihilation of communists, labor organizers, progressives, and their allies by Suharto and the United States CIA in 1965. Furthermore, Suharto forcibly repressed all Left organizing during his regime. As a result, the 1998 revolution targeted the state but in ways limited to a narrowly reformist vision; the basic material needs of the Indonesian people still have not been met. The revolution supports an argument for the continued mobilization of counterpublics against despotic states embroiled in neocolonial capitalist social relations, but also raises the further questions of *how* to confront the state and *what* demands to make on it.

Revolutionary Rehearsal, Revolutionary Criteria

It is always a challenge and a risk to advance a hypothesis contrary to fact, to make a case about "what might have been" in any given circumstance. Yet, scholars interested in social justice are rarely given straightforward positive cases on which to base their arguments about which critical theories and activist strategies to adopt. More often, we are faced with defeats and partial victories on which to model effective social movements. Furthermore, any normative critical project—that is, one that seeks not only to describe events but to argue on behalf of certain theoretical and pragmatic choices—must offer a set of extradescriptive criteria on which events are to be measured and new action is to be planned. The criteria I offer here are based on a revolutionary socialist perspective that points to the patent limits of reforms within the capitalist system and argues for the possibility of building a systematic challenge to its rule. Among my readers an objection will doubtless arise to my wanting to have it both ways. That is, the successes of the revolution up to this point evidence the partially ideological character of globalization theories and demonstrate the vitality of class struggle in today's world. Yet, the unfinished business of the Indonesian Revolution indicates that the struggle did not go far enough. Either way, a revolutionary Left model is vindicated and the example seems neither to prove nor disprove the importance of a politics of redistribution against encroachment from a politics of recognition.

To this objection I have no easy answer. All critics either lay out or imply a set of evaluative criteria. One consequence of accepting the terms of DGT/NSM theory is that revolutionary criteria are ruled out of bounds as passé and unrealistic. But let us see what kind of propositions and questions emerge from a perspective that answers the "what might have been" question with an eye toward identifying the conditions under which any given struggle could be articulated as a challenge to the system of global capitalism. This perspective also encourages critics to identify situational factors inhibiting the emergence of a system-oriented movement. I believe the Indonesian case offers insights into both aspects of this mode of critique. If nothing else, the Indonesian Revolution patently puts the question of revolution back on the table.

In 1945, when Sukarno took power on Indonesia's independence from Dutch colonial rule, the Communist Party in Indonesia, the PKI, fell into line with his program of national development and political quiescence. Thus in 1965, when a CIA-aided coup installed Suharto, the Left was in no position to defend itself against the purges Suharto led against communists, independence organizers, trade unions, and student movement leaders. An entire generation of people with the organizational skills necessary to build a movement against Suharto was wiped out. Since that time, Left organizations have been attempting to rebuild "non-state political space" in Indonesia in the face of ongoing repression (Hewison and Rodan 1994, 236).

In this light, that there was a revolution in Indonesia at all, led loosely by newly emerging forces among students, the urban poor, and workers, poses a challenge to the pessimism of globalization theory. And, in fact, there were a number of concrete gains made by and on behalf of the ordinary people who made the revolution. First among these is the push that the revolution gave the movement for an independent East Timor. Suharto's successor, B. J. Habibie, called for an unprecedented popular referendum on the question, which passed by a large margin on 30 August 1999. Although this referendum was met by brutal violence on the part of pro-military Indonesian national militias, the vote was ratified by the new People's Consultative Assembly on 20 October 1999. Habibie also freed prominent union leaders, including Muchtar Pakpahan in June 1999, and Timorese independence activists Jose Ramos-Horta and Jose Alexandre "Xanana" Gusmao in September. Alongside the new freedoms of the East Timorese, the Indonesia revolution resulted in the legalization of independent unions and other social movement organizations, which sets the stage for a more organized rebuilding of a Left counterpublic in Indonesia, one that might match the catalyst of hunger with a rhetoric that can focus future struggles.

Finally, and most important, the Indonesian Revolution deposed one of the most brutal dictators of the twentieth century and put world capital on notice that it cannot indefinitely count on its proxies in developing nations to do their bidding with regard to the provision of labor, resources, and military support for transnational capital. Suharto was responsible for thousands of deaths on seizing power in 1965, and then again for more than 200,000 murdered when Indonesia invaded East Timor in 1975. Called "our kind of guy" by a senior Clinton official in 1995, Suharto and his family became rich in the midst of his people's misery by aligning himself with United States–based firms and other corporations and their interests. If nothing else, the Indonesian Revolution will shine a spotlight on such deal-making, making it more difficult for corporations to hyperexploit workers in the developing world.[14]

The economic crisis that was the setting for the eruption of revolutionary activity in Indonesia persisted beyond the capability of international organizations or the state itself to solve. It was, in other words, a revolutionary movement that called attention to the limits of reforms and aid packages within the existing global order. However, the revolution could have and still could go further in its demands and its gains. Indeed, there is every indication that further activity will be necessary if the new regime is to be any different from the old one. There are indications that the new guard, under the leadership of Wahid and Megawati Sukarno, is still under control of the old order and its interests.

The primary indicator of this relationship is the sudden appearance of the virtually unknown Wahid (hailed in 1999 in the American press as an excellent, savvy politician) as a candidate in the presidential elections and his stunning victory over Megawati. Although Megawati was elected to the Assembly by a huge popular vote and enjoyed the overwhelming support of students and others behind the revolution, the narrower and less democratic forum of the Assembly became the place where powerful economic interests could pull strings and put in place a candidate more likely to put forward those interests.

Even Megawati, whose supporters carried banners reading "Megawati or revolution" in the run-up to the presidential election, has urged the movement not to take further steps in the democratization of Indonesia. During the revolution, she followed in her father's footsteps, preaching the philosophy of order, harmony, and unity for the good of the nation. Wahid has outlined policies that include some measures designed to alleviate the suffering of the poor. He also has proposed a new opening of relations with Israel and China. Yet his priorities still bear the stamp of the old regime. According to one press account, Wahid is appealing to transnational capital and wealthier nation-states to provide economic aid and investment. Wahid also said that he will appoint a number of representatives of Suharto's regime to his cabinet in a gesture of compromise recognizing the continuing imperative of national development (Lamb 1999).[15]

Meanwhile, former militant dissident Jose Alexandre "Xanana" Gusmao is being groomed by the U.S. Department of State as a leader who perhaps will make national development and foreign investment a key priority in the newly independent East Timor. At the time of this writing, the International Monetary Fund has withdrawn most of its aid package as a result of a banking scandal involving Suharto's cronies, and the majority of the Indonesian population remains immiserated. As described by the *Washington Post*, entrepreneurs have followed the relief workers into East Timor, replacing one kind of colonization with another, less direct but no less insidious, form (Richburg 2000).

As of December 1999, there have been serious outbreaks of religious violence between Muslims and Christians in some Indonesian provinces; at least 2,000 people have been killed. One could argue that these attacks represent misdirected scapegoating born of the inadequacy of present reforms and incompleteness of the 1998 revolution. In my view the religious strife is an obvious instance of how identity politics—the politics of recognition—emerge in the wake of redistributive defeat and therefore should not be heralded as an alternative to redistributive political projects. The down side of a cultural politics of recognition is that when it is undertaken in a context of material scarcity and inequality, it can take the form of violent scapegoating.

Thus, despite its revolutionary genesis and potential, the Indonesian Revolution remains an unfinished project, perhaps only Act I of a broader drama to unfold (Arnove 1998). The premature closure of the revolution is not unique among what socialist scholar Colin Barker (1987) calls "revolutionary rehearsals" of the twentieth century. As editor of a collection of essays on this topic, Barker includes accounts of revolutionary movements in France, 1968; Chile, 1972–1973; Portugal, 1974–1975; Iran, 1979; and Poland, 1980–1981. In each of these revolutionary moments, movements stopped short of taking control of the state and the economy on behalf of ordinary people, not because such an event was unthinkable or impossible, but because the Left in each instance demonstrated significant weaknesses of strategy and analysis. In the case of Chile, the results of revolutionary hesitation were catastrophic. When social democratic reformer Salvador Allende adopted a policy of conciliation with the Right, he left himself and his government vulnerable to the coup that deposed him and massacred more than 30,000 Leftists over a period of twelve months. In other cases, revolutionary movements died slow deaths as leaders accommodated to the capitalist system and enacted modest reforms within the parameters of that system despite their original revolutionary purpose.

The case of Indonesia is similar to these other "rehearsals," except that the Left in Indonesia was much less well developed in 1998 than the movements in the other countries Barker's book describes. The key commonality among these situations, however, is the lesson that such movements fall short not when they are confident in challenging the economy and the state on a traditional revolutionary model, but when they are weak, underconfident, or convinced by a rhetoric of invulnerable corporate dominance to settle for less than what they set out to achieve.[16] Social movement organizations that will be educating, organizing, and mobilizing oppositional counterpublics in Indonesia—as anywhere else—will need accurate theory and history in order to move the democratic struggle forward. Hunger may propel motion, but social action requires the expression of analysis and exhortation in communicative form.

OUR TASK: DISPEL THE MYTHS

If there is to be a truly democratic Indonesia (or any country, for that matter), there is a great deal of work to be done on the part of Left activists and scholars interested not only in describing revolutionary

movement but also in informing it (Cliff 1998). In contrast to the doomsday stances of some scholars today, I would like to offer a set of revolutionary socialist criteria for social movements, criteria that are based on
the lessons of the "revolutionary rehearsals" Barker describes. These criteria, which could be brought to bear on the process of forming and mobilizing oppositional counterpublics, include an emphasis on organizing
working people, who alone have the power to bring the production of
commodities, and thus corporate power, to a halt. This perspective understands capitalism as a global system, but one that can and must be challenged by a similarly internationalized revolutionary movement. A
revolutionary perspective seeks the overthrow of existing state leaders and
the corporate interests they defend and their replacement by institutions
governed by ordinary people. It puts forward the systematic critique of
exclusively reformist strategies that attempt to contain revolutionary
momentum. It calls for the defense of national, racial, and ethnic independence by oppressed nationalities or groups. Finally, it looks to build—or
rebuild—mass organizations with a revolutionary perspective in advance
of the next wave of revolutionary struggles (Barker 1987).

In a world economic system prone to crisis and founded on gross
inequalities and exploitation, there will be, of course, more waves of revolutionary struggles. As Chris Harman writes, "The very economic instability of the system ensures further upsurges of struggle and further waves of
hope. But fulfillment of these hopes is not guaranteed in advance. Professional 'mediators'—trade union bureaucrats, social democrat politicians,
repackaged Stalinists, populist demagogues—will always be available to
try to guide the struggles back into the channels of existing society"
(1998, 363). To Harman's list of "mediators" I would add the ranks of
defeatist Left intellectuals, who, wittingly or not, put forward arguments
that "guide the struggles back into the channels of existing society."

I have argued that, contrary to the claims of DGT and NSM theories, capitalism is a world system whose force and reach can be challenged. The revolution that took place in 1998 in Indonesia demonstrates
the continuing relevance of mass social movements in the confrontation
with intermeshed capital and nation-states. As Marx and Engels put it,
the social relations of modern Indonesia are products of "intercourse in
every direction, universal interdependence of nations." Real, existing
globalization today is in line with the internationalism of global capitalism as it has *always* used nation-states and blocs of nation-states to protect an international ruling class. And yet, the case of Indonesia points to
the other side of the equation identified by Marx and Engels: Like a sorcerer who cannot control his spells, the rule of corporate imperatives and
state-imposed austerity cannot contain the yearning of ordinary people

for a better life. The doing away with Suharto and the real, if incomplete, gains of the revolutionary movement show that the international ruling class can be defeated by mass movements that unite workers, students, and the poor.

As the title of this essay suggests, I believe that Suharto's reign is not the only thing that needs to be dispelled. The arguments of globalization theory summarized and critiqued here, along with the implicit or explicit "settling" for symbols inherent in New Social Movements theory, cannot account for the gains and shortcomings of this event. To the contrary, the lessons of the Indonesian Revolution suggest that, rather than abandoning the state and revolution, we should be doing the work that enables the Left in the United States and around the world to tie itself back to the revolutionary project, a project that is still viable but which also depends on confident and historically informed political leadership to make its potential real. We cannot witness the starving people of Indonesia—and the first of what will be many waves of tumultuous conflict in Asia and around the world in our time—without also recognizing the continuing relevance of a revolutionary project aimed at not just symbolic recognition but also a material justice.

NOTES

1. See Bambery (1998), Fermont (1998), and Morgan, O'Lincoln, and Fermont (1998) for background on this historic event.

2. Throughout this chapter I will use the term "counterpublic" to refer to the discursive components of social movements as defined by Sidney Tarrow. In Tarrow's terms, in a social movement, subordinated social groups move from the discursive formulation of the identities, interests, and needs to take "contentious collective action." Tarrow writes, "Collective action becomes contention when it is used by people who lack regular access to institutions, who act in the name of new or unaccepted claims, and who behave in ways that fundamentally challenge others or authorities. . . . This does not mean that movements do nothing else but contend: they build organizations, elaborate ideologies, and socialize and mobilize constituencies, and their members engage in self-development and the construction of collective identities" (Tarrow 1998, 3). In light of this passage, we may understand the formation of subaltern counterpublics as the sum of the discursively oriented moments of a social movement.

3. I believe that the commonplace claim that Marxists have not accounted for the complexities of global capitalism stems from a basic

ignorance of what Marxists have written. For example, it is probably not common knowledge among Western scholars that Lenin was a careful observer of international relations leading up to, during, and after the First World War. Based on these observations, he made some remarks that would seem prescient to today's "discoverers" of globalization: "Capitalism has grown into a world system of colonial oppression and of the financial strangulation of the overwhelming majority of the people of the world by a handful of 'advanced' countries. And this booty is shared between two or three powerful world marauders armed to the teeth (America, Great Britain, Japan), who involve the whole world in their war over the sharing of their booty" (1939, 11). I would invite my readers to compare this passage to the statistics cited from Moody, above. The central idea of his *Imperialism* is that the tendency in an international capitalist economy is the periodic concentration of production and wealth (secured by domination and violence) in monopolies and in particular countries or regions, oscillating with the cyclical eruption of competition, fragmentation, and global reorganization. Of particular interest here is his chapter on "Division of the World among Capitalist Combines," in which he concludes an analysis of the internationalizing oil industry: "The epoch of modern capitalism shows us that certain relations are established between capitalist alliances, based on the economic division of the world" (1939, 75).

4. I use the term *neocolonial* rather than *postcolonial* to designate continuity with relations of colonialism in the operations of today's transnational corporations. Likewise I refer to corporations with operations in more than one nation-state as "transnational" rather than "multinational" because most corporations exist within and depend upon a national base for their operations; their profits likewise flow back to the country of origin. Thus they cannot be described accurately as "multi-nationals."

5. For a comprehensive historical review of structural adjustment programs and statistics regarding the effects of IMF and World Bank programs in the Third World, see Geier (2000) and D'Amato and Shawki (2000). Rather than ameliorating the debt burden of poor countries, the agencies have exacerbated it. In 1990, debtor countries were 61 percent more in debt than they were in 1982, according to an Oxfam report (cited in Geier 2000, 18).

6. A third development in modern global capitalism is, of course, the emergence of electronic information technologies with global reach. An assessment of this phenomenon is beyond the scope of this paper.

7. See also Weissman (1999). At the time of this writing, similar protests had disrupted IMF and World Bank meetings in Washington, DC, and Prague, Czech Republic.

8. Furthermore, as Herrod (1997, 1999) has argued, the *globalization* of production, in which companies such as General Motors spread their production base around a series of rooted assembly plants with a set of satellite component facilities that may be either in the company's home nation or abroad, has resulted in a situation in which some sectors of industrial workers actually have *more* power to bring production to a standstill than they did before the industrial reorganization. For example, Herrod (1999) describes the 1998 General Motors strike, in which a relatively small number of workers at a component manufacturing facility managed to shut down the company's entire international operation for want of one small auto part.

9. For a feminist critique of globalization, see Gibson-Graham (1996, 120–147).

10. For arguments in social movements studies on the continuing relevance of the state as site of reform and target of revolutionary movement, see Tarrow (1996), Lambert (1991), Pitelis (1991), and Pooley (1991). For a counterargument privileging transnational social movement organizations and activities, see McCarthy, (1997), and Smith, Chatfield, and Pagnucco (1997).

11. For other instances of the turn toward identity, symbol, and the psyche as sites of social movement investigation, see Morris and Mueller (1992).

12. As a revolutionary socialist I take some issue with Fraser's conflation of the Eastern bloc and Soviet-style communism with socialism, although I appreciate her critical stance on "postsocialism" as not only an historical period but also a set of ideologies, which I would argue include globalization theory and New Social Movements theory. Fraser also argues that "the best of socialism" needs to be redeemed and reintroduced into social movement politics in the contemporary moment.

13. Ironically (from my perspective), it has become trendy to suggest that Marxist and other modernist models categorized as "old" Left are Eurocentric and elitist in orientation. As the conclusion of the foregoing paragraph suggests, I find the turn to cultural politics to be much more elitist, potentially, than a Marxist paradigm.

14. The recent national student campaign against sweatshops around the world has built on the Indonesian case.

15. At the time of this writing, Wahid's presidency is in crisis amid corruption charges, and once again students and workers are taking to the streets in protest.

16. This latter situation is called "reformism," described by Barker as "defined by its internal contradictions. It expresses a complex mixture of opposites: it arises from the structural antagonisms and conflicts of

class society, yet it also contains protest and opposition within the limits of this society. . . . It offers the promise of reforming legislation to improve the lot of workers, while accepting the overall structures of state power. It works at once within, for, and against the existing system" (1987, 221). A revolutionary perspective does not entail a rejection of struggles for reforms but rather encourages the connection of each reform effort to the broader revolutionary project.

REFERENCES

Amin, Samir. 1997. *Capitalism in the age of globalization*. London: Zed Books.

Arnove, Anthony. 1998. Indonesia: Crisis and revolt. *International Socialist Review* 5:9–17.

Aronowitz, Stanley. 1992. *Politics of identity: Class, culture, social movements*. New York: Routledge.

Bambery, Chris. 1998. Report from Indonesia. *International Socialism Journal* 80:45–52.

Barker, Colin, ed. 1987. *Revolutionary rehearsals*. London: Bookmarks.

Certeau, Michel de. 1984. *The practice of everyday life*. Berkeley: University of California Press.

Cliff, Tony. 1998. Revolution and counter-revolution: Lessons for Indonesia. *International Socialism Journal* 80:53–70.

Cox, Kevin R., ed. 1997. *Spaces of globalization: Reasserting the power of the local*. New York: Guilford Press.

D'Amato, Paul, and Ahmed Shawki. 2000. World Bank: Plunder with a human face. *International Socialist Review* 11:23–28.

Denning, Michael. 1997. *The cultural front*. London: Verso.

DuBoff, Richard B., and Edward S. Herman. 1997. A critique of Tabb on globalization. *Monthly Review* 49 (6): 27–35.

Escobar, Arturo. 1992. Imagining a post-development era: Critical thought, development, and social movements. *Social Text* 31/32: 20–56.

Eyerman, Ron, and Andrew Jamison. 1991. *Social movements: A cognitive approach*. University Park: Pennsylvania State University Press.

Fermont, Clare. 1998. Indonesia: The inferno of revolution. *International Socialism Journal* 80:3–34.

Flacks, Richard. 1994. The party's over. In *New social movements*, edited by Enrique Laraña, Hank Johnston, and Joseph R. Gusfield. Philadelphia: Temple University Press.

Fraser, Nancy. 1992. Rethinking the public sphere: A contribution to the critique of actually existing democracy. In *Habermas and the*

Public Sphere, edited by Craig Calhoun. Cambridge, MA: Massachusetts Institute of Technology Press.

———. 1997. *Justice interruptus: Critical reflections on the "post-socialist" condition*. New York: Routledge.

Friedman, Thomas L. 1999. *The Lexus and the olive tree: Understanding globalization*. New York: Farrar, Straus and Giroux.

Geier, Joel. 2000. IMF: Debt cop. *International Socialist Review* 11:16–22.

Gibson-Graham, J. K. 1996. *The end of capitalism (as we knew it): A feminist critique of political economy*. Malden, MA: Blackwell.

Giddens, Anthony. 1991. *Modernity and self-identity*. Stanford, CA: Stanford University Press.

Gordon, David. 1988. The global economy. *New Left Review* 168:24–65.

Habermas, Jürgen. 1981. New social movements. *Telos* 49:33–37.

Harman, Chris. 1996. Globalisation: A critique of the new orthodoxy. *International Socialism Journal* 73:3–33.

———. 1998. *The fire last time: 1968 and after*. London: Bookmarks.

Herrod, Andrew. 1997. Labor as an agent of globalization and as a global agent. In *Spaces of globalization: Reasserting the power of the local*, edited by Kevin R. Cox. New York: Guilford Press.

———. 1999. Finding the chain's weakest link. Paper presented at the Southern Labor Studies Conference, 30 September, Atlanta, GA.

Hewison, Kevin, and Garry Rodan. 1994. The decline of the left in Southeast Asia. In *Between globalism and nationalism: Socialist Register 1994*, edited by Ralph Miliband and Leo Panitch. London: Merlin Press.

Hirsch, Joaquim. 1999. Globalisation, class, and the question of democracy. In *Global capitalism versus democracy: Socialist Register 1999*, edited by Leo Panitch and Colin Leys. New York: Monthly Review Press.

Hirst, Paul, and Grahame Thompson. 1996. *Globalization in question*. Cambridge: Polity Press/Blackwell.

Horsman, Mathew. 1994. *After the nation-state*. London: Harper-Collins.

Jameson, Fredric. 1992. *Postmodernism, or, the cultural logic of late capitalism*. Durham, NC: Duke University Press.

———. 1998. *The cultural turn: Selected writings on the postmodern, 1983–1998*. London: Verso.

Kagarlitsky, Boris. 1999. The challenge for the left: Reclaiming the state. In *Global capitalism versus democracy: Socialist Register 1999*, edited by Leo Panitch and Colin Leys. New York: Monthly Review Press.

Kelley, Robin D. G. 1994. *Race rebels: Culture, politics, and the Black working class*. New York: Free Press.

King, Anthony. 1997. *Culture, globalization and the world system.* Minneapolis: University of Minnesota Press.

Korten, David. 1995. *When corporations rule the world.* San Francisco: Berrett-Koehler Press.

Laclau, Ernesto, and Chantal Mouffe. 1986. *Hegemony and socialist strategy.* London: Verso.

Lamb, David. 1999. New Indonesian president seeks close ties with Asia. *Los Angeles Times,* 25 October.

Lambert, John. 1991. Europe: The nation-state dies hard. *Capital and Class* 43:9–24.

Lenin, V. I. 1939. *Imperialism: The highest stage of capitalism.* New York: International Publishers.

Maheu, Louis. 1995. *Social movements and social classes.* London: Sage.

Marquardt, Michael J. 1998. *The global advantage: How world class organizations improve performance through globalization.* Houston: Gulf Publishing.

Marx, Karl, and Friedrich Engels. [1848] 1998. *The Communist manifesto.* New York: Monthly Review Press.

McCarthy, John D. 1997. The globalization of social movement theory. In *Transnational social movements and global politics,* edited by Jackie Smith, Charles Chatfield, and Ron Pagnucco. Syracuse, NY: Syracuse University Press.

McNally, David. 1998. Globalization on trial: Crisis and class struggle in East Asia. In *Rising from the ashes? Labor in the age of "global capitalism,"* edited by Ellen Meiksins Wood, Peter Meiksins, and Michael Yates. New York: Monthly Review Press.

Melucci, Alberto. 1988. Getting involved: Identity and mobilization in social movements. *International Social Movement Research* 1:329–348.

———. 1992. Liberation or meaning? Social movements, culture and democracy. *Development and Change* 23:43–77.

———. 1996. *Challenging codes: Collective action in the information age.* Cambridge: Cambridge University Press.

Miliband, Ralph, and Leo Panitch, eds. 1994. *Between globalism and nationalism: Socialist Register 1994.* London: Merlin Press.

Moody, Kim. 1997. *Workers in a lean world.* London: Verso.

Morgan, Peter, Tom O'Lincoln, and Claire Fermont. 1998. Indonesia: The anger explodes. *Socialist Review* 218:10–13.

Morris, Aldon D., and Carol McClurg Mueller. 1992. *Frontiers in social movement theory.* New Haven, CT: Yale University Press.

Ohmae, Kenichi. 1999. *The borderless world.* New York: Harper Business.

Panitch, Leo. 1994. Globalisation and the state. In *Between globalism and nationalism: Socialist Register 1994*, edited by Ralph Miliband and Leo Panitch. London: Merlin Press.

Panitch, Leo, and Colin Leys, eds. 1999. *Global capitalism versus democracy: Socialist register 1999*. New York: Monthly Review Press.

Pitelis, Christos. 1991. Beyond the nation-state? *Capital and Class* 43:131–52.

Pooley, Sam. 1991. The state rules, ok? *Capital and Class* 43:65–82.

Radice, Hugo. 1999. Taking globalisation seriously. In *Global capitalism versus democracy: Socialist Register 1999*, edited by Leo Panitch and Colin Leys. New York: Monthly Review Press.

Reich, Robert B. 1992. *The work of nations*. New York: Vintage.

Richburg, Keith B. 2000. The business of rebuilding: Entrepreneurs follow the relief workers into East Timor. *Washington Post*, 3 January.

Sassen, Saskia. 1998. *Globalization and its discontents: Essays on the new mobility of people and money*. New York: New Press.

Scott, James C. 1990. *Domination and the arts of resistance: Hidden transcripts*. New Haven, CT: Yale University Press.

Sivanandan, Ambalavener. 1997. Capitalism, globalization, and epochal shifts. *Monthly Review* 48 (9): 19–32.

Smith, Jackie, Charles Chatfield, and Ron Pagnucco, eds. 1997. *Transnational social movements and global politics*. Syracuse, NY: Syracuse University Press.

Tabb, William K. 1997a. Contextualizing globalization. *Monthly Review* 49 (6): 35–39.

———. 1997b. Globalization is an issue, the power of capital is the issue. *Monthly Review* 49 (2): 20–30.

———. 2000. After Seattle: Understanding the politics of globalization. *Monthly Review* 51 (10): 1–18.

Tarrow, Sidney. 1996. States and opportunities: The political structuring of social movements. In *Comparative perspectives on social movements*, edited by Doug McAdam, John D. McCarthy, and Mayer N. Zald. Cambridge: Cambridge University Press.

———. 1998. *Power in movement: Social movements and contentious politics*. Cambridge: Cambridge University Press.

Touraine, Alain. 1984. *Return of the actor*. Paris: Fayard.

Tsoukalas, Constantine. 1999. Globalisation and the executive committee: The myth of the weightless economy. In *Global capitalism versus democracy: Socialist Register 1999*, edited by Leo Panitch and Colin Leys. New York: Monthly Review Press.

Wallerstein, Immanuel. 1979. *The capitalist world economy*. Cambridge: Cambridge University Press.

Weissman, Robert, ed. 1999. WTO: Trading it all away. *International Monitor* 20 (10/11): 5–35.

Wood, Ellen Meiksins. 1997a. A note on DuBoff and Herman. *Monthly Review* 49 (6): 39–48.

——. 1997b. Labor, the state, and class struggle. *Monthly Review* 49 (3): 1–17.

Workers' Representatives and Socialists (WRS). 1998. Three interviews from Indonesia. *International Socialism Journal* 80:35–45.

Contributors

Robert Asen (PhD, Northwestern University, 1998) is an assistant professor in the Communication Arts Department and an affiliate at the Institute for Research on Poverty at the University of Wisconsin-Madison. His research explores issues that arise in theorizing a postbourgeois public sphere as well as relationships between social and economic inequality and public deliberation. He is the author of *Visions of Poverty: Welfare Policy and Political Imagination,* and he has published articles in such journals as *Communication Theory* and *Argumentation and Advocacy.*

Daniel C. Brouwer (PhD, Northwestern University, 2000) is an assistant professor in The Hugh Downs School of Human Communication, College of Public Programs, at Arizona State University. His research interests include studies in the public sphere, social movements, cultural performance, and rhetorical criticism, particularly as they relate to representations of HIV/AIDS. Writings on HIV tattoos and vernacular tactics of HIV discovery have appeared in *Text and Performance Quarterly* and the edited volume *Balancing the Secrets of Private Disclosures.* For nearly a decade, he has performed roles as an AIDS educator, volunteer, and activist.

Dana L. Cloud (PhD, University of Iowa, 1992) is associate professor of communication studies at the University of Texas, Austin. She is the author of a number of articles published in communication journals, in addition to her book, *Consolation and Control in American Culture and Politics: Rhetorics of Therapy* (Sage, 1998). Her current project is a book based on interviews with Boeing workers on democratic unionism in the American labor movement. A longtime member of the International Socialist Organization, Dana is active in a number of social movements, including the labor movement, the anti-death-penalty movement, and movements for gay and lesbian liberation. She lives in Austin with her daughter, Samantha, and her partner, Katie Feyh.

Erik Doxtader (PhD, Northwestern University, 1996) is an assistant professor of rhetoric at the University of North Carolina, Chapel Hill. A 1999–2000 Social Science Research Council Fellow and Honorary Research Associate at the University of Cape Town, he works and publishes in the areas of rhetorical and critical theory. Articles on argument, rhetoric, and deliberation have appeared in *Argumentation and Advocacy*. He is presently completing two books that investigate the rhetorical dynamics of South African reconciliation.

Gerard A. Hauser (PhD, University of Wisconsin, 1970) is currently on the faculty of the University of Colorado at Boulder where he is professor of communication, serves as department Chair, and is on the Board of Directors of the Keller Center for Study of the First Amendment. He has published widely on the subject of rhetorical theory and criticism and is the author of *Introduction to Rhetorical Theory* and *Vernacular Voices: The Rhetoric of Publics and Public Spheres*. He is a recipient of the Kneupper and the Hochmuth Nichols awards for research excellence and a Distinguished Teaching Award from Pennsylvania State University. Currently, he serves on the Board of Directors of the Rhetoric Society of America and is its president-elect.

Marie A. Mater (PhD, University College Cork, National University of Ireland, 1998) is an assistant professor of Speech Communication at Houston Baptist University. Her work has appeared in the *Asian Journal of Communication*, *Local Environment*, and the edited volume *Globalization and Migration: Future Worlds*. She also contributed to *Re-cycled Places: An Environmental Resource Research CD-ROM*. Her current research explores the use of new communication technologies by the United Nations and nongovernmental organizations.

Todd F. McDorman (PhD, Indiana University, 1998) is an assistant professor of speech at Wabash College in Crawfordsville, Indiana. His work has been published in the *Quarterly Journal of Speech* and *Women's Studies in Communication*. His primary research interests are legal discourse and the ways various discourse communities engage the law with respect to social and political change. These interests have been most fully explored in his PhD dissertation, "Transforming Death: The Rhetoric of Euthanasia."

Catherine Helen Palczewski (PhD, Northwestern University, 1994), director of debate and associate professor in the Communication Studies Department and Women's Studies Program, University of Northern Iowa, has previous publications on the pornography controversy, the writings of Gloria Anzaldúa, and political rhetoric in journals such as

The Southern Communication Journal, Argumentation and Advocacy, and *Women and Language.* Her present areas of inquiry include analyses of President Clinton's Race Initiative and Ward Churchill's criticism of Columbus Day Celebrations.

Catherine Squires (PhD, Northwestern University, 1999) is an assistant professor jointly appointed in the Center for Afroamerican and African Studies and the Department of Communication Studies at the University of Michigan. Her research focuses on how marginalized groups use indigenous media resources to bolster social movement efforts and debate identity issues. Her writing has appeared in *Harvard International Journal of Press/Politics*, and she is currently finishing a manuscript on the impact of Black-owned media on the Black public sphere.

Index